HEALTH CARE REFORM IN THE NINETIES

HEALTH CARE REFORM IN THE NINETIES

Edited by

Pauline Vaillancourt Rosenau

SAGE Publications
International Educational and Professional Publisher
Thousand Oaks   London   New Delhi

For information address:

SAGE Publications, Inc.
2455 Teller Road
Thousand Oaks, California 91320

SAGE Publications Ltd.
6 Bonhill Street
London EC2A 4PU
United Kingdom

SAGE Publications India Pvt. Ltd.
M-32 Market
Greater Kailash I
New Delhi 110 048 India

Printed in the United States of America

Library of Congress Cataloging-in-Publication Data

Main entry under title:

Health care reform in the nineties / edited by Pauline Vaillancourt
   Rosenau.
      p.   cm.
   Includes bibliographical references and index.
   ISBN 0-8039-5729-7.—ISBN 0-8039-5730-0 (pbk.)
   1. Health care reform—United States.   I. Rosenau,
Pauline Vaillancourt.
RA395.A3H41384   1994
362.1'0973—dc20   94-6009

94 95 96 97 98 10 9 8 7 6 5 4 3 2 1

Sage Production Editor: Yvonne Könneker

Contents

1

Health System Reform
in the United States

Introduction

PAULINE VAILLANCOURT
ROSENAU

*H*ealth care reform is central to the U.S. political agenda today. This collection of chapters considers the range of possible solutions that might be forthcoming in reconstructing our health services. We also examine how reform will affect different sectors of society. Our goal is to provide an information base for evaluating the various alternatives together with analysis by specialists that will efficiently and competently inform all those with an ongoing interest in health reform.

A broad range of opinion and substance is presented. Views vary considerably from one author to another. We begin with the experience of other countries. The political structures central to reform are explored, including the state-federal relationship and the legislative context. The public health perspective is set forth. The concerns of business and the trade unions are outlined. Gender concerns are addressed. The special needs of older Americans and the homeless are discussed as well as the normative and ethical dimensions of health reform.

Years of federal government inattention and even neglect of policy in the health sector mean that today the situation is urgent. Having been postponed so long, health system reform may necessarily break with precedent and the normal process of policy formation in the United States. We may be observing one of the most important policy experiments of our time. The legislation in question was inspired by the Health Security Act. Championed by Hillary Clinton, health reform was the product of diligent work by experts drawn from various sectors, especially university and government. Private-sector players including the American Medical Association and health insurance companies have been involved in behind-the-scenes negotiations and offered testimony at public congressional hearings. They have launched advertising campaigns in an unparalleled effort to influence the legislation. Consumer representatives have made their point of view available as well.

This attempt could result in dramatic sweeping change in any of several directions, as predicted by some authors here. Or it might yield little of substance, revealing an inability of congressional legislators to move beyond the status quo, a view defended by at least one contributor. The prognosis, however, is generally positive as crisis frees up previously bounded parameters. Institutional rigidity has softened and political actors take the challenge more seriously. The various interest groups representing the medical profession and the insurance industry were on record early on in the Clinton years as being open to compromise, but their reaction vis-à-vis specific, concrete legislative proposal has been more guarded. Nevertheless, President Clinton's successes with Congress (for example, the adoption of the North American Free Trade Agreement [NAFTA]) increase the probability of his navigating some sort of health reform package through Congress.

Promise is great and expectations are high. Even if the exact details of how health system reform will work out as it is implemented in the various states cannot be known with much accuracy, general tendencies are apparent, and we point to and explore the major issues on the national agenda.

Coming late to health system reform, the United States has the advantage of being able to learn from the experience of other modern

Western industrialized countries. Milton Roemer outlines some of these in his chapter offering summary descriptions and examples from various health systems. He traces trends across time, and he is optimistic. He points to the German example as of special importance for reforming the U.S. health system. My own concluding chapter is also informed by the experience of other countries, especially Canada where I have lived for the last 20 years.

Most of the discussion about health system reform focuses on answers, and this is essential. But at the same time, concentrating on solutions assumes the questions. Lu Ann Aday points out that the answers we are discussing may be assuming the wrong questions and that if we did not take the questions for granted, we might broaden the solutions being considered. If the goal is access to health, then the questions need to go beyond how to assure universal access to medical care. Improving the nation's health directs attention beyond the health system, into America's neighborhoods, classrooms, families—in short, toward social structures. One is left wondering if it is possible to reform the health system without taking on the concerns of social context. Joyce Lashof responds to the question. She argues that financial access to medical care, such as that envisioned by health care reform, is not sufficient, and she explains how new legislation must look at health status in the largest sense as well as considering the social environment and behavioral factors that influence it. Addressing the underlying social conditions of low income and minority populations is essential if improvement is ever to be achieved. As she points out, money saved on health care might be redirected to improve education and housing or to programs that would reduce unemployment. Philip Lee, in contrast, argues that the Health Security Act represents a breakthrough in health reform and enlarges opportunities as it supports and expands the role of public health.

Two chapters discuss federal-state relations and health reform. Colleen Grogan expects health system reform to be decentralized and to be state controlled if it follows the historical lead of parallel programs. She questions whether this will really attain the presumed goals of democratic responsiveness, innovation, and administrative efficiency. She anticipates contradictions to emerge if the federal government attempts to exert cost control mechanisms on states. Russell Hanson focuses on already existing health reform at the state level. He discusses what can be learned about the various proposed reforms: market-oriented and regulatory relief, play or pay, and various kinds of insurance. The theory of federalism and many policy experts consider the ongoing health reform record of the states to provide a wealth of information that can be employed in formulating quality federal legislation. Hanson questions this model by which the federal government selects from among the most successful state-level programs. He proposes that it is oversimplified, explaining how rivalry emerges from the different state-level experiments, perhaps making it more difficult to formulate federal-level legislation. He also asks if it is reasonable to expect that the same health system would be appropriate in all the states.

Mark A. Peterson is optimistic about the possibility of health system reform because of what he sees as significant institutional changes. The medical providers, insurance carriers, and business leaders are more divided today than in the past, he argues. They are less likely to effectively oppose reform. He also suggests that the election, in 1992, of a new Congress gives rise to enlarged opportunity for reform. His hypothesis concerning the relative increasing efficacy of Congress and the decreasing viability of interest groups is being put to the test at this very moment.

Assessments of business and labor perspectives in this volume speak to Mark Peterson's viewpoint. Linda Bergthold's analysis of the business community suggests that it is not a "community" at all. She describes less unity and more division and difference regarding health reform, outlining points of agreement and elements of contention. Cathie Martin reports on her interviews with those members of the business community who are committed to providing health insurance for their workers. Her chapter underlines the dilemma such businesses face and the constraints that limit their options. The labor perspective, presented by J. Peter Nixon, is much more unified than that of the business sector.

If the possibility of health system reform depends on there being a consensus across divergent interests, then success may be within reach. The health reform perspectives of business and trade unions presented here suggest that the differences are not that great. Their line of reasoning is not the same, but in the end, both agree on the need for reform, that "managed competition" is the likely format, that employers will play a major role, that universal access is crucial, and that cost containment is essential. Unions, however, would oppose proposals to tax health benefits, but then so would some businesses.

Three chapters discuss the coming health reform from the perspective of special, sometimes overlooked groups: older people, the homeless, and women. Older Americans consume more health care services, and efforts at cost control within the larger health reform underway may affect them substantially. Robert Binstock outlines this situation and analyzes the political role of older persons in the health reform process. He indicates how health reform laws would affect older Americans, underlining the rationing potential in provisions that permit states to fold Medicare into purchasing alliances. Michael Cousineau and John Lozier suggest that managed competition may not work for the homeless. They argue that the homeless have special needs because they use the health system differently than do those with a stable, permanent address. Comprehensive, multidisciplinary care is called for, and specific suggestions are outlined. Chris Hafner-Eaton explains what is involved in a women's health agenda. Her analysis reveals that women's needs involve those of children and men as well. She points to pressing research priorities and essential legislation that would make up for more than a decade of neglect of women's issues.

Several chapters provide background and insight on the various proposals for health reform, but none can avoid addressing, consciously or unconsciously, the Health Security Act. E. Richard Brown compares the single-payer health system model with President Clinton's proposal. He points out that by including the possibility for individual states to opt for a single-payer system, the White House proposal offers considerable flexibility. Dan E. Beauchamp and Paul Ambrose also assess the Health Security Act, arguing that it is really two different proposals, one appealing to regulators and the other to those committed to market competition. They outline three possible scenarios for the future, depending on the balance that will be achieved between these two opposed orientations. The chapter by Michael Intriligator rejects the Clinton-style employer-based managed competition and offers a straightforward alternative proposal, expanding the existing Medicare system with which Americans are already familiar and generally satisfied. It is not surprising that this intuitively straightforward and organizationally uncomplicated solution has received more attention from Congress.

My own contribution summarizes some well-known cost-conscious reform proposals and evaluates whether or not health reform suggestions take them into consideration. Most of the considerations discussed here are practically feasible. Many have been successfully implemented in other countries. Some of these propositions have not received policymaker's attention because they are complicated to carry out and/or politically sensitive. The Clinton administration has put them on the national policy agenda.

All of the authors in this special issue are painfully aware of how difficult it is to write in a time of transition and transformation. On the one hand, events might overtake us at any moment. But on the other hand, writing on the edge of events energizes as it generates a sense of urgency. Many of the contributors to this issue set aside other projects and postponed other deadlines to meet this challenge. We have the hope of informing the process of reform at the same time that we and all other scholars and practitioners in the health sector are a part of it.

President Clinton has set us on a path of health reform from which there is no return. Only a minority today suggests that anything but universal access is appropriate. Details as to the exact comprehensive benefit package may change in the future. How various states implement federal law over the coming decades cannot be known. The exact role of the federal government vis-à-vis the states may evolve. The long-term success of cost containment mechanisms cannot be known in advance. Many questions remain to be answered. How will health care and doctor-patient relationships be affected? Will all this reform affect the quality of care? Will corporate and regional alliances be attentive to their member's needs and opinions? Will plans be negotiated in good faith, bargained wisely, and prove to be fiscally sound?

We have learned from the past decade of market competition and spiraling costs in the health sector that the supply and demand dynamic does not always produce the positive outcomes predicted. Successful national health programs in the United States, such as Medicare, have been funded and closely regulated by the federal government. One hopes that the deregulation rhetoric of the 1980s has moderated. Most reform proposals anticipate a larger role for responsible government in our reorganized health system.

No matter what answers we have for health reform questions, one element is reasonably probable. Whatever "solution" we come to during the Clinton years, the programs implemented are not likely to endure for very long in the exact form in which they are initially conceived by the White House, reformulated by Congress, and finally adopted into law. They will require amendments and changes based on concrete experience. Continual learning, revision based on feedback, could make for a better health system in the future. But drawing from past mistakes to better organize the future assumes some societal accord on overall objectives. Success and failure, better and worse, are defined in terms of where we are trying to go, what we want to achieve. Although discussion and public deliberation about general civic goals is always frustrating and may even be fruitless if agreement is impossible, there is near unanimity from all quarters on one point—that what we have at the moment is not good enough.

2

National Health Systems Throughout the World

Lessons for Health System Reform in the United States

MILTON I. ROEMER

*H*ealth system reform was central to the 1992 presidential election campaign. This chapter describes the health systems of several other countries that have been more successful than the United States in providing for the needs of their citizens in these matters. They offer inspiration for reforming the U.S. health system in the months and years ahead. Every country has a national health system that reflects its history, its economic development, and its dominant political ideology. As a result of the diverse circumstances, countries have different types of health systems. The type of health system in a country depends on the characteristics of each of the system's component parts. These are examined by way of introduction.

Composition of Health Systems

Any national health system in a country at any stage of economic development may be analyzed according to five principal component parts: resources, organization, management, economic support, and delivery of services.

The resources of a health system consist of human resources (personnel), facilities (hospitals, health centers, etc.), commodities (drugs, equipment, supplies, etc.), and knowledge. Each of these may be produced or acquired in different ways and to various extents.

Health programs may be organized under diverse sponsorships. In virtually all health systems there is one principal authority of government (at several levels), other governmental agencies with health functions, voluntary health agencies, enterprises, and a private health care market. The proportions among these five major forms of organization vary greatly in different countries.

The management of health systems entails several processes: health planning, administration (supervision, consultation, coordination, etc.), regulation, and legislation. The methods of carrying out each managerial process tend to vary mainly with a country's dominant political ideology.

The economic support of the various parts of a health system usually depends on one or more financial mechanisms. These may be governmental tax revenues (at different levels), social insurance (statutory), voluntary insurance, charity, and personal households. In economically less developed countries, foreign aid may play a role. The relative proportions among these different forms of support influence many features of a health system (Roemer, 1991).

Finally, these four component parts of a health system lead to the crucial fifth part: the delivery of health services. These may be analyzed according to several main subdivisions: primary health care (preventive and curative), secondary care, and tertiary care. In most health systems, furthermore, there are special modes of delivery of health services to certain populations and for certain disorders.

The combined characteristics of these five component parts permit the designation of each national health system according to certain *types*. Although history, economic level, and political ideology determine these types, their attributes may be classified according to the degree of *market intervention by government*. The organization of every health system, it was noted, includes a private health care market. The proportions and characteristics of this market depend on the extent of intervention in the market process—supply, demand, competition, and price—by government. This may be measured, as will be seen, in different ways, appropriate to each component.

By such analysis, the national health systems in the world's approximately 165 sovereign countries may be scaled into four main types. Going from the least market intervention to the most, these health system types are entrepreneurial, welfare oriented, comprehensive, and socialist. This scaling may be applied, furthermore, to countries at high, middle, and low levels of economic development. In this chapter, I examine the lessons to be learned for health system reform mostly from industrialized countries, especially welfare-oriented, comprehensive, and socialist systems.

The United States: An Entrepreneurial Health System in Need of Reform

The United States is an entrepreneurial health system in a highly industrialized country. I begin with an assessment of what already exists in this country. There is probably no other country that belongs in this category, although Australia may have fitted into it 20 years ago.

Health resources of all sorts are relatively abundant in the United States. Physicians are plentiful (about 220 per 100,000 population), and for each physician there are 15 or 20 associated health personnel—nurses, pharmacists, dentists, technicians, physical therapists, administrators, and so forth (U.S. Department of Health and Human Services, 1990). These personnel are prepared by universities, hospitals, and other training centers that are sponsored about half by units of government and half by nongovernment agencies. Within medicine, there is a high degree of specialization so that only about 15% of doctors are generalists. Of all doctors serving ambulatory patients, about half are in group practice clinics (three or more working together). About two thirds of hospital beds are in nongovernmental institutions, and 10% of the total are operated for profit.

The major health authority of the U.S. federal government is the Department of Health and Human Services, which promotes disease prevention and gives medical care to selected population groups. In the 50 U.S. states and 3,100 counties, there are local public health authorities engaged in environmental sanitation, communicable disease control, preventive service for mothers and infants, and certain other functions. Voluntary health agencies, focusing on certain persons, diseases, or services are especially numerous. The largest channel for providing health care, however, is the private market of thousands of independent medical practitioners, pharmacies, laboratories, and so on.

Economic support for the U.S. health system comes predominantly from private sources—about 60% of the vast expenditures in 1990 of $2,566 per capita (Koch, 1993, p. 300). Of these health funds spent in the private sector, about half are derived from voluntary insurance, sold by hundreds of commercial or nonprofit companies. The public sector of 40% is derived partly from social insurance (social security legislation) and partly from federal, state, and local tax revenues. Charity and industrial management contribute only a small fraction (under 5%) of health system costs. As a share of gross national product (GNP), U.S. health expenditures consume 11.5%—the largest percentage of any country. Still, some 15% of the population are without adequate economic protection for health care costs.

Because the U.S. health system is so pluralistic in structure and function, primary health care is not delivered in a uniform way. Most is provided by private practitioners, who are paid fees for each service rendered—whether the source of payment is private or public. The largest governmentally sponsored programs of medical care are Medicare for the elderly and totally disabled and Medicaid for the poor (see Binstock's chapter in this volume); under both of these programs, doctors and other practitioners are paid by the fee-for-service method, administered with much elasticity (Koch, 1993, p. 315). This applies to services in hospitals, which usually have "open" medical staffs, as well as to care of the ambulatory patient.

In spite of these highly entrepreneurial characteristics, the U.S. health system has been undergoing rapid changes, and it is likely to continue to do so into the Clinton years because this administration is so committed to health system reform. The long-term trend of economic support has been toward increased financing through collectivized mechanisms. The delivery of health service has also been subjected to various patterns of organization so that teams of health personnel working in clinics and community health centers, as well as in hospitals, are becoming increasingly common.

Notes for the Future Debate on Health Care Reform in the United States in the 1990s

The prominent feature of debate in the United States in the 1980s has been the role to be played by private health insurance plans. With the election of Democrat Bill Clinton in 1992, it may be assumed that enrollment in approved health insurance plans (AHIPs) will be mandatory. For small employers, the costs will be softened by tax deductions or tax credits.

It is likely that a state government health insurance fund will be available for employment groups that do not wish to enroll in any available AHIP. The private insurance industry, meanwhile, will undergo substantial reform so that all premiums will be "community rated," without adjustment for insurance risks.

The fate of the Medicaid program is not clear. Is it to be continued with more generous funding, or will it be absorbed into health insurance coverage? Will it continue as a responsibility of each state, or will it be nationalized, like Medicare? Other chapters in this collection attempt to answer these questions (e.g., see chapter by Intriligator).

As a general estimate of the future, the new national government is likely to retain administrative practices of the past as much as possible. The Clinton White House will probably attempt to avoid controversy as much as possible. This will mean reform of the most entrepreneurial practices in private health insurance operations, while expecting insurance companies to serve as the chief carriers and agents for financing health care.

Aside from financing, there is wide consensus that the delivery of health services should be shaped in patterns of managed care. In the interests of quality, prevention, efficiency, and effectiveness, managed health care should become the norm, according to most health leaders. Various inducements—in financial terms and in conditions of work—can be offered to encourage medical participation in managed care. Remuneration of doctors by salary, varying with productivity and responsibility, is becoming commonplace—a reflection of the social organization of health services.

Various legislative strategies are being actively debated to achieve universal population coverage for health services in the United States. Political prediction is a hazardous game, but it is safe to say that the costs of U.S. medical care today, accessibility to it, and control of its quality have all become political issues. Canada started its movement to national health insurance by action at the level of one prairie province; this was Saskatchewan, where a program launched in 1947 became nationwide by 1958 (Taylor, 1990, chap. 7). Rhode Island, incidentally, enacted a social insurance law to cover catastrophic medical costs in 1974 (Taylor, 1990, chap. 7). The same year,

Hawaii enacted a social insurance law for much broader medical care protection of all employees in that island state (Dukakis, 1992, p. 1092). In the legislatures of many states, numerous bills for mandatory insurance coverage have been introduced, with important enactments in Minnesota, for example (see Hanson's chapter in this volume). With so much brewing at both state and national levels, one can expect that the United States will soon lose its dubious distinction of being the only industrialized nation on earth whose people lack the protection of a social insurance program for general health service.

Welfare-Oriented Health Systems

Many health systems of Western Europe are welfare oriented, as are the systems of Canada, Japan, and Australia. The health system of the Federal Republic of Germany has mobilized economic support to make health service available to practically all of its people, for the longest period of time. It is especially pertinent in terms of its example for health care reform in the United States today.

After many years of voluntary health care insurance organizations among low-income workers, Germany enacted mandatory legislation for such insurance in 1883. The kinds of workers covered and the scope of health services provided were gradually broadened. The insurance is now carried by several hundred relatively small "sickness funds" that are regulated by government as to their costs, benefits, and methods of administration. The principal governmental responsibility for this social insurance is the Ministry of Labor and Social Affairs in the central government and also in each of the nine provinces. Preventive public health work is done by the Ministry of Youth, Family Affairs, and Health, working in local communities.

Education of physicians and other health personnel takes place in universities and schools sponsored entirely by units of government. Hospitals are also sponsored mainly (52.3% of beds in 1980) by units of government; of the nongovernmental hospital beds, two thirds are under voluntary nonprofit agencies and one third are proprietary. The medical staffs of the proprietary hospitals are open to any qualified local physician, but in government and voluntary nonprofit facilities, there are "closed" medical staffs of salaried physicians.

The payment of nonsalaried physicians for their services is a complex process, resulting from long historical developments. Experience from this system would be worthwhile for the Clinton administration to examine. The sickness funds enter into contracts with associations of physicians, which are paid periodic per capita amounts, according to each fund's membership. Then the medical association reviews and pays the fees charged by physicians. If in a quarter year, the fees charged exceed the money available, less than the full amount of each fee may be paid; alternatively, certain doctors (suspected of overservicing patients) may be underpaid. To safeguard the earnings of specialists in private practice, *hospitals do not offer outpatient services*, except for emergency cases.

In the United States, regulations on the approval of pharmaceuticals are being liberalized (deregulated), and we can look to the German experience here too.

The German pharmaceutical industry, largely an offshoot of the dye industry, is especially robust. Hundreds of new or slightly modified drugs are produced each year and dispensed by private pharmacies. The tragedy of thalidomide—causing severely defective babies when taken by the pregnant woman—occurred in West Germany in the 1960s and led to more regulatory drug legislation in Germany and many other countries. On the other hand, one must recognize that the principle of chemotherapy originated in 1912 in Germany (Paul Ehrlich and "Salvarsan"), and the sulfonamides were first synthesized by German chemists.

In contrast to the United States, the entire health system in Germany required expenditure of 8.2% of the gross domestic product (GDP), as of 1987. Of this amount, 77% was derived from programs under government and only 23% came from the private sector. Most of the public sector funds came from the social insurance, administered by the sickness funds. In spite of Germany's period of brutal fascism and the experience of defeat in two world wars (1914-1918 and 1939-1945), the German health system has continued to serve well the great majority of the population to the present time (Roemer, 1991; Sigerist, 1943).

The other welfare-oriented health systems of Western Europe are similar to Germany, and these too are of interest to the United States. Local insurance organizations administer the health service financing in many of these countries. In France, for example, the patient must make a payment for services directly to the physician and then seek reimbursement from his or her *caisse de maladie* according to a "nomenclature" (fees negotiated between the government and the medical association). Typically, the reimbursement is for 80% of the charges, so that the patient copays 20%. Administrative mechanisms in Belgium, the Netherlands, and Austria differ in other ways (Roemer, 1991).

My own assessment is that the German example is more of interest to the United States than are others because it has local sickness funds that parallel the U.S. coverage through insurance companies. The welfare-oriented health systems of Australia and Canada are more fully under the umbrella of government, without use of intermediary insurance agencies. In Australia, there was no history of worker's insurance funds, so that health insurance is managed by a single national government authority. In Canada, the key administrative bodies are the provincial governments, with partial funding by grants from the federal government. In both countries, funds come mainly from general revenues, rather than earmarked employer/employee contributions, to finance the programs. Most of the health services are still provided by private doctors, who are paid by negotiated fees, and hospitals are paid by prospective global budgets. In Australia, most hospitals are sponsored by local governments, and in Canada, the majority are controlled by churches or other voluntary bodies.

Comprehensive Health Systems

Health system reform in the United States is unlikely to lead to a government-sponsored public system as is the case in many other Western countries. It is important to look at these examples just the same because the results have been impressive. National health systems that were welfare oriented for some years underwent further political development after World War II and became comprehensive in type. This has meant that 100% of the national population has become entitled to complete health service, and the financial support has shifted almost entirely to general tax revenues. Larger proportions of doctors and other health personnel have come to work in organized frameworks on salary. Almost all health facilities have come under the direct control of government (Raffel, 1984; Roemer, 1976, 1991, chap. 7).

Great Britain adopted this comprehensive type of health system soon after World War II, pursuant to planning done during the war (Sidel & Sidel, 1977). The Scandinavian countries did likewise in the 1950s; Italy enacted "national health service" legislation in the 1970s, and somewhat less sweepingly, this was done in Greece and Spain (Raffel, 1984; Roemer, 1976, 1991). The British National Health Service (NHS) has had a worldwide impact, so it is useful to describe this comprehensive health system in more detail. The lesson for the United States is that even a relatively well-organized health care system cannot function adequately if it is drastically underfunded. Limited insurance for general practitioner services and drugs had covered low-wage manual workers in Great Britain since 1911 (Beveridge, 1942). With the 1946 legislation, this program was expanded to provide all ambulatory treatment services and to become the first pillar of the NHS. Because of the war, British hospitals had been organized into regional groups, and these, headed by regional hospital boards, became the second organizational pillar. Local public health authorities, along with visiting nurse and ambulance services, became the third pillar (Forsyth, 1973; Lindsay, 1962). Finally, a special administrative channel was reserved for teaching hospitals, affiliated with medical schools. In this three- or four-part administrative structure, policies on professional remuneration varied pragmatically. General medical practitioners were paid by capitation, according to the persons enrolled with each one. Dentists were paid by fees for each unit of service. Specialists (or consultants), who were hospital based, were employed by the regional boards and were paid by salaries.

In 1974, the British NHS was reorganized to achieve greater administrative integration. After a preliminary period, all health services were placed under unified management in some 200 health districts. At this level, a well-trained specialist in management was supported by a specialist in community medicine (including epidemiology). The regional hospital boards were converted into regional health boards and became the conduits for money from the central government. At all levels, there were "community health councils," which were made up of leading consumers and providers, for advisory purposes (Kinnaird, 1981; Roemer, 1991).

Popular opinion in Great Britain has been highly favorable toward the NHS, although there are complaints about long waiting lists for elective (nonemergency) surgery in hospitals. The explanation of these delays is fundamentally that the resources provided by government for this large comprehensive health system are inadequate. In 1987, when the United States was spending 11.2% of GDP on health and Sweden was spending 9.0%, Great Britain was spending only 6.1% of its smaller overall GDP. Of this expenditure, 87%

came from government and 13% from the private sector. (In 1975, however, only 9% of British health expenditures had been private, and Conservative government policy has encouraged greater private spending.)

The development of comprehensive health systems in the Scandinavian countries was more gradual. The local workers' health insurance funds were simply converted into branch offices of the national government, and services became available to everyone. The demand for health services in Norway and Sweden does not appear to be so high as in Great Britain, and yet both human and physical resources are relatively greater. In Sweden, for example, the health spending in 1987 amounted to 9.0% of GDP, of which 91% came from public sources and 9% from private sources. This was an increase from 8.0% of GDP in 1975, of which—in contrast to Great Britain—10%, a slightly greater fraction, had previously come from private sources (Borgenhammer, 1983; Roemer, 1976, 1991). The Swedish government, in other words, has responded to rising demand by strengthening the public sector. This is an example the United States is very unlikely to follow.

The fact that some developing countries have achieved comprehensive health systems, which have entitled 100% of their populations to complete health services, should inspire the United States because other less developed countries have managed it. Costa Rica, a middle-income-level country, which in 1948 abolished its military establishment and then gradually extended its social security coverage for medical care to everyone, is an example (Casas & Vargas, 1980). Another country of very low income level (GNP per capita of $400 in 1986) is Sri Lanka, a tropical island south of India.

In 1986, Sri Lanka had 16,100,000 people, with the same sort of vast disparities in family wealth as most developing countries; the richest 20% of households earned 50% of the total income, whereas the poorest 20% earned only 6% of the income. Yet the government health services made available to all of these people are remarkably complete. For governance, the country is divided into 25 districts, each headed by a centrally appointed medical officer. Within each district, there are about 10 divisions, averaging 60,000 people, with a medically staffed "divisional health center." Even more peripherally, there are "subdivisional health centers," staffed wholly by auxiliary personnel, including assistant medical practitioners with two years of training in primary health care. Voluntary health agencies are also strong in Sri Lanka, especially the Red Cross, the Cancer

Society, and the Family Planning Association (American Public Health Association, 1979; De Silva, 1986; Perera, 1985; Roemer, 1991).

The supply of modern physicians in Sri Lanka is quite modest—13.4 per 100,000 in 1981—because many are Tamils, who faced ethnic discrimination and therefore emigrated. The stock of Ayurvedic practitioners is three times as great, and these are virtually all in private practice. Government health needs for human resources in Sri Lanka are met largely by auxiliary personnel (Gunatilleke, 1985).

Nutrition policy in Sri Lanka has been a major factor contributing to health. Soon after independence in 1947, a weekly ration of rice was provided free to every family; even when this was altered in the 1970s, it was continued for very poor families, along with free lunches for all school children. General education has also had high priority in Sri Lanka. Nearly all girls as well as boys go to primary school, and in 1985 adult literacy was 91% for men and 83% for women (De Silva, 1986; Roemer, 1991).

The Sri Lanka Ministry of Health in the mid-1980s estimated that health services were accessible to 93% of the population. Because of the shortage of modern physicians, Ayurvedic practitioners are consulted extensively; many of these make use of penicillin and other scientific drugs in their practice (De Silva, 1986; Marga Institute, 1984).

Because of its closeness to India and its cultural similarities, Sri Lanka's health record has often been compared to India's. In 1985, when India's infant mortality rate was 105 per 1,000 live births, the rate in Sri Lanka was 36 per 1,000. In 1987, life expectancy at birth in India was 59 years and in Sri Lanka 71 years. Strong programs of nutrition and education have doubtless contributed importantly to these achievements, but the comprehensive health system has surely played a substantial part (Ministry of Health and Family Welfare [India], 1988; Roemer, 1991).

Socialist Health Systems

Health system reform in the United States will emphasize the private sector. But from the historical experience of the socialist countries we learn that government-organized systems can function quite satisfactorily in the health sector. In countries that have had a revolution to install a socialist economic order, the health systems have become socialist in structure and function. This has meant that practically all physical and human resources have been taken over by government, and health services have theoretically become available to everyone, at least until 1989 and 1990 when certain basic changes were brought about in these socialist economies.

After the Russian Revolution of 1917, the Soviet Union became the first country with a socialist health system. The changes into a socialist system did not occur overnight but were essentially completed by 1937. By then, virtually all doctors, nurses, and other health personnel had become public employees, and all hospitals and other health facilities were taken over by government. The private pharmaceutical industry was nationalized; medical schools were removed from the universities and put under the Ministry of Health as academic institutes. Health science research was carried out in other special institutes, also under the Ministry of Health (Hyde, 1974; Sigerist, 1937).

All services were free of charge to every Soviet resident, except drugs, which had to be purchased in government pharmacies. Certain life-saving compounds, however, and all drugs for certain persons (military veterans or pensioners) were dispensed without charge. To provide accessible ambulatory care, hundreds of polyclinics—staffed by generalists, pediatricians, gynecologists, and others—were established in the cities, and hundreds of smaller health centers were constructed in rural areas (Field, 1967, 1972; Sigerist, 1947). The Soviet *feldsher*—trained since the 19th century—was one of the world's earliest forms of medical assistant, serving mostly in rural areas where physicians were too few (Sidel, 1968).

The Soviet health system has turned out enormous numbers of physicians so that in 1986 there were 430 per 100,000 population. Nurses, midwives, and feldshers were also plentiful, but technicians were relatively less numerous than in other industrialized countries (USSR Ministry of Health, 1987). Diagnostic and therapeutic equipment in hospitals was generally less developed than in Western European countries—a deficiency that then-President Gorbachev's *perestroika* (restructuring) was expected to correct (Galin, 1987; Gorbachev, 1987). Certain exceptionally well-equipped and -staffed hospitals and polyclinics, however, were established to serve high Communist Party officials. Such "preferred care" is provided for "important persons" in most national health systems, but in an egalitarian socialist society it has caused much popular resentment.

Since about 1960, private out-of-hospital health service has expanded slightly in the Soviet Union for those who can afford to pay private fees. These "paying polyclinics" are staffed by hospital-based specialists, who work in them a limited number of hours per week. As a general backup for all polyclinics and hospitals, all large Soviet cities have well-developed emergency services, staffed by physicians and feldshers and equipped with modern ambulances. Calls to a central telephone exchange lead to the dispatch of ambulances from various locations in large metropolitan areas (Ryan, 1978).

The health of the population in the Soviet Union improved markedly after the 1917 Revolution for about 50 years. The infant mortality rate declined, and the life expectancy at birth increased significantly. Then in the 1970s, these indices changed, and health conditions clearly deteriorated. Various explanations were offered, but most important seemed to be the Cold War and the vast military expenditures it entailed. The funds remaining for health services were seriously inadequate (Knaus, 1981; Nelson, 1988; Venediktov, 1973; Zhuk, 1976).

Soviet health system expenditures in the 1970s and 1980s were less than 4.0% of national wealth (as calculated by economists from international agencies). This was much lower than in any Western industrialized country and far below the health needs. As part of perestroika, health expenditures were expected to increase, but the effects of this would take time to see. In the other socialist countries of Eastern Europe (Poland, Hungary, etc.), the health systems were modeled largely after that of the Soviet Union, and the transformations toward a free market pattern were occurring somewhat earlier in the 1980s (Roemer, 1991).

As of 1992, it is striking to see that in Poland and Hungary the health systems are continuing as before, as when the economies were socialist in character, and very little change is observed. This is of interest because other sectors of these countries have been so dramatically transformed. These countries seem to cling to the old systems regarding the health sector, and only 5% of this sector has been privatized. Yet health systems in these countries are underfinanced. But the basic structure remains the same.

General Trends

In all four types of national health system in industrialized as well as developing countries, certain general trends have been evident over the past 50 years, and the United States is no exception. The resources, both human and physical, have been greatly expanded. As more people have survived to older age groups and as educational levels have improved, the demands for personal health care everywhere have risen. Every country has responded by developing larger resources and new kinds of health personnel. Pharmaceutical products have also increased in quantity, variety, and effectiveness.

The organization of health systems, largely under government, has increased and grown more complex. Agencies, both public and private, have multiplied, and, in general, the strength and scope of ministries of health have been enhanced. Public health authorities have grown at various jurisdictional levels—local and provincial as well as national. Nongovernmental voluntary agencies have also grown to promote health efforts regarding certain persons, certain disorders, or certain services.

The management of national health systems has become generally more sophisticated, as the interests of more groups of health care providers and consumers become defined. Administrators are trained, record systems are formulated, consumers are given a stronger voice, and decision making has become a more democratic process. To limit abuses in the private market, regulatory powers have been extended. More and more aspects of health are being subjected to legislative intervention—from reducing the sale of harmful tobacco products to the mobilization of funds for supporting the costs of prevention and treatment.

As a share of national wealth, the money devoted to health systems has increased steadily, except perhaps in the European socialist countries. It has grown both in public and private sectors, although in all but a few countries more rapidly in the public sector. Of all the health services, those in hospitals have absorbed the most rapidly expanding proportion (Roemer, 1991, chap. 19) to provide the benefits of advanced technology to an aging population with chronic diseases. With the objective of meeting the health needs of more people, rural and urban, the World Health Organization (1984) has stressed everywhere a higher priority for primary health care.

In the patterns of delivery of health care, the key concept has become teamwork. The importance of this has long been recognized in hospitals, and it is now appreciated in ambulatory care as well. The socialist countries first demonstrated the value of polyclinics and health centers to provide integrated preventive-curative services to general populations, and all countries with other types of health systems have to some extent acted likewise. There is a generally increased application of these organized frameworks, from the entrepreneurial to the welfare oriented to the comprehensive and to the socialist types of health system. The United States might take note of this trend with reference to its own poverty-level populations who have no insurance under the present system. These developments in all components of national health systems add up to the attainment of greater health care equity in the world. The constitution of the World Health Organization (1978) stipulates that the highest attainable standard of health is a fundamental right of every human being, without regard to race, religion, political belief, or economic or social condition.

Implementation of this ideal may lie in the future, but the developments in national health systems throughout the world over the last half-century give grounds for confidence about its ultimate achievement. The United States for its part is set to carry out important health system reform. It will not be an easy task. The obstacles are clear. But the potential gains are enormous.

References

American Public Health Association. (1979). *A health and population brief: Republic of Sri Lanka*. Washington, DC: Author.

Beveridge, W. (1942). *Social insurance and allied services*. New York: Macmillan.

Borgenhammer, E. (1983). *Health services in Sweden*. Goteberg: Nordic School of Public Health.

Casas, A., & Vargas, H. (1980). The health system in Costa Rica: Toward a national health service. *Journal of Public Health Policy, 1*, 258-279.

De Silva, U.H.S. (1986). *A review of the national health development network of Sri Lanka*. Colombo: Ministry of Health.

Dukakis, M. (1992). The states and health care reform. *New England Journal of Medicine, 327*, 1090-1092.

Field, M. G. (1967). *Soviet socialized medicine—An introduction*. New York: Free Press.

Field, M. G. (1972). Taming a profession: Early phases of Soviet socialized medicine. *Bulletin of the New York Academy of Medicine, 48*(1), 83-92.

Forsyth, G. (1973). United Kingdom. In I. Douglas-Wilson & G. McLachlen (Eds.), *Health service prospects: An international survey* (pp. 1-35). London: *The Lancet* and Nuffields Provincial Hospitals Trust.

Galin, L. (1987, November 11). "Glasnost" boosts health care: Soviet MDs. *Medical Tribune*, p. 10.

Gorbachev, M. (1987). *Perestroika: New thinking for our country and the world*. New York: Harper & Row.

Gunatilleke, G. (1985). Health and development in Sri Lanka—An overview. In S. B. Halstead, J. A. Walsh, & K. S. Warren (Eds.), *Good health at low cost* (pp. 111-124). New York: Rockefeller Foundation.

Hyde, G. (1974). *The Soviet health service: A historical and comparative study*. London: Lawrence & Wighort.

Kinnaird, J. (1981). The British National Health Service: Retrospect and prospect. *Journal of Public Health Policy, 2*, 382-412.

Knaus, W. A. (1981). *Inside Russian medicine: An American doctor's first-hand report.* New York: Everest House.

Koch, A. (1993). Financing health services. In S. J. Williams & P. R. Torrens (Eds.), *Introduction to health services* (4th ed., pp. 299-331). Albany, NY: Delmar.

Lindsay, A. (1962). *Socialized medicine in England and Wales: The National Health Service 1948-1961.* Chapel Hill: University of North Carolina Press.

Marga Institute. (1984). *Intersectoral action for health: Sri Lanka study.* Colombo: Author.

Ministry of Health and Family Welfare, Government of India. (1988). *Health information of India.* New Delhi: Nirman Bhavan.

Nelson, H. (1988, May 15). Massive reforms—Soviet goal: Resuscitate health care. *Los Angeles Times,* pp. 1, 16.

Perera, P.D.A. (1985). Health care systems of Sri Lanka. In S. B. Halstead, J. A. Walsh, & K. S. Warren (Eds.), *Good health at low cost* (pp. 93-110). New York: Rockefeller Foundation.

Raffel, M. W. (Ed.). (1984). *Comparative health systems: Descriptive analyses of fourteen national health systems.* University Park: Pennsylvania State University Press.

Roemer, M. (1976). *Health care systems in world perspective.* Ann Arbor, MI: Health Administration Press.

Roemer, M. (1991). *National health systems of the world: Vol. 1. The countries.* New York: Oxford University Press.

Ryan, M. (1978). *The organization of Soviet medical care.* Oxford: Blackwell.

Sidel, V. W. (1968). Feldshers and feldsherism: The role and training of the feldsher in the USSR. *New England Journal of Medicine, 278*, 934-939.

Sidel, V., & Sidel, R. (1977). *A healthy state: Great Britain. Equitable entitlement.* New York: Pantheon.

Sigerist, H. E. (1937). *Socialized medicine in the Soviet Union.* New York: Norton.

Sigerist, H. E. (1943). From Bismarck to Beveridge: Development and trends in social security legislation. *Bulletin of the History of Medicine, 13*, 365-388.

Sigerist, H. E. (1947). *Medicine and health in the Soviet Union.* New York: Citadel.

Taylor, M. (1990). *Insuring national health care: The Canadian experience.* Chapel Hill: University of North Carolina Press.

U. S. Department of Health and Human Services. (1990). *Seventh report of the President and Congress on the status of health personnel in the United States* (DHHS Publication No. HRS-P-OD 90-1). Washington, DC: U.S. Government Printing Office.

USSR Ministry of Health. (1987, November 27). The basic plan for the development of health care and for reorganization of the healthcare system of the USSR in the twelfth five-year plan and for the period until the year 2000 (C. Kaylin, Trans.). *Meditsinskaya Gazeta, 96*, 4749.

Venediktov, D. (1973). Union of Soviet Socialist Republics. In I. Douglas-Wilson & G. McLachlen (Eds.), *Health service prospects: An international survey* (pp. 231-254). London: *The Lancet* and Nuffield Provincial Hospitals Trust.

World Health Organization. (1984). *Strengthening ministries of health for primary health care* (Publication No. 82). Geneva: Author.

World Health Organization and United Nations Children's Fund. (1978). *Primary health care* (Report of the International Conference on Primary Health Care). Geneva: Author.

Zhuk, A. P. (1976). *Public health planning in the USSR* (DHEW Publication No. NIH 76-999). Washington, DC: Fogarty International Center.

3

Should Single-Payer Advocates Support President Clinton's Proposal for Health Care Reform?

E. RICHARD BROWN

Many advocates of health care reform have worked for years—even decades—for national health insurance, a publicly run single-payer system that excludes the insurance industry. Should they now support President Clinton's proposal for a market-based reform, a system of coverage through private insurers and health plans?

Before we answer these questions, we must answer three other questions. First, what goals would a single-payer system achieve? Second, how well would the Clinton proposal achieve these goals? Third, what political alternatives are available?

EDITOR'S NOTE: This chapter is from the *American Journal of Public Health* (February 1994): 182-185. Reprinted with permission from the American Public Health Association and the author.

What Goals Would a Single-Payer System Achieve?

A single-payer system is, most simply, a public program that collects most of the money that goes into health care and pays it out to those who provide health services. A single-payer system is a means to achieving certain social goals; it is not an end in itself.

The Canadian system has many advantages that are attractive to Americans (Blendon & Taylor, 1989; Evans et al., 1989; Fuchs & Hahn, 1990; Hayes, Hayes, & Dykstra, 1993; U.S. Congressional Budget Office, 1993b; U.S. General Accounting Office, 1991; Woolhandler & Himmelstein, 1991). The American Public Health Association (APHA), for example, based its principles for national health reform on expectations of what a Canadian-style single-payer approach could achieve.

We can examine President Clinton's proposal against the standard of five broad reform principles established by single-payer advocates—universal coverage, comprehensive benefits, affordability, freedom of choice, and public accountability—and an additional criterion—political prospects for enactment. I also will assess how closely the President's proposal parallels S. 491, the Canadian-style proposal introduced into the U.S. Senate by Senator Paul Wellstone (D-MN), and how much it would improve current conditions.

How Well Would the Clinton Proposal Achieve These Goals?[1]

Principle 1. Universal Coverage

President Clinton's proposal covers all citizens and legal residents of the United States, thus extending coverage to the great majority of the 37 million uninsured Americans.

The Clinton proposal, like the present system, retains the financial link between health insurance coverage and the workplace, but for most people it breaks employers' control over choice of plans. Unlike the present system, it requires all employers to pay at least 80% of the cost of coverage. All workers, part-time as well as full-time, will receive coverage—an important reform for the millions of uninsured Americans, more than 8 of 10 of whom are workers and their families. This mandate is a critically important reform for those who are now uninsured and for the effectiveness of the health care system itself.

All nonelderly persons are required to enroll in health plans offered through their regional health alliance, a large health insurance purchasing cooperative. Very large firms (those with 5,000 or more employees) may form their own "corporate alliance" for their employees. Persons who change jobs will not need to change plans if they are covered by regional alliances, but those covered by corporate alliances may have to change plans and providers. The President's proposal also reforms the insurance market, banning the industry's most egregious practices such as excluding persons with preexisting conditions or not covering such conditions, charging higher rates to groups that include people with health problems, and redlining certain occupations.

In contrast to the Clinton proposal, a single-payer system eliminates much of the medical insurance market, rather than reforming it, and completely separates coverage from employment. It thereby ensures uninterrupted coverage, facilitates greater equity, permits greater efficiency in collecting revenues and paying providers, and asserts public control over the funds.

Despite their commitments to universal coverage, neither the Clinton proposal nor the Wellstone bill extends entitlement to undocumented immigrants. Explicit coverage of this population, it is widely believed, would politically doom any reform proposal.

Principle 2: Comprehensive Benefits

The Clinton proposal covers a comprehensive range of health services, including clinical preventive services, outpatient prescription drugs, dental care, and mental health and substance abuse services. The reform also establishes a system of home- and community-based long-term care for the elderly and nonelderly disabled, although it does not cover nursing homes.

The proposal limits some services, such as mental health and substance abuse treatment, rehabilitation services, and dental care for adults. The Wellstone bill benefits are more comprehensive.

The Clinton reform also proposes to increase health care access for underserved populations. Building on the extension of coverage to most of the population, access initiatives will provide additional funding targeted to increase the supply of practitioners and services in underserved rural and urban areas; provide supplemental services not covered by the required health benefits; and overcome cultural, linguistic, and other nonfinancial barriers to service.

The reform also includes public health initiatives intended to improve the health of communities. They promise to increase federal support for the public health infrastructure throughout the country, focusing additional funds and technical support on core public health functions, developing an integrated public health data system, and addressing preventable health problems prioritized at the community level. Health care reform will enable public health departments in many states to shift their emphasis from providing clinical services to public health activities, although this shift will be limited in states and areas with large numbers of undocumented immigrants who will not be covered by health alliances. Nevertheless, designation of "essential community providers" and continued funding for categorical programs, such as community and migrant health centers, may reduce current medical care financial burdens on most local health departments.

Although the public health reforms are very broad, they depend on the generosity of annual congressional appropriations. A public health "set aside" of a small percentage of medical care funds, advocated by APHA and included in the Wellstone bill and some other proposals (Brown, 1992), would provide more secure funding for disease prevention and health promotion.

These public health and health care access initiatives are important elements of a comprehensive health system, adding to the reform's development of long-term care and required benefits that, despite some limitations, are indeed comprehensive.

Principle 3: Affordability

President Clinton's proposal requires employees to pay up to 20% of the cost of their premiums, and it requires the self-employed and nonworkers to pay 100% of the cost. However, it subsidizes those with family incomes up to 150% of the federal poverty level, and it limits most families' share of premium costs to 3.9% of family income.

Employers must pay at least 80% of the health alliance's premium for each employee, but their costs are capped at 7.9% of payroll. Contributions of small firms with low average wages (fewer than 75 employees and average wages less than $24,000 a year) are capped at 3.5% to 7.1% of payroll.

To reduce financial barriers to using health services, the Clinton proposal, like the Wellstone bill, prohibits "balance billing"; doctors

x cannot
but

and other providers must accept as payment-in-full the fees paid by health plans. Required out-of-pocket cost sharing, however, may impose a significant burden on many low- and moderate-income people. Total annual out-of-pocket limits on cost sharing ($1,500 per individual and $3,000 per family) are not income related, although low-income people who enroll in a low-cost-sharing plan would be unlikely to reach these limits. People who choose the low-cost-sharing option (mainly health maintenance organizations [HMOs]) pay no deductible, but they face copayments of $10 per visit, except for preventive services, to the plan's network of doctors, and higher co-insurance if they use nonnetwork providers. Medicaid recipients pay $2 per visit, but other low-income persons must pay the full copayment. The proposal requires patients in a high-cost-sharing plan to pay 20% co-insurance for all benefits except preventive services, a general deductible, plus separate deductibles for outpatient prescriptions, dental care, and inpatient mental health services. Cost sharing is also substantial in the long-term care program. The Wellstone bill, in contrast, bans cost sharing of any kind for covered benefits, effectively eliminating all financial barriers to care.

adm

The Clinton reform's financing and administration lack the simplicity of a single-payer approach. Although the proposal streamlines the fee-for-service (FFS) payment system by requiring all insurers to use a single claims form, FFS plans probably will still rely on utilization review and other controls on volume of services to keep their premiums competitive. Only states that opt for prospectively budgeted payment systems, added onto universal fee schedules, would be likely to eliminate these costly utilization controls. Furthermore, as many as several hundred health alliances will be created throughout the country, adding substantial administrative costs to the system. Although the Clinton proposal is likely to reduce today's extraordinarily high administrative costs, it will not save nearly as much as would the Wellstone single-payer bill (Wellstone & Shaffer, 1993).

The President's proposal attempts to control total health spending by managing the health insurance market and by restraining the economic demand for health care. But it rejects the "pure" market approach advocated by managed-competition purists, which would bypass proven methods of controlling health spending and would compromise access and quality of care for low-income people (Rice, 1992; Rice, Brown & Wyn, 1993; U.S. Congressional Budget Office, 1993a). The Clinton proposal makes health care more affordable for individuals, business, and society by limiting the rate at which insurance premiums may increase, requiring health alliances to establish fee schedules used by all FFS health plans, giving states the authority to impose prospective budgets on FFS plans, and allowing health alliances to reject plans whose premiums exceed the average of all plans by more than 20%. States also have the power to establish a single-payer system, which can control health spending more effectively (U.S. Congressional Budget Office, 1993b).

To protect the public purse, the administration's proposal caps total subsidy funds for low-income families and employers. If costs exceed this subsidy cap, Congress must either vote for increased taxes (an unlikely event), reduce benefits or payments to plans (also unlikely because it would harm the middle class), or reduce subsidies (more likely because it would affect only lower-income groups). The reform's affordability for low-income people and their employers thus depends on both the growth of health spending and the number of people who need subsidies not exceeding the administration's expectations. The subsidy cap thus negates for low-income people the reform's entitlement to health care coverage.

Principle 4: Freedom of Choice

The Clinton proposal requires all persons entitled to the guaranteed benefit package to enroll in a health plan offered by their health alliance. Regional and corporate health alliances must offer a choice of plans and pay the plan the same premium for every person who enrolls in it—regardless of whether the enrollee's contribution is fully paid by employer-employee payments, is subsidized, or is paid by Medicaid. All low-income persons thus will be eligible to enroll in the same plans as the nonsubsidized population.

Enrollees who join a plan that charges less than the average premium may reduce their premium contribution below the standard 20% share, whereas those who join a more expensive plan pay the additional premium charges with their own funds, unless their employer pays this added cost. Enrollees probably will have to pay more for FFS plans and HMOs that provide more choice of doctors, shorter waits for appointments with primary care doctors and specialists, and more conveniently located providers. The higher premiums for such plans are likely to restrict lower-income enrollees to plans with more limited choice of providers. President Clinton's reform thus falls short of giving equal choice of health plans and doctors to all Americans.

The Clinton proposal, nevertheless, provides important protections of choice and access. It requires health alliances to pay health plans the weighted-average premium for every enrollee. Enrollees who are eligible for Medicaid or other subsidies will be able to choose among health plans that charge the weighted-average premium or less, reducing the potential for segmentation of the market into two tiers, a serious risk to low-income persons under most managed-competition strategies (Rice et al., 1993).

The President's proposal also includes substantial efforts to increase access to primary care. It provides more funding to encourage the development of health services in underserved urban and rural areas. Finally, the reforms prohibit discrimination by health plans, preventing plans from limiting choice by barring enrollees with health problems.

The Clinton proposal will give more choice of plans to many Americans whose employers offer their workers only one plan. But increasing numbers of Americans will find themselves in managed-care plans that limit their choice of physician to the plan's practitioners unless they can afford to pay more costly co-insurance to use nonplan doctors. The Clinton proposal merely accelerates the already rapid shift toward HMOs, whose enrollments have grown from 10.8 million in 1982 to 41.4 million in 1992 (Pear, 1993). The Wellstone bill, based on FFS payment, would probably reverse this trend and preserve the institution of private practice medicine.

Principle 5: Public Accountability

The reform establishes new structures and defined responsibilities that may increase accountability to enrollees and to public agencies. Plans must report data on access and quality. Health alliances will disseminate these data to inform individuals' enrollment decisions, a modest form of market accountability. Effective use of such information depends on enrollees having real alternative plans from which to choose and the financial ability to enroll in their preferred plan.

Health alliances will monitor plans' marketing materials, and plans must develop grievance procedures and due process protections for enrollees. Health alliances and the states would have substantial responsibilities and powers to monitor the quality of plans and to ensure that enrollees' rights are protected. How effectively they will do so is uncertain (Rice et al., 1993). Although health alliances must be nonprofit private or public agencies governed by a board of enrollees and employers, alliances may not adequately represent vulnerable populations. Their mission to control health spending may conflict with their quality assurance responsibilities, which are somewhat limited in any case. Although the Clinton proposal may incrementally increase health plans' accountability to enrollees and watchdog agencies, the Wellstone bill dramatically increases public accountability, including far stricter public regulation of HMOs (Wellstone & Shaffer, 1993).

Finally, the reform allows states to choose the single-payer option, a more fully accountable system than the managed-competition approach. States can eliminate intermediary insurers and pay directly doctors, hospitals, other providers, and organized health systems—all with just one waiver required to integrate Medicare beneficiaries into this system. This important option will permit states to develop health care financing systems that maximize equity and effective control over health care spending. Although the Wellstone bill would create a single-payer system throughout the country, the Clinton proposal would permit its development state by state, very much as Canada's national health insurance system began. Building on state experiences can demonstrate that this approach provides the best access to quality health care and effectively controls costs.

What Political Alternatives Are Available?

The Clinton proposal will have a far-reaching impact on the U.S. health care system, although it falls short of what a single-payer reform could achieve. Yet it is not sufficient merely to assess the proposal's strengths and weaknesses. After numerous failed efforts to enact national health insurance during this century, it is important to take stock of political possibilities.

We have arrived at a rare moment of opportunity for health care reform. Health care reform appears politically possible now because the major problems of the current system—rapidly rising costs and declining rates of coverage—hurt nearly every sector of American society. A large coalition of labor, senior citizen, and grassroots groups has forced health care reform onto the national political agenda, although the coalition lacks sufficient political power to enact a single-payer system. The traditional opponents of reform—organized medicine, the insurance industry, hospitals, and the drug

industry—are divided, with few points of political consensus beyond their opposition to dominance of the public sector; some even
support modest reforms. Important business sectors have concluded
that reform is essential because they cannot control health benefit
costs (Cantor et al., 1991). The President is strongly committed to
reform, and a unique First Lady is asserting political leadership. The
Democratic majorities in both houses of Congress are committed to
enacting reform, and the Republican minorities proclaim their support as well. Medicare and Social Security were enacted under similar conditions.

The United States is plagued, however, by a political system that
makes it difficult to enact significant reform. Our political institutions divide legislative and executive power, whereas controversial
reforms require concentrated political power. Our political parties
are weak and have little control over politicians. The country lacks
a strong labor movement and a labor party, elements historically
important in other countries' development of national health insurance (Morone, 1990; Navarro, 1989; Weir, Orloff, & Skocpol, 1988).

These political weaknesses foster interest group dominance of political institutions and impede enactment of progressive social programs. The ability of the congressional Democratic majorities to enact
the Clinton reforms is weakened by the Conservative Democratic Forum
members, who oppose employer mandates and government-imposed
cost controls. Republicans in both houses also oppose employer mandates and cost controls. Despite some employer support for reform,
small business groups are opposed to an employer mandate. Medical
interest groups are expected to spend many tens of millions of dollars
to defeat cost controls and other reform elements that they oppose.
Even the HMO industry, which can expect to prosper if the Clinton
reforms are enacted, opposes reform elements that would restrict their
premium charges or increase their public accountability (Pear, 1993).
The combined resources of the Clinton administration's health care
reform campaign, the administration's allies, and the single-payer
movement are likely to be overwhelmed by the media, direct mail, and
even the grassroots campaigns of the medical industries, small-business
coalitions, and conservative political groups.

Prospects for a single-payer system may improve if business and
other groups conclude that market reforms will not work and if they
overcome their ideological attachment to market solutions. By that
time, however, the political window may have closed. We may not
have a Democratic president and Democratic congressional majori-

ties, a combination that was essential to enacting Medicare and Social Security. Further suffering of the American people and further draining of the American economy may increase the need for reform, but they may not provide the necessary political alignments and opportunity to enact a single-payer reform.

• Single-payer advocates should continue to mobilize support for the Wellstone proposal, but they also should lobby to improve the Clinton proposal. They should insist that it provide full equality of choice regardless of income, expand benefits to meet more fully the needs of all people, and make cost sharing for premiums and services more affordable to those with low and moderate incomes. They especially should insist that the budget cap on subsidies be eliminated and that the public health and access initiatives be adequately funded. Some of the greatest political efforts in the Congress will be needed, however, to defend progressive elements already in the Clinton proposal, including the employer mandate and cost controls, both of which are essential to ensure universal coverage and limit the medical care drain on personal incomes and public coffers. Advocates will need to vigorously defend the right of states to choose freely the single-payer option.

• Advocates must ensure that the current political debate is between a national single-payer system, the Clinton proposal, and far more limited reforms. In the end, however, the real political choice is likely to be between the Clinton proposal and far more limited reforms. This should not be a difficult choice for single-payer advocates. Although President Clinton's proposal is not the ultimate fulfillment of health care reform, with some improvements, it will be an extraordinarily important reform that deserves and needs the support of single-payer advocates. •

Note

1. This analysis is based on the October 27, 1993, legislative draft of the Clinton proposal.

References

Blendon, R. J., & Taylor, H. (1989). Views on health care: Public opinion in three nations. *Health Affairs, 8*(1), 149-157.

Brown, E. R. (1992). Health USA—A national health program for the United States. *Journal of the American Medical Association, 267*(4), 552-558.

Cantor, J. C., Barrand, N. L., Desonia, R. A., Cohen, A. B., & Merrill, J. C. (1991). Business leaders' views on American health care. *Health Affairs, 10*(1), 98-105.

Evans, R. G., Lomas, J., Barer, M. L., Labelle, R. J., Fooks, C., Stoddart, G. L., Anderson, G. M., Feeny, D., Dafni, A., Torrance, G. W., & Tholl, W. G. (1989). Controlling health expenditures—The Canadian reality. *New England Journal of Medicine, 320*, 571-577.

Fuchs, V. R., & Hahn, J. S. (1990). How does Canada do it? A comparison of expenditures for physicians' services in the United States and Canada. *New England Journal of Medicine, 323*, 884-890.

Hayes, G. J., Hayes, S. C., & Dykstra, T. (1993). Physicians who have practiced in both the U.S. and Canada compare systems. *American Journal of Public Health, 83*, 1544-1548.

Morone, J. A. (1990). *The Democratic wish: Popular participation and the limits of American government.* New York: Basic Books.

Navarro, V. (1989). Why some countries have national health insurance, others have national health services, and the U.S. has neither. *Social Science and Medicine, 28*, 887-898.

Pear, R. (1993, October 18). HMO leaders express doubts on health plan. *The New York Times*, pp. A1, A9 (national edition).

Rice, T. (1992). Containing health care costs in the United States. *Medical Care Review, 49*(1), 19-65.

Rice, T., Brown, E. R., & Wyn, R. (1993). Holes in the Jackson Hole approach to health care reform. *Journal of the American Medical Association, 270*, 1357-1362.

U.S. Congressional Budget Office. (1993a). *Managed competition and its potential to reduce health spending.* Washington, DC: Author.

U.S. Congressional Budget Office. (1993b). *Single-payer and all-payer health insurance systems using Medicare's payment rates* (CBO staff memorandum). Washington, DC: Author.

U.S. General Accounting Office. (1991). *Canadian health insurance: Lessons for the United States* (GAO/HRD-91-90). Washington, DC: Author.

Weir, M., Orloff, A. S., & Skocpol, T. (1988). *The politics of social policy in the United States.* Princeton, NJ: Princeton University Press.

Wellstone, P. D., & Shaffer, E. R. (1993). The American Health Security Act—A single-payer proposal. *New England Journal of Medicine, 328*, 1489-1493.

Woolhandler, S., & Himmelstein, D. U. (1991). The deteriorating administrative efficiency of the U.S. health care system. *New England Journal of Medicine, 324*, 1253-1258.

4

Managing the Contradictions in the Clinton Health Plan

DAN E. BEAUCHAMP
PAUL M. AMBROSE

What needs to be understood about President Clinton's health care reform proposal, the Health Security Act, is that it is not one plan but two—with two different theories of cost control, two different theories of politics, and two different institutional psychologies.

Characteristically, the President has chosen to compromise by bridging the gulf between regulators and competitors among health care reformers. Each group sees in the President's plan some gains for their side: Competitors see managed competition and the rejection of certain direct controls as support for the market approach to health care reform. Regulators see the partial vindication of regulation in the national character of the program, in the idea of spending ceilings, and in the threat of direct controls. As might be expected, each group is deeply disturbed by the inclusion of features backed by the opposing camp. Rather than engendering broad-based support from both sides, the plan seems to be alienating many regulators, competitors, and even many of those advocating centrist policies. The plan has accentuated the fragmentation even within the Democratic Party.

Will the President's plan work? The answer won't be found in the debate between those advocating managed competition or a single-payer system. Rather, the answer lies in probing more deeply the new plan's hybrid institutional logic and in whether the President's decision to marry markets to traditional features of national health plans is institutionally viable.

How Health Plans Work

What do national health plans do, and how do they work? It is precisely because the President is attempting to modify substantially how health plans work that we need answers to this question. Oddly, our knowledge of this is very incomplete. National health plans provide universal coverage; they also provide mechanisms for limiting spending. As the U.S. General Accounting Office reports (Bowsher, 1991), national health plans also institute uniform payment rules for health care services, and they standardize insurance across a population, including the rules for eligibility, benefits, and estimating risk.

We argue that to know how national health plans work is to know them as institutions.[1] As institutions, health plans seek to introduce commonalty and similarity in how people think about, fix responsibility for, and hold together for health care (and across other conflicts in society). Health plans are dominant structures for community and social integration, and they have a profound influence on individual and group behavior.

a. As institutions, health plans *think*—which is to say that health plans foster sameness and similarity in how the public thinks about health care.[2] National health plans promote the view of health care as a social good rather than a commodity.[3]

b. Health plans *fix responsibility*. Health plans clarify the lines of responsibility between the public and public officials, and they narrow the choices faced by the electorate. In England and Canada, health officials are government officials; in Germany, responsibility for collective health security and stability in health care spending is shared by private and public officials (Reinhardt, 1990).

c. Health plans *hold people together*. They organize the power of the public around a common national institution. This public power acts as a countervailing force against the concentrated political power of health providers, drug manufacturers, and other special interest groups. Health plans mobilize national voter and taxpayer solidarity, thereby protecting the plan from political attack and unaffordable rates of growth.

d. Health plans *dominate*.[4] They seek to make preeminent the meanings and forms of common provision (as opposed to market competition) throughout the health sector, and they forbid or severely limit competition from rival forms of provision, such as private or commercial insurance.

Clinton's Two Plans

The Clinton plan contains elements of this classic form of health plan, in its goal of establishing a *national program* of universal entitlement; a single card; a common benefit; a stable, affordable growth path for the entire system; and so forth. However, it also contains a very different institutional logic for a national plan—a *managed competition program*. The critical issue is whether this combination of two strongly dominant and opposed institutional logics—markets versus communal logics—will result in protracted conflict within an unstable system, or a new, and unique, hybrid institution.

The National Program

The first part of the plan—the national program—was signaled when the President, in the middle of his October 1993 speech to Congress, held up the single national health insurance card. The card stands for far more than a simpler, easier-to-use system. It also symbolizes a national program of universal coverage, making insurance benefits uniform nationally, and setting national (and state) spending ceilings.

When Clinton held the card up, he came very close to FDR and Harry Truman and to the New Deal. The New Deal's theory of political reform was not just to change health care but also to change American politics (Beer, 1978). The national health plan would mobilize a powerful new majority and national opinion for universal coverage and for holding the line on spending. It would help shift the center of politics to a more progressive point.

This approach to universal health care was called, simply, *social insurance*, or national health insurance. National health insurance took as its goal the construction of a new, national institution whose purpose was to reform health care, and politics as well. Beer (1978), referring to Galbraith's (1952) notion of countervailing power, suggests that the new institution would be nonmarket in character and would define health care as a social good. The new institution would help serve as the countervailing political force to outweigh the power of the vested interests—to increase the "power of a numerous and disadvantaged group obliged to deal with a smaller and more advantaged group" (Beer, 1978, p. 11). The new institution was to be strong enough, and politically secure enough, to overcome regional, ideological, or racial divisions weakening public support for common provision.

National health plans are strategies for facing the health care system as a group—group methods are used to solve group problems and to foster group loyalty to common provision. President Clinton's national program would become the principal group backbone of the new plan. The national program's job is to instill in every American a sense of collective or group security guaranteed and protected by the national government. Although improving the health and the security of individuals are the plan's primary goals, the plan would, it is hoped, also help strengthen the "we," or communal, side of American society.

The national program appeals to the National Democrats in the President's party, Democrats who are still strong supporters of a strengthened role for the federal government in much of public policy. It also appeals to the health regulators inside and outside the Clinton administration, who take heart from the fact that, of the principles announced in the plan—security, simplicity, savings, choice, responsibility, and quality—all seem to be based on the national program.

Managed Competition

It is the second part of the Clinton speech—the managed competition program—that represents Clinton's fundamental break with the New Deal and his ambivalence toward its theory of politics and institutions.

Managed competition is a cost control strategy rooted in a more market, or individual, theory of national health care reform. It would use extensive government regulation to make these individual incentives dominant in the way we think about and act toward health care as a good. It relies on new organizations called *health alliances* (or buyers' cooperatives for small groups and businesses), accountable health plans (including managed care plans such as health maintenance organizations [HMOs]), and cost-conscious consumers to stem the health care system's high rate of inflation.

Managed competition is an attempt to radically alter the politics of health care and to recast the psychology at the core of national plans as institutions. Market power is created by moving much of the population into competing accountable health plans and by using the purchasing power of health alliances to bargain on behalf of public employers, small groups, and individual purchasers. Market power and financial incentives, instead of public power, would be used to break up the stranglehold that high-priced specialists, insurance companies, and hospitals have on American medical care.

Managed competition appeals to the New Democrat side of Bill Clinton. This is the side of the Democratic Party that is less national in its orientation, the side that favors competition and market-based solutions over central planning and public sector controls in solving problems, whenever possible. It is consistent with his plans to "reinvent government"—to propose novel and tradition-breaking solutions to old problems.

Realms of Contradiction

The Health Security Act is neither fish nor fowl: It is both the market and its power, and a new national program mobilizing public power. The Clinton strategy of "managing contradictions" by merging them into a new institution is both daring and highly risky.

We speak of the conflict between market and regulation as though they are ideal types, a view that is clearly overly simplistic. Managed competition relies on a high dose of regulation as well as market incentives, but the balance is tilted toward the market side and to a process designed to achieve somewhat uncertain ends. Therefore, we see managed competition as market-dominant.

Similarly, regulatory approaches typical of national plans are outcome oriented in that the results, such as overall health care expenditures, are intended and predetermined. This is not to say that national plans are devoid of competition but that they rely more heavily on direct control. The real issue is whether and how market and control systems, with their different dynamics and their natural struggle for dominance, can fit together.

Two Theories of Cost Control

The regulators' approach to cost control would emphasize national, state, and hospital budgets, or the old-fashioned strategy—setting hospital reimbursement rates and creating physician fee schedules. Those advocating a more market-dominant approach for the Clinton plan would prefer to let market incentives limit cost growth, and they resist budgets and price controls for hospitals and doctors. The differences in opinion within the managed competition camp warrant a brief diversion into the historical development of managed competition as theory.

Managed competition was invented by Alain Enthoven in the 1970s. Although not an advocate of a free market for health care (Enthoven, 1988b), Enthoven wanted to promote universal coverage financed through a new kind of social insurance and with care provided through a delivery system driven by market forces (Starr, 1993).

Enthoven took up the growing interest in HMOs, initiated under the Nixon administration, and made it bolder. HMOs would compete with each other for customers, based on an annual, prospective fee to cover all costs for each patient. HMOs would be at risk to deliver that care for the promised annual price. Citizens or corporations who wanted more expensive conventional care (fee-for-service) would have to pay for it, out-of-pocket and without tax benefit.

In the mid-1980s, Enthoven (1986) modified his plan to add sponsors (later to be called *health insurance purchasing cooperatives* and health alliances)—new organizations that would pool individuals and groups into larger purchasing units to make insurance more equitable and to distribute purchasing power more widely. Aggregating individuals and small groups into larger insurance purchasing pools would give them the leverage needed to negotiate better premium rates with insurers.

Enthoven's ideas were likely strongly influenced by a book written earlier by Charles Schultze (1977), a moderate Democrat who had served under Lyndon Johnson and who was President Carter's chairman of the Council on Economic Advisers. Schultze advocated the use of the market to "reduce the need for compassion, patriotism, brotherly love, and cultural solidarity" (p. 17). He suggested that without relinquishing their social goals of protecting the environment or rebuilding the slums, the Democrats ought to use market incentives, rather than direct government regulation. In the antiregulatory climate of the period, a lot of people read Schultze's book and quoted it.

Schultze seemed to urge Democrats to forget their suspicion of the market and to be both pro-social policy and promarket. By keeping the social policy ends of national Democrats and by using the market as the means, Schultze seemed to have shown a way for the party to move into the future.

The trouble with Enthoven's idea of managed competition is that he used the market not only as a means but also as an end. In a major part of his plan that has never changed, Enthoven (1988a) makes efficiency, not cost control, a goal of the national health plan. "The ' essence of *managed competition* is the use of available tools to structure cost-conscious consumer choice between health plans in the pursuit of equity and efficiency in health care financing and delivery" (p. 28).

· *Efficiency*, as a technical economic term, denotes the competitive character of markets and the avoidance of wasteful allocation of resources. It doesn't always mean the lowest possible cost that can be squeezed out of health care spending.[5] An efficient health care system would approach that level of spending achievable by competitive markets in which informed consumers choose cost-consciously. Clearly, Enthoven believes that that level would not be as low as the one achieved by direct regulation but would sharply reduce the present rate of growth in health spending (Enthoven, 1988a).

The President's chief advisers on managed competition, Paul Starr and Walter Zelman, reject the outright use of broad-based and direct price controls, but they part company with Enthoven in that they advocate global limits on expenditure growth as a backup for competition. They claim that the stakes are too great to risk a failure of cost controls that are strictly market based (Starr & Zelman, 1993).

> Some may ask why, if we believe competition will work, we also see a need for global budgets. One might as soon ask the designers of a

new airplane if their specification of a second engine demonstrates a
lack of confidence in the first. Good designs often build in redun-
dancy. If competition is a complete success, the provisions for global
budgets will turn out to be superfluous. But, given past experience,
a backup system of cost control seems prudent. Moreover, if employers are going to give up control of health benefits, they are going to
expect strong guarantees of cost containment. Global budgets are that
guarantee. (pp. 13-14)

The critical institutional point is that the President's new plan
does not resolve finally this dispute—he does not declare whether
market efficiency or direct cost control is dominant. Instead, he
proposes a compromise: Managed competition will be tried first,
with direct regulation serving as a backup. According to an article
by Paul Starr (1993), rate setting would be used only for fee-for-
service provider plans that remain in the reformed health care insurance system.

Two Kinds of Politics

There are also two kinds of political power in the Clinton plan.
Although managed competition mixes regulation and market incentives, the market side is clearly dominant. According to New Democrats, one of the chief virtues of market-based policies is that they
shift the onus for painful social change away from politics and
elected officials and more to impersonal market forces.

For example, one of the most attractive features of Enthoven's
managed competition model, as a form of politics, is that it would
allow the market to hold down spending each year and to sharply
shrink the demand for medical specialists in the American health
care system. If accountable health plans grow in influence in most
health care markets and if, as predicted, they replace specialists with
primary care practitioners, the plans, not the politicians, would
revolutionize the balance of specialists and generalists in American
medicine. President Clinton's approach also seeks to limit or adjust
the mix of primary care providers and specialists graduating from
medical schools through the end of the decade and beyond.

A more control-dominant plan would leave little to process and
chance, and the results might be more immediate. The federal government would specify in advance how much money must be put

into the system and the appropriate mix of primary care physicians and specialists. '

Enthoven (1993) argues that our politics are incapable of making difficult choices and that limiting spending will mean closing hospitals and putting surgeons out of work. As Enthoven notes, quoting Charles Schultze (1977), "Under the social arrangements of the private market, those who may suffer losses are not usually able to stand in the way of change. As a consequence, efficiency-creating changes are not seriously impeded" (Enthoven, 1993, p. 40).

Government controls, on the other hand, tend to freeze industries in place. Thus we find it extraordinarily difficult to close an unneeded school or air base. Actually, although it is true that we do find it difficult to close military bases or to cut defense spending, we are, in fact, doing both of those things (Tallon & Nathan, 1992), and we have done both of those things at many different times in our history.

This is not the only way the Clinton plan proposes to overturn the traditional politics of national health plans. The political logic of national health insurance, and of Clinton's national program, is to nationalize political conflict. But managed competition would make the distribution of resources and health risks an explosive state and local issue as well (Fossett, 1993). For example, in New York, the state would have to decide whether to combine the city and the surrounding suburban counties into one large health alliance, to help spread the high costs of the city's medical centers and the costs of treating its poor and sick residents, or whether to create a single state alliance. (New York has many citizens who want a single-payer system for the state; New York Health, a Canadian-style health plan has passed the New York Assembly.) The upstate versus downstate, Long Island versus New York City, are the traditional fault lines of New York politics, and, like other states, New York will likely have great difficulty in resolving these conflicts unless the national government intervenes more forcefully than the health alliance system now contemplates.

Two Psychologies

As institutions, national health plans influence how individuals and groups think about and behave within the health care system. Traditionally, health plans form what might be called *taxpayer solidarity*. Consumers, as taxpayers and premium payers, are united in opposing significant increases in their spending on health care, just as taxpayers oppose general increases in taxes. Under taxpayer solidarity, the group, including both the sick and the healthy, holds together in resisting spending increases beyond a fixed amount.

Clinton's national program moves toward taxpayer solidarity with its stated goals of limiting overall spending and in treating the sick and the healthy on an equal basis. Clinton's national program wants Americans to wear their taxpayer hats, to see health care as a social good, to see spending as necessitating collective limits, to develop solidarity with the sick and the elderly, and to hold together in loyalty for the new plan. In other words, the national program fosters a "we" or more communal psychology.

The opposing psychology, that underlying managed competition, is the psychology of the cost-conscious consumer—a "me" psychology. Managed competition and its advocates among competitors want each American to wear a consumer's hat, to see health care as a commodity much like automobiles, to shop for bargains, to distrust government, to blame even the new plan for interfering with the "health market," and to question why the healthy should pay as much as the sick for health coverage.

It is not clear whether the Clinton health plan designers have given much thought to which of the two psychologies built into their plan should be, or will prove to be, dominant. Perhaps they envision a new psychology, one that blends to the two approaches, a kind of public consumer—a citizen of two minds who understands that he or she is both united with other citizens, whether sick or healthy, in supporting ceilings on spending for health care and at the same time looking out for himself or herself, shopping around for the most efficient health plan, one that does a good job of avoiding too many sick or poor people.

However, this rosy scenario seems psychologically naive. The health care consumer will be told by accountable health plans and insurance companies that lower costs depend on competition not government prices; indeed, the two will be seen as incompatible. This is already occurring, as national advertising campaigns from the insurance industry (at the present writing) are all over television opposing direct price controls. Even Enthoven has rejected the President's Health Security Act because of its reliance on government-imposed price controls. Many New Democrats have expressed support for a plan proposed by Rep. Jim Cooper (D-TN), who claims that his more market-oriented version of managed competition is the real middle ground in the reform debate, and he charges that the Clinton plan relies too heavily on government regulations and mandates.

Three Possible Outcomes

We see three plausible outcomes of Clinton's union of market and public institution: the Happy Marriage, the Great Divorce, and the Marriage From Hell.

The Happy Marriage

The most optimistic scenario for American health care reform is that competition and regulation will come together to form one plan, not as separate realms, but as logics that are increasingly seen as interdependent. Although we remain deeply skeptical, this could happen. There is an increasingly influential school in economics that sees regulation as a powerful tool for promoting efficiency and sees the need for studying not just competitive markets but also institutions. This could be the ground for compromise—a Happy Marriage.

We might see competitive health care markets operating within a framework of regulation that ensures fair competition while protecting social and public interests. In this version of the Happy Marriage, the ideological conflict begins to die down, competitors consent to global budgets, and single-payer advocates become reconciled with a reasonable form of competition. The struggle for dominance between market and communal modes of provision proves to be a false issue.

Henry Aaron (1993), the Brookings economist and former assistant secretary for planning and evaluation of the Department of Health, Education and Welfare under President Carter, argues that there is a way to marry budgets and managed competition: by putting hospitals on budgets and allowing accountable health plans to compete for the rest of the market. Such an arrangement would likely be far more plausible and realistic as a cost control strategy, and it would place a powerful and expensive part of the health system under direct spending limitation. It would also help place a more marked boundary between primary and routine care on the one hand and the hospital sector on the other, a strategy that is central to cost control in most European systems.

We suspect that Aaron's idea would represent a substantial improvement in the President's plan, precisely because it would measurably strengthen the regulator's hand and make the direct control of growth in the health sector dominant in minds of both the public and hospital managers. It would clearly reduce the scope of competition (and threats to regulatory dominance). Whether it would prove enough to secure a happy marriage of market and communal incentives is hard to predict.

The political scenario of the Happy Marriage, or the belief that competition and regulation can be joined at the spine, is, in our view, the most unrealistic of the three scenarios. Those predicting a Happy Marriage scenario include Clinton's White House advisers Ira Magaziner, Paul Starr, and Walter Zelman. All apparently believe that the opposition of market and government that shapes the health care debate everywhere in the world, including here, is a figment of our collective imaginations.

Unfortunately, the political conditions for merging competition and regulation in health care hardly exist in the United States. Both competitors and regulators view the opposing camp with deep suspicion. The embrace of competition by many moderate and conservative Democrats is not because of vast experience with managed care and HMOs—indeed, in most of the American South, HMOs are almost nonexistent. In fact, the track record of managed care in limiting spending is mixed, at best (Congressional Budget Office, 1993; Rice, Brown, & Wyn, 1993).

The heart of the matter is this: In both markets and communal realms, there is a powerful strain toward dominance. If market mechanisms are to be introduced successfully into common provision, it must occur where the logic of communal provision is strongly dominant and widely accepted and understood among the public, and where public officials across the two parties are in accord.

The Clinton reformers are right to attack the idea that markets are pure examples of competition and that communal realms contain no competitive dynamics; the future promises market and communal realms that have mixed incentives. But the Clinton plan refuses to clarify which is dominant—market or community—thereby encouraging intense political conflict with deep ideological roots throughout its design and implementation.

The Great Divorce

The second scenario, the Great Divorce, is actually the more hopeful one. This is likely the outcome predicted by many within the

Clinton camp, such as Bruce Vladeck and Judy Feder of the Department of Health and Human Services, who have in the past, at least, indicated that they are much more strongly proregulation than President Clinton's plan. This camp believes that major elements of managed competition will be tried and will fail and that a more traditional system of controls—waiting in the wings as "backup"—will be the final system. That is, the national program and its direct controls will prove dominant.

This is a more likely scenario than the Happy Marriage, in our view. As opposition from the wide variety of interests materializes over the next several months, the President will likely be forced to rely, increasingly, on the national program and its far more simple architecture to sell his approach. Presidents need simple themes and ideas to sell a complex plan. The President is already highlighting the importance of the threat to reform from "special interests." To swing public opinion behind his plan, he will likely stress more and more the need to limit what insurers, hospitals, and doctors charge— a core tenet of the regulators. He will stress the single card and government accountability—another regulator's point. He will likely continue to defend the marketplace and competition as critical, but as attacks grow against the way managed care plans limit choice, he clearly will have to mute the managed competition side of the plan. Thus the President's need to mobilize public opinion may threaten managed competition more than it does regulation.

The Great Divorce could happen. If the Clinton plan passes and costs continue to escalate, it becomes a likely outcome. Over time, as costs continue to rise, the President could gradually move his plan to a de facto victory for the regulators.

The Marriage From Hell

We should also all be worried that something more bleak and unpromising might develop—this is the Marriage From Hell. The President's strategy of keeping global budgets in the closet as a backup, just in case competition fails, could very well lead to such a scenario—a forced marriage of suspicious and resentful partners.

In this scenario, neither the regulators nor the competitors will win a decisive victory—competition half succeeds and half fails. Cost growth falls off but not enough to reduce the increasing panic among federal and state officials struggling with budgets. Neither side proves dominant. The goals of achieving universal coverage and eliminating Medicaid are stretched out. Medicare is cut, but private insurance controls prove less effective in stemming spending. The regulators want to move hospitals to budgets, but the competitors want more years to show that competition can work—if only it is given a chance. The United States approaches 20% of gross domestic product (GDP) on health care spending. Health economists feverishly pen articles arguing that a high level of spending on health care is not necessarily the enemy of economic prosperity.

The public will likely be terminally confused. Given the constant fighting that occurs between competitors and regulators, they will wonder what their roles will be, and for good reason. Are they to stand fast, as taxpayers, and demand global budgets and other direct controls, or are they to throw their lot in with the competitors?

The competitors, in particular, will likely take their case to the public and to the media. Along with the tidal wave of advertising for health plans that managed competition will likely bring, the competitors will likely also appeal to the public, as cost-conscious consumers, that their way is better.

Meanwhile, the surge in public spending puts more and more pressure on curbing Medicare and Social Security. The original appointees to the Clinton administration begin to leave. The virtues of a two-tier or three-tier health care system are openly discussed. Health reform lies mostly dead in the water, and millions of Americans are stranded in huge health plans, watching their choices go up in smoke.

How the President Can Strengthen His Plan

The most dramatic thing the President could do to strengthen his plan would be to make Medicare the platform for the national program instead of leaving it outside. This, coupled with other changes, would make it clearer that the national program is dominant among the two parts of the system.[6]

We suspect that it may be already too late for this big a change, at least for now. The President's compromise has mobilized powerful forces for a procompetitive system, and we will likely have to live with this as a major feature of the plan for the next period of years.

The fallback position would seem to be to assure that the national program and regulation as a cost control strategy become clearly dominant within the plan. The most important step to achieve this goal would be to begin to prepare now to place hospitals on budgets. Although procompetition forces will resist the move to confine competition to the primary care sector, this seems a reasonable compromise. This system, coupled with direct ceilings on spending for primary care each year, would likely be a substantial improvement over the President's present design.

Also, the President should make the new information technology much more central to his plan. The new clearinghouse and card technologies may introduce a capacity for change and innovation into the system that will far surpass what more traditional forms of competition will accomplish. Indeed, standard competition between plans will likely hinder, rather than help, the development of the information highway for health care. The new technology will enable the President to quickly institutionalize the single card in the new system, will provide dramatic reductions in paperwork, and will provide a sharp increase in data for controlling health care spending (Beauchamp, 1993; Beauchamp & Rouse, 1990).

More than anything, we need to know that in marrying markets and national health plans we are attempting something very difficult and filled with unknowns. Albert Hirschman (1970), in *Exit, Voice, and Loyalty,* argued that the combined effects of markets (exit) and regulation and monopoly (voice) need to be far better understood. Mixing the two offers opportunities but also many pitfalls. Indeed, in a somber conclusion to his book, Hirschman argues that there is no "firm prescription for some optimal mix of exit or voice . . . it is very unlikely that one could specify a most efficient mix of the two that would be stable over time" (p. 124). If political leaders are hopeful that managed competition, combined with direct regulation, will prove more stable over time and more ideal for the American political context, Hirschman offers them little hope.

Notes

1. We appreciate that the institutional perspective that lies behind our chapter represents something of a departure from the way we ordinarily talk about national health plans. However, it seems logical and urgent that we think more clearly about how health plans become "institutionalized," or how they instill a common pattern of beliefs, values, and practices across a huge sector such as health care. The literature on institutionalism is too vast to summarize here. The classic study is Philip Selznick's *Leadership in Administration* (1957). See the critical review in Charles Perrow's *Complex Organizations: A Critical Essay* (1986). See in the same book (Perrow, 1986) Perrow's

excellent discussion of the contributions of March and Simon (1958) and the concept of "bounded rationality," which has reworked institutional models and all organizational theory. There is a strong revival of institutionalism or "neoinstitutionalism" (see Friedland & Alford, 1991). As Glaser (1993) correctly notes, the economists and others who were so influential in the New Deal period were all institutionalists.

2. The phrase "how institutions think" is from Mary Douglas's (1986) fine book, *How Institutions Think*. Douglas argues that institutions provide the rules and the classification schemes for citizens to think about the practices they share in common. Although her book is a scathing attack on the "economic" or "individualistic" theory of institutions, it actually stands somewhat in the mainstream of contemporary thinking about the functions of institutions in "bounding rationality."

3. The notion that health care is a social good, which is a staple of the social insurance and social ethics literature, takes on a new twist here. Health plans as institutions have the job of promoting the view of health care as social goods. The perspective here is that new health plans, like new policies, promote new patterns of thinking. More than this, the institutionalist perspective that we are advocating sees new policies and new institutions promoting a new pattern of politics. See the classic statement of this position in T. Lowi (1964).

4. The idea of dominance is taken from several sources. Michael Walzer (1983) employs the idea in his *Spheres of Justice*, to imply the ways in which separate spheres exhibit symbolic coherence, governing modes of provision (commodities versus communal goods) and are defended against rival symbols and modes. Parallel ideas are found in Roger Freidland and Robert R. Alford's (1991) "Bringing Society Back In: Symbols, Practices and Institutional Contradictions." Also, Fred Hirsch (1975), in *The Social Limits to Growth*, uses the idea of "commodity bias" in much the same way as "dominance."

5. Enthoven (1988b), in his *Theory and Practice of Managed Competition in Health Care Finance*, says that efficiency "should not be confused with minimizing or containing health care expenditures. . . . [A] lower percentage of GNP spent on health care does not necessarily mean greater efficiency. If the reduced share of GNP is achieved by denial or postponement of services that consumers would value at more than their marginal cost, then efficiency is not achieved or enhanced by the cut in spending" (p. 11).

6. As the 80-year-old mother of one of us (Beauchamp) put it not long ago, "I don't understand all of this. Why don't they just extend Medicare to all Americans?" We would only add, Why didn't the Clinton administration consider some variant of this, including the American Association for Retired Persons Plan (AARP) (1992) of using private insurance, and conforming it to a new and strengthened Medicare program? (See also Intriligator in this volume.) Why Clinton ignored this option is a mystery, especially when it could be accomplished by using private insurance as proposed in the AARP plan.

We won't know the whole story, perhaps ever, but we suspect that it comes down to a few key facts. Clinton, as a former governor and as a southern governor active in the National Governors Association, was well aware that there wasn't much enthusiasm among many moderate and conservative Democrats in the House of Representatives for a more unified, national program. Certainly, the doctors and the hospitals would not welcome an all-Medicare program, largely because it is known to have effective methods for limiting spending.

What helped Clinton in this choice is that the Medicare option was overshadowed by the pro-Canada forces. Whatever the gains that came with equating a single-payer approach with the Canadian health care system, it became a convenient foil for the competitors fighting off an effective, popular alternative to managed competition. Glaser (1993) points to the American debate surrounding Canada's public financing method as indicative of "the poverty of US policy thinking" (p. 981). He aptly labels this argument a red herring. It would have been far more difficult for Clinton, and for southern Democrats, to attack Medicare as the vehicle for reform.

References

Aaron, H. J. (1993, Fall). Budget limits and managed competition: Allies, not antagonists. *Health Affairs, 12*(3), 132-136.

American Association of Retired Persons. (1992). *Healthcare America*. Washington, DC: AARP National Legislative Council.

Beauchamp, D. (1993, March). *MacPlan: Managing the contradictions of health care reform*. Paper presented at Health Care Reform in Rural Areas, a Conference on President Clinton's Health Care Reform Plan, sponsored by the Robert Wood Johnson Foundation, Little Rock, AR.

Beauchamp, D., & Rouse, R. (1990). Universal New York Health Care: A single-payer strategy linking cost control and universal access. *New England Journal of Medicine, 323*(10), 640-644.

Beer, S. H. (1978). In search of a new public philosophy. In A. King (Ed.), *The new American political system* (pp. 5-44). Washington, DC: American Enterprise Institute for Public Policy Research.

Bowsher, C. A. (1991, April 17). *U.S. health care spending: Trends, contributing factors, and proposals for reform* (Statement before the Committee on Ways and Means of the House of Representatives). Washington, DC: General Accounting Office.

Congressional Budget Office. (1993). *Managed competition and its potential to reduce health spending*. Washington, DC: U.S. Congress.

Douglas, M. (1986). *How institutions think*. Syracuse, NY: Syracuse University Press.

Enthoven, A. C. (1986). Managed competition in health care and the unfinished agenda. *Health Care Financing Review, 5*(Suppl.), 105-119.

Enthoven, A. C. (1988a). Managed competition: An agenda for action. *Health Affairs, 7*(2), 25-47.

Enthoven, A. C. (1988b). *Theory and practice of managed competition in health care finance*. Amsterdam: North-Holland.

Enthoven, A. C. (1993). The history and principles of managed competition. *Health Affairs, 12*(Suppl.), 24-48.

Fossett, J. W. (1993). *States and national health reform: Implementation problems and prospects*. Working paper, SUNY at Albany, Department of Public Administration and Policy, Nelson A. Rockefeller College of Public Affairs and Policy, Albany, NY.

Freidland, R., & Alford, R. R. (1991). Bringing society back in: Symbols, practices, and institutional contradictions. In W. W. Powell & P. J. DiMaggio (Eds.), *The new institutionalism in organizational analysis* (pp. 232-263). Chicago: University of Chicago Press.

Galbraith, J. K. (1952). *American capitalism: The concept of countervailing power*. Boston: Houghton Mifflin.

Glaser, W. (1993). The United States needs a health system like other countries. *Journal of the American Medical Association, 270*(8), 980-984.

Hirsch, F. (1975). *The social limits to growth.* Cambridge, MA: Harvard University Press.

Hirschman, A. O. (1970). *Exit, voice and loyalty.* Cambridge, MA: Harvard University Press.

Intriligator, M. D. (1993). A way to achieve national health insurance in the United States: The Medicare expansion proposal. *American Behavioral Scientist, 36*(6), 709-723.

Lowi, T. (1964). American business, public policy, case-studies, and political theory. *World Politics, 16,* 675-715.

March, J. G., & Simon, H. A. (1958). *Organizations.* New York: John Wiley.

Perrow, C. (1986). *Complex organizations: A critical essay.* New York: McGraw-Hill.

Reinhardt, U. E. (1990). *West Germany's health-care and health-insurance system: Combining universal access with cost control* (Report prepared for U.S. Bipartisan Commission on Comprehensive Health Care).

Rice, T., Brown, E. R., & Wyn, R. (1993). Holes in the Jackson Hole approach to health care reform. *Journal of the American Medical Association, 270*(11), 1357-1362.

Schultze, C. (1977). *The public use of private interest.* Washington, DC: Brookings Institution.

Selznick, P. (1958). *Leadership in administration.* New York: Harper & Row.

Starr, P. (1993, Winter). Healthy compromise: Universal coverage and managed competition under a cap. *American Prospect,* pp. 44-52.

Starr, P., & Zelman, W. (1993). Bridge to compromise: Competition under a budget. *Health Affairs, 12*(Suppl.), 7-23.

Tallon, J., & Nathan, R. P. (1992). A federal/state partnership for health system reform. *Health Affairs, 11*(4), 7-16.

Walzer, M. (1983). *Spheres of justice.* New York: Basic Books.

5

A Way to Achieve National Health Insurance in the United States

The Medicare Expansion Proposal

MICHAEL D. INTRILIGATOR

The Crisis in Health Care in the United States

The current crisis in health care financing and delivery in the United States has made health care reform once again a subject of considerable interest and debate (Aaron, 1991; Lundberg, 1991; Mariner, 1992). Health care costs have soared dramatically in recent years. From the viewpoint of the national economy, the cost of health care, which had represented about 6% of national income in 1950, has

AUTHOR'S NOTE: The author acknowledges, with gratitude, the valuable suggestions of Lu Ann Aday, Evelyn Cederbaum, Stephen Cederbaum, Eric W. Fonkalsrud, Milton Roemer, Pauline Vaillancourt Rosenau, and Stuart Schweitzer and the research assistance of Jill Perry.

risen to the point where it now represents over 14% and is still rising. In fact, health care represents a significantly higher proportion of national income in the United States than it represents in any other industrialized nation. U.S. health care spending was over $840 billion in 1992, up 11.5% from 1991, and, according to the Department of Commerce, it is expected to grow by 12% to 15% annually during the next 5 years unless there are significant changes in the health care delivery system.

From the viewpoint of industry, employers have frequently, and with good reason, cited the cost of providing health insurance to their employees as a major factor in the "restructuring" layoffs in large firms in the 1990s. In many industries, health care costs are among the highest reported costs, and these costs have risen to the point where some companies simply cannot afford to include the cost of health care as part of their cost of business. In fact, recent huge reported losses posted by General Motors, Ford, and other large U.S. corporations are largely due to the costs of covering long-term benefits for active and retired employees, and business pays more than a third of total health care costs (see the chapter in this volume by Linda Bergthold). High health costs are also a significant factor in the slower growth of small business as compared to earlier periods. It is also a factor in the lack of competitiveness of U.S.-made products and services as compared to those of other industrialized nations because U.S. employers must pay for health care while they are competing with firms in other nations in which health costs are covered under a more broadly financed system of national health insurance.

It is important that this crisis in health care financing be seen not simply as one of financing and costs but as a real problem in the allocation of resources to health, reflecting the organization of the health care delivery system. The monetary measures in terms of prices and costs are just the financial manifestation of a more fundamental problem, namely, the failure to establish an efficient system of health care delivery for the entire population. The problem of lack of access is another aspect of the failure to establish an efficient system of health care delivery. This failure stems, to a large extent, from the many complicated and varied forms of health insurance, both private and public, that currently exist. In particular, it is largely a consequence of the heavy reliance on employer-provided, private health insurance in the United States. Many of the monetary and real problems in the system of health care financing and delivery stem, directly or indirectly, from this reliance on employer-provided health insurance, so these problems would not be alleviated by those currently proposed policy initiatives that retain this system, including managed competition.

This chapter analyzes the problems with the present system, discusses the various reform proposals currently under discussion, and proposes an alternative system of health care reform built around an expansion of the current Medicare program. The Medicare program is an ideal starting point from which to build an alternative system of health care delivery because it is a national system that is already in place and working, one that has been accepted by hospital and physician providers, and one that is regarded as successful by all parties. The Medicare expansion proposal would build a national health insurance system via phased changes in the age of eligibility for the Medicare program, starting with the enrollment of preschool children, until eventually it would cover the entire population. It would involve both a single payer and a single collector for basic health care, and it would be financed and managed by the government through the Social Security program. The chapter considers the issues of cost containment, access, and quality of care under this reform of the health care system and discusses the issues of single payer versus multiple payer and single collector versus multiple collector. It presents a specific proposal on how the present Medicare system might be expanded in phases so that it gradually becomes a system of national health insurance by the year 2000, and it suggests a role for the private insurance industry under such a system. It concludes that now may be an appropriate time to consider such a fundamental restructuring of the health care delivery system, which would eliminate its inherent problems of constantly escalating costs and ever more limited access.

Employer-Provided Health Insurance

The U.S. system of health care financing relies heavily on employer-provided health insurance, in which employers pay health insurance premiums. This system is one that began during World War II when, because of wartime restrictions, employers could not raise wages. As an alternative, they began to provide fringe benefits, including health insurance, that were accepted in spite of wartime wage and price controls. Health insurance grew rapidly, and the majority of the U.S. population is now insured by private carriers. Currently, the United States is the only advanced industrialized nation, other than South Africa, not to have a governmental system of national health insurance.

Unfortunately, this system of employer-provided health insurance has several inherent problems. Its basic problem is that it is not universal and thus leads to limited access to health care. Because it is a voluntary system of health insurance, those who are not enrolled—currently, some 37 million people—are left uninsured. In fact, it has been estimated that more than 60 million people are without health insurance benefits at some time during each year (Weil, 1992). The uninsured include the unemployed and people in jobs without health insurance benefits, especially lower-paid jobs, transitory jobs, and jobs in small firms. In fact, the number of uninsured people is growing due to the restructurings of large firms, which leads many to lose their health insurance coverage; the shift from full-time work, with health benefits included, to part-time, temporary, and independent consultant type work, without such benefits; and the fact that many entry-level jobs do not have health insurance included as a fringe benefit. Employer-provided health insurance can also terminate after retirement, and there is no guarantee of its continuity when people change jobs. There is also active discrimination against those with health conditions that could potentially lead to expensive treatment, with some insurers unwilling to provide coverage for bad risks. In addition, under this type of insurance, health benefits can be reduced or eliminated altogether without notification, even retroactively, by the employer and the carrier, as seen in recent cases involving reduced coverage for AIDS or the elimination of benefits for retirees (Mariner, 1992). The health insurance trade association, the Health Insurance Industry Association, appears to have recognized some of these problems in its call, in December 1992, for a new federal law that would require universal coverage with a government-defined essential set of benefits that all insurers would agree to provide regardless of medical history (Pear, 1992).

Another basic problem with the current system of employer-provided health insurance is its cost to the national economy and to industry. As a result of employer-provided health insurance there have been enormous increases in the demand for medical care without offsetting increases in supply or controls over health care use. The increases in demand follow directly from the nature of the insurance program. If consumers pay only a small fraction of the cost of health care, they are given an incentive to consume as much as possible. At the same time, if providers, whether hospitals or physicians, are paid for virtually all services rendered, they are given an incentive to prescribe services to the point of waste, as in the case of defensive medicine stemming from fear of malpractice suits. The result is an outward shift in the demand curve for health services due to the behavior of both consumers and providers under the current system of insurance. Although there has also been some outward shift in the supply curve for health services as a result of the establishment of additional providers and increases in their efficiency, the shift in demand has basically outstripped the shift in supply, the result being huge increases in the prices and costs of health care (Intriligator, 1981). There have also been substantial increases in the overhead costs of providing coverage without offsetting increases in efficiency. The result of both these trends has been very substantial increases in the cost of medical care at both national and industry levels.

Precisely because of the increases in costs to employers of providing health insurance, many employers are trying to save money by reducing or eliminating certain benefits or increasing copayments and deductibles. The result has been an erosion of the level of coverage in the system and a shift of costs to the employees or to government programs, including state Medicaid and county health programs, which are themselves underfinanced. Nevertheless, employer-provided health insurance premiums continue to rise at more than twice the overall rate of inflation, frequently by more than 20% a year.

Yet another problem with the current system is that it involves substantial subsidies because health benefits provided through employment are not taxed and health insurance costs are fully deductible for employers in computing their taxes. The result is that employers are given an incentive to buy too much health insurance via regressive tax subsidies. All of these problems exist in the current system of employer-provided health insurance, and most would not be eliminated by those reforms that retain this system. These problems could, however, be overcome by a system of national health insurance that would eliminate the tax subsidies altogether. Rather than patchwork fixes, the problems with employer-provided health insurance call for fundamental reform, with the current system replaced by a new system of national health insurance.

Current Proposals for
Reforming the Health Care System

Some are calling for various incremental reforms of the health care system to make it more cost-effective and equitable (Lundberg, 1991). Others, however, are calling for more radical reform that would lead to the introduction of a system of national health insurance (Berki, 1990; Etheredge, 1990; Fuchs, 1991; Himmelstein & Woolhandler, 1989; Kinzer, 1990; Relman, 1989; Weil, 1992). A major issue, however, is precisely how to establish such a system, given the complicated and varied forms of health insurance that currently exist and, in particular, the current heavy reliance on employer-provided health insurance.

Many of the proposed reforms of the health care delivery system retain employer-provided health insurance (American College of Physicians, 1992; Bipartisan Commission on Comprehensive Health Care [the Pepper Commission], 1990; National Leadership Commission on Health Care, 1989; Pauly, Danzon, Feldstein, & Hoff, 1991; Simmons, Rhoades, & Goldberg, 1992). Several seek universal coverage within the system by requiring employers to offer health insurance and providing various additional requirements to cover those still not otherwise included. One such proposal, "pay or play," would require employers either to provide such health insurance or to pay into a pool that would provide it. Such reforms requiring employers to pay for health care costs run the risk of either providing only very limited coverage or forcing marginal firms out of business. In general, retaining the system of employer-provided health insurance would maintain all of its drawbacks, including the inefficiencies of multiple payers and multiple collectors.

One of the most popular of the current proposals calls for setting up a system of managed competition (Ellwood, Enthoven, & Etheredge, 1992; Enthoven, 1988; Enthoven & Kronick, 1989; Relman, 1990, 1993; Simmons et al., 1992). Under this system, consumers would be organized into large groups run by a sponsor with the knowledge and leverage to negotiate successfully with private insurers. Sponsors could include large employers, clusters of small employers, or local governments. The sponsors would, in principle, set standardized benefit packages and require insurers to offer coverage even to high-risk consumers at nondiscriminatory rates. They would also encourage the development and use of organized delivery systems of providers, including health maintenance organizations (HMOs) that would offer coverage via prepaid capitated premiums rather than fee-for-service type coverage. Prepayment would, in principle, change the incentives to providers so as to foster more preventive care and less wasteful services. Managed competition, including competing HMOs, appears to be a good idea in reaping the benefits of competition, and it has some powerful advocates. Nevertheless, it should be carefully evaluated on the basis of a benefit-cost analysis. Such an analysis would indicate that there are substantial fixed costs in organizing such groups and HMOs in the first place, that there are substantial administrative costs in managing such groups and HMOs, that a proliferation of such entities would interact with the existing proliferation of payers and collectors to add to costs, and that past experience with HMOs might not be representative because they tend to enroll relatively healthier working-age people. It is also questionable whether the sponsors could really do all that is expected of them. Furthermore, such a system makes little sense in the absence of a critical mass of health care consumers, such as in rural regions, representing over 20% of the population, where consumers are scattered. In such regions, it is already difficult to find any providers, much less providers who could be organized to compete with one another, yet such competition among providers is the heart of the managed-competition system. All in all, there may be value in competition in terms of both controlling costs and ensuring quality of care, but these benefits are likely to be swamped by the costs of setting up and operating the system, which would probably accelerate rather than contain national health costs.

Other popular current proposals call for "managed care," through preferred-provider insurance, under which insurers coordinate and have oversight over networks of physician and hospital providers that serve large groups of workers and their dependents (Boland, 1991; Iglehart, 1992). Managed care involves close scrutiny of providers, including utilization review, and directing patients to efficient providers who are responsible for giving appropriate medical care in a cost-effective setting. It is, in theory, able to reduce costs, but again there are substantial capital investments needed to organize such networks and large costs involved in maintaining them, which may more than offset any cost containment achieved by such a system. Furthermore, the freedom of the consumer to choose physicians and hospitals is restricted because they must use providers that promise lower levels of costs.

An Alternative: National Health
Insurance via Medicare Expansion

If employer-provided health insurance has inherent problems, which are growing in significance, then now may be the time to abandon this system altogether in favor of an alternative one. An attractive alternative is that of structuring a new national health insurance system around an already existing system, namely, the Medicare program. Presently, Medicare applies only to a particular targeted sector of the national population: those over 65 years of age. Although not perfect, it is tested and proven in having operated for a long time, and it is operational. Furthermore, the Medicare program is supported and regarded as successful not only by the over-65 population but also by physicians, hospitals, the government, and the population as a whole. The history of the Medicare program shows that physicians and hospitals can adjust to such a system and continue to provide quality care. It also shows that the government, through the Social Security program, can successfully administer a major system of national health insurance that covers an important subpopulation. The Medicare program has also been improving over time, as more experience has been gained in managing such a large program. For example, a new payments schedule has been recently implemented based on the new Resource-Based Relative Value Scale, which increases payments for preventive medicine and lowers payments for most high-tech procedures. Medicare provides a single payer for basic health care costs and a single collector of the funds needed to cover these costs for this particular population.

A way to achieve national health insurance in the United States would be through Medicare expansion, by gradually changing the age of eligibility in the Medicare program until eventually it would cover the entire population. In that way, it would eventually provide a package of basic health services not only to those covered by employer-provided health insurance but also to those covered by Medicaid and other programs, reducing the burden on the states and counties. Such a change would be relatively easy to make from an administrative standpoint because age is easy to verify and the basic system is already in place and functioning. Changing the age of eligibility is much easier, for example, than making certain groups, such as the self-employed, the unemployed, or the retired, eligible for the program, because the matter of eligibility for these other categories would be much more difficult to verify. Compared to other proposals, this one is the most evolutionary of any in building on existing institutions and networks.

Coverage under Medicare expansion would continue to be similar to that under the Medicare program, subject to certain limitations, as in the current program. These limitations, such as present Medicare limits on days of inpatient hospital care, would be adjusted as experience is gained with the enlarged program. Even with these limitations, the resulting system would provide a comprehensive benefit package of basic levels of coverage to all those enrolled in the program and allow choice of physician and hospital by the patient. Financing would be largely through an increase in Social Security taxes, including increases in the taxes paid by both employer and employee and a substantial increase in the maximum income subject to this tax, which would provide sufficient funding to cover the costs of providing basic levels of coverage to those enrolled in the program.

One of the advantages of establishing a system of national health insurance through the Medicare program is that it can act not only as a direct payer (through a fiscal intermediary) but also as a contractor, so that it could introduce innovative systems of care. One such possibility might, for example, be the use of HMOs or other institutional arrangements, where those enrolled who choose coverage through these other forms of care might accept some limitations in convenience in exchange for increased services covered.

Medicare expansion would not entirely displace private health insurance coverage. Supplemental coverage could, as today, be offered by private carriers to provide coverage going beyond the basic program, such as additional days of care, long-term care, and private rooms. The present system cannot and should not be changed immediately to a system of national health insurance, because the system would then be overloaded and could not function effectively. With a phased and predictable evolution of this system into one of national health insurance, however, it could plan for the designated changes and be prepared to handle them. For example, the Medicaid population and other subpopulations now receiving various levels of care would gradually be included in the new system, with private health insurance gradually changed to supplemental coverage.

At the same time that the Medicare program is expanding into a system of national health insurance, it should set standards for certain basic levels of coverage for all enrolled in the program. These standards would be set in the light of the levels of services that could be provided by the health care system, with clear criteria for coverage established under the program. These standards can and should be set so that those enrolled would receive basic health coverage, with additional treatment and services provided through supplemental coverage. Setting standards so that all enrolled are treated equally and reasonably would avoid such irrational situations as are seen today, where many children have no coverage and do not have even access to immunizations, yet enormous sums are provided to prolong by a few days or weeks the lives of insured people with hopeless prognoses. Such situations would be avoided by enrolling children early in the program and by limiting the care provided in hopeless cases to providing comfort. Setting standards and thereby controlling use of health care will ensure an efficient allocation of health resources and successful cost containment.

Cost Containment, Access, and Quality Under National Health Insurance

Any reasonable reform of the present system of health care in the United States must contain costs or at least the increase in costs. It would be better, of course, if it could even roll back some of these costs, in the process providing some sort of "health dividend" as the capital and labor resources released from the health care system become available for use in other areas such as education and communications. Cost containment cannot be the sole criterion for reform, however, as any reasonable reform must also extend access to care by providing coverage to those not now insured. It must, in addition, maintain or increase the quality of care provided.

A national system of health insurance would satisfy all of these criteria for reform. Costs could be contained through limiting those services provided under the program to basic care and through review of care. Cost increases would also be moderated through the scale efficiencies realized by having a single payer for basic care, as opposed to multiple payers; by having a single collector of the funds needed to provide this basic care, as opposed to multiple collectors; and by establishing centralized medical records. In fact, the Medicare program itself has demonstrated that a single payer can establish reimbursement procedures leading to lower medical fees. A national system can also be the basis for rationalizing the allocation of health resources, including greater use of preventive medicine than the present system provides, thus decreasing the need for more expensive acute care. It would also place more emphasis on primary care and less on high-tech care and limits on the life-prolonging treatment of patients who have conditions such as advanced cancer with a very poor prognosis so as to allocate health resources in a cost-effective way. Unlike some of the other proposals for reform, it would (a) use existing hospital facilities, without any need for new construction; (b) provide care for rural as well as urban areas; and (c) entail minimal costs of marketing and middle management. For all these reasons, such a system would reduce the overall cost of health care.

Equally important, such a system would greatly increase the access to care by providing health insurance to those groups who are not now covered, representing some 15% of the population. Of particular importance is the coverage of children, representing almost a third of those not currently covered by health insurance. Preventive care in the form of immunizations for children, many of whom are not currently receiving such treatment, would simultaneously extend access and lower costs of providing health care through reducing the need for acute care. Thus Medicare expansion would provide greater access to care at the same time that it is reducing the overall cost of health care.

As to the quality of care, a national system should have guidelines and requirements that would bring all health service up to a minimum standard of care. It would involve a fundamental principle of the "most favored member," comparable to that of the "most favored nation" in international trade, whereby each member of the plan receives the benefits of the most favored member. Thus, unlike the present system where there are certain favored subpopulations who happen to belong to a particular insurance plan, whether private or public, once the system is in place everyone enrolled in it would receive equal treatment, and basic care would be provided for all.

Organization: Multiple Payers Versus a Single Payer

The organization of the present system of health care involves more than 2,400 different payers of provider claims, most of which are private health insurance carriers for employer-provided health insurance. The fact that there are so many different payers adds enormously to costs. First, providers and patients have to cope with different procedures, different requirements, different forms, and so forth, all of which contribute to costs of providers, including hospitals and physicians. Many have to hire specialized personnel just to cope with the myriad of forms that must be completed for payment. Second, there are fixed costs associated with just setting up a payment system, including capital costs, management costs, and employee costs, all of which add to the costs of health care.

A more rational and efficient system of organization would involve a single payer, with uniform negotiated fees for all private providers and standardized procedures, forms, and so on that would greatly simplify its administration, as in the case of the Canadian system and those in other countries that are able to provide comprehensive coverage at lower costs than those in the United States. Such a system would reduce administrative expenses, which have been estimated to be as much as 20% of overall health costs (Ginzberg, 1989). It should both reap the rewards of scale economies and avoid the fixed costs associated with thousands of different payers. The logical single payer should be a government agency with nationwide experience in paying health claims, such as the Medicare program.

Financing: Multiple
Collectors Versus a Single Collector

Although the value of a single payer is frequently recognized, there is also a comparable argument for a single collector of the funds to support basic health care, as opposed to thousands of collectors. Health premiums are currently collected by more than 2,400 different private insurers so as to provide payments for the health coverage of their enrollees. It would not make sense to move to a single payer and not also move to a single collector because then the value of scale economies and avoiding fixed costs would not be realized.

The most efficient single collector, in fact, is the federal government, with government taxes financing the costs of basic health care, as in the case of other industrialized economies. In the United States, a very efficient system of collecting most of the funds required to pay for health care is that of the Social Security system, which, because it is a broad-based tax, is an efficient mechanism for collecting premiums from all age groups and is currently used for the Medicare program. By uncoupling health insurance from employment status, the financing of health care would shift from the employment base to a broad tax base, involving all payrolls. The Social Security system already provides for many individuals from the general population, not just the retired population. It can be used to collect the funds needed for a truly national system of national health insurance by increasing the rate paid by both employees and employers and by substantially raising the highest income subject to the Social Security tax. By increasing the payments and the benefits of this tax, it would finally live up to its name by providing a form of social security to the entire population—by giving the population access to health care. Because the current high costs to employers of providing health care are largely passed on to consumers, higher Social Security taxes would, to some extent, be offset by reduced prices as health costs are shifted from employer costs and prices to taxes.

The Specific Proposal:
National Health Insurance by the Year 2000

The specific Medicare expansion proposal calls for having the present Medicare system expand into a complete system of national health insurance by the year 2000. The first step would be to enroll all preschool children under 5 years of age and pregnant women in the program so that both groups would be covered by the end of 1995, amounting to about 20 million people (Spencer, 1989). The remaining population, between ages 5 and 65, would then eventually be covered by the end of the decade through a series of phased changes in the age of eligibility. In the next phased change, by the end of 1996, 5 years of age would be added to both the younger and older covered population, so that everyone other than those between ages 10 and 60 would be covered. This change in the age of eligibility would add another 29 million people. In the next phased change, by the end of 1997, 5 more years would be added to both the younger and the older covered population, so that everyone other than those between ages 15 and 55 would be covered, adding another 31 million people. Similarly for subsequent years, by the end of 1999, adding 35 million people in 1998 and 37 million people in 1999, everyone other than those between ages 25 and 45, would be covered. Finally, by the end of 2000, by adding the remaining 81 million people between 25 and 45, everyone would be covered. Although there would be some inequities dependent on age, they would eventually disappear and are less discriminatory than the present system, under which there are great disparities depending on whether and where one is officially employed. Added people would be enrolled on their birthdays, so that the new enrollments would occur on a gradual basis each year.

This incremental and predictable way of converting the current Medicare program into a system of national health insurance would enable the entire system of health care delivery to respond to these phased changes and learn by experience. The new system would be the basis for rationalizing the allocation of health resources, thereby reducing the overall cost of health care.

The Role of Private Insurers

The size, political influence, and substantial current role of the private health insurance industry must be taken into account in any plan for reform of the health care system. There are now more than 2,400 private commercial and nonprofit carriers that have enrolled a majority of the American people through their employers (or the employers of their spouses or parents). The industry commands enormous capital resources and employs substantial numbers of people. What will be the role of this industry if a complete system of national health insurance is built around the present Medicare system? In fact, the industry could have a significant role to play under such a reform and could gain from such a system (Kerr, 1992).

First, the private health insurance industry would continue to provide supplemental coverage, as it now does via Medigap coverage for the population eligible for the Medicare program. This would be an enormous market, and it involves less risk than the industry currently faces.

Second, the Medicare program will need substantial help in implementing its transformation into a complete system of national health insurance, even if done on the proposed phased basis. The private health insurance industry can assist in this transformation by acting as intermediaries for the expanded Medicare program, including processing claims as subcontractors. Enrolling the 37 million people who have no coverage will create a substantial new market, where the service demands of the enlarged Medicare program can be met by private industry, including private health carriers. Conducting this use of the more efficient private carriers on a competitive basis and using standardized forms will ensure that administrative costs are kept to a minimum.

Very low rates of return appear to be earned in the health insurance industry (Pear, 1992, refers to profit margins of only 1% or 2%). Thus the alternatives suggested here for its role under a system of national health insurance should be welcomed by the industry because they might even provide a way for it to obtain a higher return at lower risk.

Conclusion: A Time for Action

The crisis in health care in the United States should lead to a search for alternative systems of health care delivery. The problems are deep and involve not just the question of financing health care but, more fundamentally, the organization of the whole health sector. Patchwork fixes of the present system will not be adequate, because the problems call for fundamental reform. It is not by accident that almost every industrialized nation has such a system, which provides health insurance to the entire population at reasonable cost. The United States is the exception in this area, and by relying heavily on employer-provided health insurance, it suffers in terms of both high cost and lack of access to health care. Now may be the time finally to establish a system of national health insurance in the United States. A national health insurance could be established by Medicare expansion, with consumers, providers, and health insurers gradually adjusting to this program and realizing its benefits without undue costs. In fact, among the biggest advantages of this proposal are its simplicity and its ease of implementation. The resulting system, established by Medicare expansion, would be both cost-effective and equitable in that it would both control costs and provide quality health care to all Americans.

References

Aaron, H. J. (1991). *Serious and unstable condition: Financing America's health care.* Washington, DC: Brookings Institution.

American College of Physicians. (1992). Universal insurance for American health care: A proposal of the American College of Physicians. *Annals of Internal Medicine, 117,* 511-519.

Berki, S. E. (1990). Approaches to financing care for the uninsured. *Henry Ford Hospital Medical Journal, 38*(2-3), 119-122.

Bipartisan Commission on Comprehensive Health Care (the Pepper Commission). (1990). *A call for action: Final report.* Washington, DC: U.S. Government Printing Office.

Boland, P. (1991). *Making managed health care work.* New York: McGraw-Hill.

Ellwood, P. M., Enthoven, A. C., & Etheredge, L. (1992). The Jackson Hole initiatives for a twenty-first century American health care system. *Health Economics, 1*, 149-168.

Enthoven, A. C. (1988). *Theory and practice of managed competition in health care finance.* Amsterdam: North-Holland.

Enthoven, A. C., & Kronick, R. (1989). A consumer-choice health plan for the 1990s—Universal health insurance in a system designed to promote quality and economy. *New England Journal of Medicine, 320*(1), 29-37; *320*(2), 94-101.

Etheredge, L. (1990). Universal health insurance: Lessons of the 1970s, prospects for the 1990s. *Frontiers of Health Services Management, 6*(4), 3-35.

Fuchs, V. R. (1991). National health insurance revisited. *Health Affairs, 10*(4), 7-17.

Ginzberg, E. (1989). Harder than it looks. *Health Management Quarterly, 11*(4), 19-21.

Himmelstein, D. U., & Woolhandler, S. (1989). A national health program for the United States—A physicians' proposal. *New England Journal of Medicine, 320*(2), 102-108.

Iglehart, J. K. (1992). The American health care system—Managed care. *New England Journal of Medicine, 327*, 742-747.

Intriligator, M. D. (1981). Major policy issues in the economics of health care in the United States. In J. van der Gaag & M. Perlman (Eds.), *Health, economics, and health economics* (pp. 355-368). Amsterdam: North-Holland.

Kerr, P. (1992, December 4). Insurers stand to profit big from a health care overhaul. *The New York Times*, p. 11.

Kinzer, D. M. (1990). Universal entitlement to health care—Can we get there from here? *New England Journal of Medicine, 322*, 467-470.

Lundberg, G. D. (1991). National health care reform: An aura of inevitability is upon us. *Journal of the American Medical Association, 265*, 2566-2567.

Mariner, W. K. (1992). Problems with employer-provided health insurance—The Employee Retirement Income Security Act and health care reform. *New England Journal of Medicine, 327*, 1682-1685.

National Leadership Commission on Health Care. (1989). *For the health of a nation: A shared responsibility.* Ann Arbor, MI: Health Administration Press Perspectives.

Pauly, M. V., Danzon, P., Feldstein, P., & Hoff, J. (1991). A plan for responsible national health insurance. *Health Affairs, 10*(1), 5-25; comments and responses, *10*(2), 223-228.

Pear, R. (1992, December 6). Leading health insurers into a new age. *The New York Times*, p. 11.

Relman, A. S. (1989). Universal health insurance: Its time has come. *New England Journal of Medicine, 320*, 117-118.

Relman, A. S. (1990). Reforming the health care system. *New England Journal of Medicine, 323*, 991-992.

Relman, A. S. (1993). Controlling costs by "managed competition"—Would it work? *New England Journal of Medicine, 328*, 133-135.

Simmons, H. E., Rhoades, M. M., & Goldberg, M. A. (1992). Comprehensive health care reform and managed competition. *New England Journal of Medicine, 327*, 1525-1528.

Spencer, G. (1989). *Projections of the population of the U.S. by age, sex, and race: 1988-2080* (U.S. Department of Commerce, Bureau of the Census, Current Population Reports, Series P-25, No. 1018). Washington, DC: U.S. Government Printing Office.

Weil, T. P. (1992). A universal access plan: A step toward national health insurance. *Hospital & Health Services Administration, 37*(1), 37-51.

6

Health Care Reform
A Public Health Perspective

JOYCE C. LASHOF

*T*he current debate on health care reform has centered almost exclusively on how best to insure universal comprehensive health insurance at a cost that society can afford. This is a laudable goal, and, indeed, it is essential for a civilized society to assure that all persons have access to medical care. What has been lacking in this discussion, however, is how best to improve the health status of the population. To address that question, a change in emphasis will be needed. One look at our nation's health indices and major health problems make it apparent why this is so.

The major killers today—circulatory diseases, cancer, and injuries—account for three quarters of the deaths in this country, but many of these deaths are postponable. A panel of experts assembled at the Carter Center in 1984 examined the 13 leading health problems in the United States. They estimated that 66% of the deaths that occurred in 1980 were postponable if all the social, environmental, and behavioral factors leading to death and disability were effectively controlled (Amler & Eddins, 1987). Smoking, alcohol, and occupational exposure to carcinogens accounted for approximately 17% of all cancer deaths in 1980 (Rothenberg, Nasca, Mikl, Burnett, & Reynolds, 1987). In the 1980s, death rates declined for the three leading causes of death—heart disease, stroke, and motor vehicle crashes. Much of the 40% decline in heart disease mortality since 1970 has been attributed to increased detection and control of hypertension, decreased smoking, and dietary changes. Similarly, the 50% reduction in stroke reflects gains in hypertension control and reductions in smoking. Traffic fatalities have decreased by one third in the past 15 years, highly influenced by the use of seat belts, lower speed limits, and diminished alcohol abuse (Mason & McGinnis, 1990). But 100,000 deaths due to illnesses and injuries related to alcohol still occur each year, and although smoking has declined, approximately 400,000 deaths a year can be attributed to tobacco. The toll that AIDS and intentional and unintentional injury are taking on young adults, although preventable, continues unabated.

And of special concern is the fact that people of low income have death rates that are twice the rates for people above the poverty level. Thirteen percent of black infants and 6% of white infants are born at low birth weight. The risk of heart disease is more than 25% higher for low-income people than for the overall population. The incidence of cancer increases as income decreases, and survival rates are lower for low-income cancer patients (Public Health Service, 1991).

Some of the disparity in health status will be decreased by improved access to health care, but to really change the health statistics of rich and poor alike will require that we focus our attention on the determinants of health and on health promotion and disease prevention. The Lalonde report, *A New Perspective on the Health of Canadians*, published in 1974, served to refocus our attention on the multifactorial nature of the causes of disease and stimulated a new look at the determinants of health (Lalonde, 1974).

There is now a growing body of literature that explores the interplay between genetics, lifestyle, environment, and medical care on health status (Blum, 1981, pp. 2-30; Evans & Stoddart, 1990; Stachtechenko & Jenicek, 1990). And although a great deal of the emphasis in the early work on health promotion was on individual lifestyle, there is increasing recognition of the importance of the social and economic environmental influences on health behavior. In fact, it is clear that one cannot examine any of the determinants independently of the others nor look for single causes of disease any more than one can write a simple prescription for health. It is from this perspective that the health strategy initiated in 1979 with the publication of *Healthy People: The Surgeon General's Report on Health Promotion and Disease Prevention* was developed (Public Health Service, 1979) and expanded on with publication of the 1990 health objectives. Examining all of the health data available and building on knowledge gained in pursuing the 1990 health objectives, *Healthy People 2000: National Health Promotion and Disease Prevention Objectives* was developed and released in 1991. The purpose of *Healthy People 2000* is to commit the nation to the attainment of three broad goals that are essential for us to reach our full potential—namely, to increase the span of healthy life for Americans, to reduce health disparity among Americans, and to achieve access to preventive services for all Americans (Public Health Service, 1991).

The Year 2000 Objectives identify 22 priorities and present over 300 objectives to chart the direction for public health. These are presented under three categories: health status objectives, risk reduction objectives and services, and protection objectives. The latter two are clearly supportive of the objectives dealing with health status. Although 40% of the objectives fall into the category of services and protection, only 8% relate to preventive care that physicians give individual patients.

A review of the objectives clearly reveals the number whose attainment is dependent on the interplay between race and socioeconomic status and all that that entails, such as low education, poor nutrition, poor housing, and poor social conditions, generally, and adverse health behaviors, such as use of alcohol and tobacco and drug abuse. Among the 300 health items listed, there are 79 different health status objectives for 50 of which there are either specific targets based on socioeconomic or minority status or for which these factors are known to be of importance.

Until this nation deals with these underlying social conditions, it is unlikely that progress will be made in improving the health status of low-income and minority populations. A much better understanding of the manner in which social and economic factors influence health status is essential. Recent studies have shown that there is a continuous gradient in health status from lowest to highest income, not just from the extremes (Smith & Egger, 1992). But, of course, the difference between the richest and the poorest is the most dramatic. Although it is beyond the scope of health care reform legislation per se to deal with all of the social, economic, educational, and environmental factors that are key, it does offer the opportunity to integrate the public health perspective with medical care.

Health care reform offers the opportunity to focus on the health of populations and make meeting the objectives set out in *Healthy People 2000* the goal of the health care system. A nonprofit organization, Partnership for Prevention, founded in 1991 to increase prevention's priority in national policy and practice, outlined three essential elements of prevention—namely, public policy for health promotion and disease prevention, community-based health promotion and disease prevention, and clinical preventive services (Partnership for Prevention, 1993). Health care reform legislation that goes beyond assuring that everyone has health insurance and builds into the health care system incentives and resources to address each of these elements would make it possible to actually have health care reform rather than just medical care reform. To accomplish this, however, will require (a) a strengthened public health infrastructure; (b) a coordinated approach to public policy directed toward improving health and involving multiple agencies using regulatory, legislative, and tax initiatives; and (c) community participation in decision making and a system of accountability that focuses on the health status of communities, not just performance measures of health plans.

Whether competition between managed-care health plans is compatible with such an approach remains to be seen. Theoretically, a capitation payment system provides an incentive to prevent disease and promote health, but without cooperation and the building of partnerships and coalitions at the community level to deal with the multiple factors influencing health, little will be accomplished. Health care reform must address these issues as an essential component of the plan and assure the funding necessary to implement a truly comprehensive public health approach to improving the health of populations.

The proposal that President Clinton has submitted to the Congress does provide for payment for clinical preventive services and includes provisions dealing with core public health functions and public health initiatives to help overcome some of the nonfinancial access barriers to medical care. But funding for the latter two activities is limited and administered primarily through competitive categorical grants. It is thus unlikely to be effective in shifting the emphasis from payment for clinical services to the broader goal of addressing the health needs of communities. And, sadly, discussion of these issues has not even been part of the public debate.

But probably the most important potential accomplishment of health care reform would be the control of medical care costs so as to allow government spending to be redirected toward social policies designed to deal with unemployment, education, and housing. Only when that is possible will there be a real improvement in the health of the people.

References

Amler, R. W., & Eddins, D. L. (1987). Cross-sectional analysis: Precursors of premature death in the United States. In R. W. Amler & H. B. Bulls (Eds.), *Closing the gap: The burden of unnecessary illness* (pp. 191-187). New York: Oxford University Press.

Blum, H. (1981). *Planning for health: Generics for the eighties.* New York: Human Sciences Press.

Evans, R., & Stoddart, G. (1990). Producing health, consuming health care. *Social Science Medicine, 31,* 1347-1363.

Lalonde, M. (1974). *A new perspective on the health of Canadians.* Ottawa: Information Canada.

Mason, J. O., & McGinnis, J. M. (1990). Healthy people 2000: An overview of the national health promotion and disease prevention objectives. *Public Health Reports, 105,* 441-446.

Partnership for Prevention. (1993). *Prevention is basic to health reform: A position paper from an expert panel.* Washington, DC: Partnership for Prevention.

Public Health Service. (1979). *Healthy people: Surgeon General's report on health promotion and disease prevention.* Washington, DC: U.S. Department of Health and Human Services.

Public Health Service. (1991). *Healthy people 2000: National health promotion and disease prevention objectives* (DHHS Publication No. PHS 91-50212). Washington, DC: U.S. Department of Health and Human Services.

Rothenberg, R., Nasca, P., Mikl, J., Burnett, W., & Reynolds, B. (1987). Cancer. In R. W. Amler & H. B. Bulls (Eds.), *Closing the gap: The burden of unnecessary illness* (pp. 39). New York: Oxford University Press.

Smith, G. D., & Egger, M. (1992). Socioeconomic differences in mortality in Britain and the United States. *American Journal of Public Health, 82*(8), 1079.

Stachtechenko, S., & Jenicek, M. (1990). Conceptual differences between prevention and health promotion: Research implications for community health programs. *Canadian Journal of Public Health, 81,* 53-59.

7

Reinventing Public Health

President Clinton's Health Security Act

PHILIP R. LEE

*I*n a special message to Congress: "Advancing the Nation's Health,"
on January 7, 1965, President Lyndon Johnson began: "In 1787,
Thomas Jefferson wrote that 'without health there is no happiness.
An attention to health, then should take place of every other object.'
That priority has remained fixed in both private and public values
in our society through generations of Americans ever since."

While health has been a priority, it has not been at the top of the
domestic policy agenda since the enactment of Medicare in 1965. In
1993, health and health care reform are back at the top of the domestic
policy agenda. Issues are being considered and discussed that will

EDITOR'S NOTE: The opinions expressed in this chapter are those of the author. They
are not official and do not represent the views of the U.S. Department of Health and
Human Services. This chapter was written by a government employee as part of official
duties, therefore the material cannot be copyrighted and is in the public domain. This
chapter was originally presented as the closing address of the 121st Annual Meeting of
the American Public Health Association, October 23, 1993, San Francisco. Some of the
material may have been slightly altered or omitted at the time of delivery.

move us forward into the 21st century in a way that will both improve the health of all the population and close the gap between socioeconomically disadvantaged populations and the rest of the population.

We are reexamining not only the personal health care delivery system but the paradigm that currently defines public health in the United States. And in the process, we are reinventing public health.

History

Public health has traditionally been viewed as separate from personal medical care. Medical treatment focused largely on diagnosing, treating, and caring for individuals. An old friend of mine—a French physician—once described our system of medical care as a "one ill, one pill, one bill" system. Public health, by contrast has traditionally focused on nonpersonal health services, targeted largely at the environment or the community as a whole. Public health was viewed as a public sector or governmental activity. In recent years, however, as the health insurance system failed more and more Americans, the responsibilities of public health broadened to include personal preventive medical services for high-risk or vulnerable groups.

In its very important report, "The Future of Public Health," the Institute of Medicine adopted this view and limited public health to "organized community efforts aimed at the prevention of disease and the promotion of health." A broader view was advocated by Dr. Julio Frenk in his brilliant paper "The New Public Health," published this year in the *Annual Review of Public Health*. Dr. Frenk introduced his paper from a Jeffersonian perspective:

> Health is a crossroad. It is where biological and social factors, the individual and the community, the social and the economic policy all converge. In addition to its intrinsic value, health is a means to personal and collective advancement. It is, therefore, an indicator of success achieved by a society and its institutions of government in promoting well-being, which is the ultimate meaning of development.

Dr. Frenk's concept of public health was based on the notion that "the essence of public health is that it adopts a perspective based on groups of people or populations." He added that "this population perspective inspires the two facets of public health as a field of inquiry and as an area for action."

In both of these areas—research and practice—Dr. Frenk's ideas about a population perspective have guided the development of many of the policies proposed by the President in the Health Security Act transmitted to Congress yesterday.

Health Security Act

In his address to the Joint Session of Congress on September 22, 1993, President Clinton outlined the six principles that form the basis for the Health Security Act. They are security, savings, quality, simplicity, choice, and responsibility. While the words "public health" do not appear in this list of principles, it is part and parcel of all of them and in the concept of health security.

By changing the paradigm, public health will be reinvented. We are not scrapping the old model but building a new one—one that addresses three broad areas. First, serving the needs of both the personal health care system and the population-based public health system. This includes improving the quality of health data and simplifying the process of collecting and analyzing data; focusing on health research, especially prevention research; and making major changes in the health care workforce. The second overarching area is assuring access to care for underserved populations. And the third area is strengthening the core functions of public health and meeting the health needs of regional or national significance.

Public Health Research

Let me begin with public health research and then move on to public health practice as they are included in the reform and in our vision of reinventing public health.

Health research include three broad areas—biomedical, clinical, and public health research. The Health Security Act proposal by President Clinton includes support for expanded research in all three of these areas. Dr. Frenk's topology for public health research includes epidemiological research and health systems research. Epidemiological research includes research of determinants and research of consequences. Health systems research includes research on health systems organization at the micro level and health policy research at the macro level. Research on health systems organization consists of health services research and health resources research. Public health research shares equally with biomedical and clinical research in our plans for the future. They are not mutually exclusive but are often linked.

They differ principally in their level of analysis, not in the object of analysis. Public health research, particularly in epidemiology, must be closely tied to the biological sciences. In all areas of public health the social and behavioral sciences are also critical.

Public Health Practice

The public health policies incorporated in the Health Security Act submitted to Congress by President Clinton incorporate the concept expressed so well by Dr. Frenk. "As an area for action," he wrote, "this modern conception of public health goes beyond fragmenting dichotomies, such as personal vs. environmental services, prevention vs. curative activities, and public vs. private responsibilities. Instead of lending itself to these dichotomies, the new public health addresses the systemic efforts to identify health needs and to organize comprehensive services with a well-defined population base."

This is precisely the strategy adopted in the Health Security Act. The Health Security Act as proposed by President Clinton changes the focus of the health system; restructures the personal-care delivery system and restructures the public health system.

Changing the focus of the health system means—putting health back into our system as a priority. To do that, we need to focus on what the long-term as well as the short-term objectives of a health system are. Americans need to know and see the big picture. In a system that promotes health, primary, secondary, and tertiary prevention must be emphasized as well as treatment service. In a system that promotes health, total patient care must be emphasized as well as individual services and organ systems. Populations as well as individuals must be considered as patients. And health professionals must work together as teams. And they must be held responsible and accountable for keeping patients healthy.

Restructuring the personal-care delivery system means making it an active participant in achieving public health objectives. There are four basic problems that prevent the personal-care delivery system from doing so now. Not everyone has insurance coverage and access is not universal. And even when an individual has insurance coverage, no one is responsible or accountable for making sure that

practice sites, including rural and public hospitals. In addition, it will improve access to specialty care in underserved areas—and reduce practitioner isolation—by linking members of the practice networks with each other and with regional and academic medical centers through information systems and telecommunications.

The second new approach will be a grant program that provides isolated, culturally diverse, hard-to-reach persons not served by other programs with the supplemental services they need to obtain access to medical care and to use the health care system effectively. Targeted grants to public and private nonprofit entities cover outreach and enabling services—for example, transportation, translation and interpretation, and child care. Supplemental services would be covered along with linkage of individuals to health plans, community health services, and social services. Also covered in this grant program are advocacy and follow-up services. This new program complements the provision of enabling services already provided through existing PHS programs, such as family planning, maternal and child health, community and migrant health centers, health care for the homeless, Ryan White care for people with HIV / AIDS funds, and substance abuse and mental health clinics.

In order to assure access and continuity of care during the transition, the President's plan calls for the designation of providers in these existing programs as essential providers that practice in underserved areas. Health plans will be required to contract with these essential providers for a minimum of 5 years or until they are established and well integrated into the delivery system.

In addition to expanding the capacity to provide health services in rural and inner-city areas, the Health Security Act addresses some other crucial issues. One of them is adolescent school-based and school-linked health services. This needs to be done nationwide because many adolescents, despite the fact that they have health insurance, are underserved. We found from studies here in San Francisco, as others have found, that high school students, more than anything, wanted somebody to talk to about their emotional problems, their family problems, their social situations. So mental health services—counseling services—are an essential part of those primary care services at middle and high schools.

Another area the Health Security Act expands is the National Health Service Corps, which has been downsized in recent years. We plan to see the program expanded to provide health professionals to serve in rural and urban underserved areas.

The Health Security Act also strengthens and expands the Indian Health Service. The Indian Health Service does an absolutely outstanding job of providing services to Indian populations with limited resources. Urban Indians will be served by the standard benefits package they will have access to under health care reform.

Finally, reinventing public health means revitalizing the essential core functions of public health and supporting national and regional priority prevention initiatives. In order to fulfill the public health system's essential role, core health functions must be revitalized.

These functions—data for surveillance and monitoring; protection of the environment, housing, food, and water; investigation and control of both infectious and chronic diseases, as well as injuries; public information and education; accountability and quality assurance; public health laboratory services; training and education; and leadership in policy development and administration—must all be supported at the national, state, and local level.

These core functions are all key to protection and prevention and our best hope for a healthier nation. Again, when public health fails, people and communities suffer and personal health care costs increase.

Finally, health problems of regional or national significance require resources above and beyond the need for the core public health functions and the existing categorical prevention programs of the PHS. For example, tobacco use, violence, and chronic illness are problems that do not face the entire population uniformly but call for tailored, community-based prevention programs. Rather than spreading our resources around like water, we need to focus them on those communities and those populations groups hit hardest. We must better position public health to maintain a strong defense against preventable disease and conditions that affect local communities. If carried out effectively, this public health role promises vital support for the personal health care delivery system.

Conclusion

Universal insurance for personal health care alone will not assure access to appropriate and necessary services, nor will access to these services protect and promote the public health. But we can't solve them without universal access.

Achieving the goals of increasing the span of healthy life for all Americans and reducing the health disparities depends on universal access to the personal health care delivery system supported by a strong foundation of public health and population-based programs.

Achievement of health care reform depends on acceptance of shared responsibilities, among government at every level, health professionals, private and voluntary sectors, communities, families, and individuals.

Our challenge is to set aside partisan and selfish special interest. We have got to keep our eyes on the long term. We must focus on what is best for America. Our personal security as well as our nation's economic security depends on health care reform. Only when we fix on what is best for America will we produce the consensus needed to build a health care system that is not just the best for some Americans but a system that is the best for all Americans.

The President has committed his administration to achieving health care reform. We certainly have a lot to do.

8

Equity, Accessibility, and Ethical Issues

Is the U.S. Health Care Reform Debate Asking the Right Questions?

LU ANN ADAY

*T*he current health care reform debate in the United States regarding how to assure more universal access to medical care has posed an array of answers, but is it asking the right questions?

The debate principally addresses the pros and cons of competing proposals for extending public or private health insurance coverage. This chapter argues that both the focus and the scope of the debate are too narrowly defined and the answers being offered therefore inadequate. The question implicitly or explicitly being addressed is how to assure more universal access to *medical care*. An alternative

AUTHOR'S NOTE: This chapter is based on selected areas of my book, *At Risk in America: The Health Care Needs of Vulnerable Populations in the United States*, copyright © 1993 by Jossey-Bass, Inc. Used by permission.

focus for an informed health policy debate is how best to assure more universal access to *health*.

The Clinton administration has argued for expanded and fundamental investments in the social and economic infrastructure of U.S. society—schools, jobs, housing, and neighborhoods—and in encouraging grassroots, community-oriented involvement in the political and infrastructure rebuilding process. The President has also called for a serious-minded effort at health care reform that has, as defining tenets, the commitment and means to control the spiraling costs of medical care. He has not, however, articulated a coherent policy framework that considers the extent to which these or other policy initiatives are likely to succeed in ultimately improving either individuals' or the nation's health.

The argument offered here is that fundamental investments in enhancing the economic and social well-being of American families and neighborhoods may offer the greatest long-term possibilities for improving their physical, psychological, and social health and well-being. Providing more universal access to medical care may have some, but a more limited, effect in terms of improving individuals' and the nation's health. Competing universal health insurance proposals should be evaluated in terms of these effectiveness, as well as equity and efficiency, criteria. Ultimately, this chapter argues that a coherent and effective policy framework for improving the nation's *health* requires a broader vision and set of objectives than simply reforming methods of paying for *medical care*.

Values Framework: From Individual Rights to the Common Good

The values underlying policy debates about how to improve access to medical care have traditionally focused on the principles of distributive justice (or equity) that justify societal assurances of a right to medical care. Thus far, no such universal assurances of a legal right to care exist in the United States. The current U.S. health care reform debate regarding universal health insurance alternatives may be viewed, at base, as deliberating whether a right to care should be more broadly extended and assured (Aday, Begley, Lairson, & Slater, 1993; Dougherty, 1988).

Some countries already have well-established systems for the universal financing of medical care. Critics posing reforms in the United States have often borrowed directly from models in place in other Western democratic countries (most particularly, Canada, Germany, and Great Britain). The primary values underlying the formulation of these nations' policies do, however, differ from those that Americans are likely to endorse. The normative underpinnings for more universal modes of financing medical care in other countries are more often rooted in a shared sense of social solidarity or responsibility for the health or common good of the nation's citizenry rather than in the individual rights of those deserving of societal investments in their well-being, as is the case in the United States (Anderson, 1989; Fuchs, 1991; Glaser, 1991; Priester, 1992; Saltman, 1992).

The language of both *individual rights* and the *common good* have both historically been components of U.S. social and political discourse. Political liberalism, rooted in the writings of John Locke and John Stuart Mill, among others, has focused on the norms of autonomy, independence, and individual well-being underlying the individual rights perspective. Communitarian sentiments, as articulated by Michael Sandel, Alisdair MacIntyre, Amitai Etzioni, and Michael Walzer, are, on the other hand, based on the competing norms of reciprocity, interdependence, and public responsibility that are formative of commitments to the common good. Political liberals caution against the liberty-limiting potential of centralized, governmental, bureaucratically controlled policy alternatives ("welfare state"). Communitarians, in contrast, criticize the unchecked self-interest that they argue characterizes pluralistic, private, business-dominated policy alternatives ("market competition") underlying the more liberal rights-oriented perspective (Bellah, Madsen, Sullivan, Swidler, & Tipton, 1985, 1991; Mulhall & Swift, 1992).

Currently, liberal political philosophy in the United States is under a siege of criticism from critics arguing that liberal sentiments and the semantics of individual rights have come to dominate and silence community-oriented norms and the associated language of the common good. The political and social consequences of this imbalance are, they argue, manifest in increasingly atomized and socially isolated individuals, diminished political participation, and exacerbated vulnerability to harm and neglect associated with the absence or abandonment of caring others. The dominance of the language of individual rights has led to the perverse and unintended consequence of mitigating rather than enhancing individuals' well-being as a result of enforcing punitive and adversarial divisions between individuals and groups. The result has been a seemingly insoluble series of moral impasses in legal and ethical debates over the rightness of competing claims (related to abortion rights, civil rights, patient vs. provider rights, etc.) (Barber, 1984; Glendon, 1991; Kymlicka, 1989; Mulhall & Swift, 1992).

Substantial evidence exists that the current system of providing and paying for services in the United States fails to assure either individuals' rights to medical care or improvements in the nation's health. Many Americans have little or no access to preventive services that are known to have beneficial health effects, such as prenatal care or childhood immunizations. Others, however, have access to high-cost, technology-intensive care that may have limited or adverse effects on health and well-being, such as elective or high-risk surgery and prescriptions for multiple, counterindicated pharmaceuticals. Further, health and medical care are consuming an increasing share of the nation's gross national product (GNP) that could well be devoted to other individual or societal goals (e.g., education, housing, and jobs) (Aaron, 1991; Aday, 1993; National Center for Health Statistics [NCHS], 1992). The Clinton administration has pointed out the importance of reducing the accelerating costs of medical care to free up resources to invest in these and other productive components of the U.S. economy.

This chapter attempts to discern, translate, and give voice to the second language of the *common good* that has characterized U.S. social and political discourse, as well as the policies in other countries that U.S. health care reformers have sought to emulate or adopt. The implicit or explicit focus of the current U.S. health care reform debate (how to assure more universal access to medical care), the means for achieving this goal (medical care financing reform), and the ethical underpinnings underlying proposed solutions (individual rights) may be inadequate for ultimately enhancing both individuals' and the nation's health. A debate encompassing the language of the common good may well shift the implicit or explicit question posed (how to assure more universal access to health), the means for achieving this goal (a national *health* policy), and the ethical underpinnings underlying proposed solutions (shared responsibility).

The argument is not that the second language (of the common good) should dominate or override the first (individual rights) but that the questions posed in an informed debate about reform of the U.S. health care system should be more broadly framed and that the concepts and principles that both distinguish and translate these contrasting languages of U.S. social and political discourse be more clearly illuminated, to ultimately enhance both individuals' and the nation's health.

Individual Rights Tradition

Different theories of distributive justice highlight alternative principles or criteria for a fair distribution of benefits and burdens as the foundation for defining the nature and limits of a right to medical care (Dougherty, 1988).

Robert Nozick's (1974) *entitlement* theory emphasizes that fairness is rooted in the freedom to possess and use one's property and resources as one chooses. Rights to medical care under this perspective are facilitated by policies that serve to maximize consumer choice and satisfaction (preferences) in the medical care marketplace. The *egalitarian* point of view, developed by Robert Veatch (1981) and others, argues that what is primary is the perspective that each individual is of equal worth and should be treated equally. Considerations of rights to medical care from this point of view focus on how to narrow or eliminate subgroup disparities in health and medical care.

John Rawls's (1971) *contractarian* theory is based on an argument regarding what reasonable people would decide if they were asked to come together to derive a set of fair principles for distributing societal goods. Rawls reasoned that such individuals would endorse, in order of importance, (a) maximizing everyone's rights to liberties compatible with a similar system of liberty for everyone, (b) assuring fair equality of opportunity for people with similar abilities and skills, and (c) making sure that those who are worst off benefit. This perspective focuses on assuring that the rights of those who are least likely to be able to buy care or be cured are considered.

Norman Daniels's (1985) *needs-based* theory of justice points out that medical care is necessary to address minimal human needs for "normal species functioning." Rights to medical care are justified in terms of their role in assuring that there is a fair equality of opportunity for living a normal life. This perspective prompts consideration of what such needs might be and the basic decent minimum set of services that should be provided to meet them. *Utilitarian* theory has its roots in the writings of David Hume, Jeremy Bentham, and John Stuart Mill (Dougherty, 1988). The principal goal underlying this theory is that of maximizing utility—to promote the greatest good for the greatest number. Cost-benefit- and cost-effectiveness-oriented decision making and market-oriented policies are rooted in the utilitarian perspective. Rights to medical care from this perspective emphasize assuring access to those services for which the measured benefits (in terms of health, well-being, or productivity, for example) would be maximized relative to what it costs to provide them (Culyer, 1992).

Communitarian Tradition

The communitarian (community-oriented) paradigm has characterized traditional public health policy and practice, with its focus on community welfare and the use of medical police power (public health regulations, inspections, quarantines, etc.) to protect the public's health.

The "second public health revolution," which began in the mid-1970s in the United States in response to the surgeon general's *Healthy People* report, placed more of a focus on individual lifestyle-oriented interventions than on community ones to promote and protect the nation's health. Sylvia Tesh (1988), in *Hidden Arguments: Political Ideology and Disease Prevention Policy*, argues that this second public health revolution has inappropriately redirected public health research and practice from a more community- and social-structural-oriented paradigm to a more individualistic one, which could result in a failure to identify and address the fundamental social and economic origins of illness.

Dan Beauchamp (1988), in his book, *The Health of the Republic: Epidemics, Medicine, and Moralism as Challenges to Democracy*, applies the communitarian critique developed by Michael Walzer to translate the public health perspective into principles of social justice and equality and argues that public health, not medical care, should be at the center of a theory of equality to serve the common good. Beauchamp's analysis does, however, fail to adequately define the framework and policy process for translating these principles into a reformed U.S. health care policy.

The discussion that follows argues that focusing on improvements in the nation's health would be a defining tenet of a U.S. health policy rooted more explicitly in the *notion of the common good*. An explanatory paradigm regarding the social origins and consequences of illness is presented to assist in identifying fundamental and relevant points of intervention outside the medical care system. Criteria for evaluating universal health insurance proposals would assess their health-related, as well as equity, implications.

Policy Perspective:
A Focus on the Nation's Health

Implicit in the U.S. health care reform debate is the assumption that enhanced access to medical care will lead to improved health. Ample evidence is available, however, to suggest that (a) substantial variation exists in how medical care is practiced, (b) many clinical protocols and technologies have little or ambiguous effects on health outcomes, (c) the overuse of medical care services leads to as many or more adverse health effects as does underuse, and (d) a variety of factors other than medical care per se (e.g., genetics, lifestyle, and environment) contribute to producing and maintaining an individual's health (Carlson, 1975; Fuchs, 1991; Illich, 1975; Knowles, 1977; Milio, 1983; NCHS, 1992).

In spite of this clinical and epidemiological evidence, the current debate over alternatives for more universal financing of care fails to adequately consider or challenge the assumptions underlying the role of medical care per se in enhancing individuals' health, as well as whether a policy of promoting access to medical care alone is sufficient for improving aggregate statistical indicators of the nation's health, such as infant mortality rates, the incidence of preventable diseases, or prevalence of long-term disability.

There is no paucity of conceptual and policy-oriented frameworks for identifying and integrating the variety of factors that contribute to health. Canadian Marc Lalonde's (1975) field concept, as well as subsequent adaptations and modifications of his perspective, have highlighted the greater importance of lifestyle and environmental factors, relative to biologic factors or medical care, in ameliorating many of the major health problems that plague contemporary Western (including U.S.) society (Evans & Stoddart, 1990).

Other social and health care critics have looked more deeply at the social-structural origins of the variations in health risks and related health outcomes associated with varying access to social and economic resources as a function of age, gender, race, or social class in U.S. society, as well as other societies (Tesh, 1988). For example, persistent and substantial social class variations in health status in England continue to be documented, although access to basic medical care services has historically been more universally assured in that country than in the United States (Gray, 1982). On the other hand, many of the statistical, aggregate indicators of health status in the United States (such as infant mortality) continue to compare unfavorably to other nations, as well as mirroring wide and persistent differences between race and income groups (NCHS, 1992).

The World Health Organization and the Public Health Service in the United States, Canada, and other countries have sought to formulate achievable national (Year 1990 and 2000) health objectives. Models for achieving these goals have highlighted Lalonde's (1975) field concept and, to a lesser extent, the policy changes required to ameliorate the social-structural correlates and consequences of poor health (McBeath, 1991; McGinnis, Richmond, Brandt, Windom, & Mason, 1992).

The current debate regarding health care reform in the United States appears to be largely proceeding without consideration of these more fundamental arguments and evidence regarding the extent to which assuring access to medical care assures access to health and, if so, based on how much and what types of services. A more broadly defined debate would pose challenging questions regarding what medical care should appropriately be covered under expanded universal access alternatives, but perhaps more important, how should limited societal resources be allocated among medical care versus other more promising public health, social, or economic reforms?

U.S. policymakers are struggling, in the context of the current health care reform debate, with how to enhance *access to medical care*. The abundant alternatives being proposed nonetheless fail to address whether these or other options are most likely to enhance Americans' *access to health*.

The United States currently has no national *health* policy. The scope of the current debate over health care reform could, however, be more widely and wisely focused to encompass consideration of the principles, objectives, and programs to guide the formulation of such a policy. Reform options could then be evaluated and new means perhaps be revealed for formulating approaches to attaining the shared and mutually beneficial objective of improving the nation's health.

Explanatory Paradigm: The Social Origins and Consequences of Health and Illness

Vulnerable populations are *at risk* of poor physical, psychological, and/or social health. Underlying this definition of vulnerability is the epidemiological concept of risk, in the sense that there is a *probability* that an individual will become ill within a stated period of time. Community and corresponding individual characteristics are *risk factors* associated with the occurrence of poor physical, psychological, and/or social health. Risk factors refer to those attributes or exposures (e.g., smoking, drug use, and lead paint poisoning) that are associated with or lead to increases in the probability of occurrence of health-related outcomes (Aday, 1993).

Relative risk refers to the ratio of the risk of poor health among groups that are exposed to the risk factors versus those that are not (Last, 1983). The concept of risk assumes that there is always a *chance* that an adverse health-related outcome will occur. Correspondingly, we are *all* potentially at risk of poor physical, psychological, and/or social health. People may, however, be more or less at risk of poor health at different times in their lives, whereas some individuals and groups are apt to be more at risk than others at any given point in time.

Being in poor physical health (such as having a debilitating chronic illness) may also make one more vulnerable (at risk) to poor psychological (depression) or social health (few supportive social contacts). The risk of harm or neglect would be increased for those who are in poor health and have few material (economic) and nonmaterial (psychological or social) resources to assist them in coping with illness.

The beginning point for understanding the factors that increase the risk of poor health originates in a macrolevel look at the availability and distribution of community resources (see Figure 8.1). Individuals' risks vary as a function of the opportunities and material and nonmaterial resources associated with (a) the personal characteristics (age, sex, and race/ethnicity) of the individuals themselves; (b) the nature of the ties between them (e.g., family members, friends, and neighbors); and (c) the schools, jobs, incomes, and housing that characterize the neighborhoods in which they live. The corresponding rewards and resources available to individuals as a function of these social arrangements include social status (prestige and power), social capital (social support), and human capital (productive potential).

Social status is associated with positions that individuals occupy in society as a function of age, sex, or race/ethnicity and the corollary socially defined opportunities and rewards, such as prestige and power, that they have as a result. Minorities often have poorer health

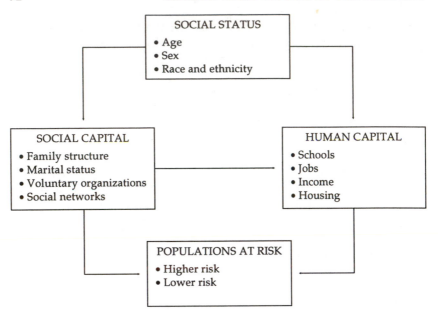

Figure 8.1. Predictors of the risk of poor health.

SOURCE: From *At Risk in America: The Health Care Needs of Vulnerable Populations in the United States* (Figure 1.2, p. 7) by L. A. Aday, 1993, San Francisco: Jossey-Bass. Copyright © 1993 by Jossey-Bass, Inc. Used by permission.

and fewer material and nonmaterial resources to meet their needs than do majority-race individuals. The prevalence of certain types of illness and the need to depend on others for assistance due to poor health differs at different stages of life (infancy, adolescence, adulthood, and old age). Women report higher rates of many types of illness than do men, which has been variously attributed to women's differing health needs, the stress associated with the complex of deferential and demanding roles that women play, and its being more socially acceptable for women to admit their vulnerability (see chapter by Chris Hafner-Eaton in this volume). However, men may also be placed at greater risk of poor health outcomes as a function of working in hazardous jobs or being influenced by societal sex role expectations regarding heavy drinking or the use of violence to settle disputes. Those individuals with a combination of statuses (poor, minority, elderly women or young males) that put them at a high risk of having both poor health and few material and nonmaterial resources are in a highly vulnerable position (Kaplan, 1989).

Social capital resides in the quantity and quality of interpersonal ties between people. Families provide social capital to members in the form of social networks and support and associated feelings of belonging, psychological well-being, and self-esteem. The value of social capital to individuals, say, single mothers, is that it provides resources, such as having someone to count on for child care, they can use to achieve other interests, such as going to school or working. Social support has been found to be an important resource for individuals in coping with and minimizing the impact of negative life events or adversity on their physical and mental health. Physical, psychological, and social well-being are directly enhanced for people who have supportive social networks. Communities constitute the reservoir in which social capital resources are both generated and drawn on by individual community members. Those who are likely to have the least social capital (or the fewest social ties to count on) are people living alone or those in female-headed families, those who are not married or in an otherwise committed intimate relationship, people who do not belong to any voluntary organizations (such as churches or volunteer interest groups), or those who have weak or nonexistent social networks of family or friends (Coleman, 1990; Gore, 1989).

Human capital refers to investments in people's skills and capabilities (such as vocational or public education) that enable them to act in new ways (master a trade) or enhance their contributions to society (enter the labor force). Social capital can also enhance the generation of human capital through, for example, family and community support for encouraging students to stay in school. Neighborhoods that have poor schools, high rates of unemployment, and substandard housing reflect low levels of investments in the human capital (or productive potential) of the people who live there. Similarly, individuals who are poorly educated, unemployed, and poorly housed are likely to have the fewest resources for coping with illness or other personal or economic adversities (Coleman, 1990; Hornbeck & Salamon, 1991).

An informed *health* policy acknowledges the central role that social and economic, as well as medical care and public health, policies play in attenuating the risks and consequences of vulnerability through investing in individuals and the supportive ties between them.

Social and economic policy to ameliorate vulnerability would focus on mitigating the socially and legally sanctioned power and *social status* differences, based on age, sex, and/or racial or ethnic group membership. Family-centered public policy directed toward strengthening those social units and households concerned with the mutual care and support of members represents an effort to invest in the maintenance and enhancement of *social capital* resources. Related efforts would attempt to build cooperative bridges between the variety of public health, medical care, and human and social service agencies required to meet the needs of multiproblem families and individuals. Those initiatives that are likely to be most successful in enhancing social capital formation are ones in which neighborhood residents are directly involved in the needs identification and program development process.

The availability of social capital directly affects the level of investments in *human capital*. Family or other community support is important in encouraging children to stay in school or assisting with child care to facilitate individual family members' participation in the workforce. Health-oriented social and economic policy acknowledges the importance of investing in those community institutions and resources that are both directly and indirectly supportive of the generation of human capital—schools, jobs, housing, and associated family and individual economic safety nets.

To begin to both envision and attend to the dimensions and scope of the problem of vulnerability to poor physical, psychological, and/or social health in the United States, policymakers must come to understand the role that communities play as well as the normative compass that such a perspective provides.

Payment Principles: A Shared Responsibility

A plethora of proposals for health care financing reform have emerged in recent years. They are lodged primarily in the individual rights-oriented objective of enhancing equity of access to medical care.

The major equity criteria underlying these proposals include (a) maximizing *consumer* choice; (b) not discriminating on the basis of age, sex, race, or ability to pay; (c) assuring some minimum standards for everyone; (d) making sure that those who need care get it; and (e) providing high-quality care at an affordable cost. These commonly applied *norms of distributional fairness* parallel ethical principles derived from the major theoretical perspectives on indi-

Table 8.1 Criteria for Evaluating Universal Health Insurance Proposals in Terms of Equity of Access to Medical Care

	Focus		
Criteria of Equity	*Plan*	*Patients*	*Providers*
Freedom of choice			
Minimize constraints on consumer choice of providers		X	
Similar treatment			
Provide universal coverage	X		
Minimize disparities between private and public plans	X		
Use community rating	X		
Use progressive methods for determining consumer contributions		X	
Limit or cap consumer out-of-pocket costs		X	
Use same reimbursement rates for all payers			X
Limit or cap provider reimbursement			X
Decent basic minimum			
Cover core benefits	X		
Primary care			
Acute care			
Long-term care			
Need, cost-effectiveness			
Prioritize benefits, based on outcomes	X		
Primary prevention			
Secondary prevention			
Tertiary prevention			

vidual rights reviewed earlier: (a) freedom of choice (libertarian, contractarian), (b) similar treatment (egalitarian, contractarian), (c) decent basic minimum (needs based), (d) need (needs based, contractarian), and (e) cost-effectiveness (utilitarian). Conflicts in the interpretation or operating definitions of these norms and the relative importance or values assigned to each underlie debates regarding how to design a fair and equitable universal health insurance plan (Aday et al., 1993).

Table 8.1 summarizes how these criteria could be translated and applied in specifying features of the plan itself as well as the distribution of benefits and burdens between patients and providers with respect to enhancing *equity of access to medical care.* Applying more community-oriented norms would also focus on the extent to which they are likely to enhance *equity of access to health.*

The discussion that follows highlights the extent to which the American Health Security Act proposed to Congress by the Clinton administration incorporates these principles (Task Force on National Health Care Reform, 1993).

The Plan

Equity-based criteria for evaluating features of a universal health insurance plan include (a) the universality of coverage, (b) minimization of disparities between public and private tiers of payers, (c) the use of community rating as a basis for determining premiums, and (d) the provision of a decent basic minimum set of (e) medically effective services.

Those plans that cover *everyone* in a *similar* fashion and use a broad, rather than a narrow, actuarial base in computing risks are most likely to assure equity of access, based on egalitarian norms. The former minimizes the disparities in the type or extent of coverage provided, and the latter assures that the burdens and benefits are spread more widely and evenly.

Community rating refers to the fact that the basis for computing actuarial risks and the attendant impact on premiums is based on broad, rather than narrow, population groupings. *Experience rating,* in contrast, bases the setting of rates on a narrowly defined group of eligibles. This latter strategy provides incentives to limit eligibility and enrollment to those most likely to require the least or least expensive care so as to keep the price of premiums down. The result is that those most in need (those with serious health problems or at risk of developing them, such as persons who are HIV-positive) are likely to be excluded or charged very high rates for coverage.

Need and effectiveness norms focus on whether certain procedures or services have been demonstrated, in the aggregate, to improve patient functioning or well-being. Such a perspective would underlie the entire range of prevention-oriented, treatment-oriented, and long-term care services for vulnerable populations. Existing and proposed models for providing and paying for care should be evaluated in the context of their adequacy in providing a decent basic minimum set of services *across* this caregiving continuum.

The American Health Security Act proposes to maximize universal coverage for the U.S. population, with the exception of undocumented persons, who would continue to receive Medicaid coverage for emergency services. The plan calls for other Medicaid-eligible individuals to be folded into regional health alliances. States have the option of including Medicare enrollees but only if benefits are equal to or better than current coverage and a fee-for-service plan is offered. Community rating would replace experience rating as the basis for determining premiums paid by consumers, but payments to a participating health plan by the alliances would be adjusted to account for variations in risk for individuals actually enrolled. Further, individuals could not be excluded from plans because of preexisting health problems.

Overall, the Clinton proposal reflects significant progress in implementing the similar treatment norm through extending more universal coverage, attempting to minimize disparities between private and public insurers (particularly statewide variation in Medicaid), and employing community rating as a basis for premiums.

Considerable discretion, however, is left to the states in setting up the alliances, which may still result in substantial interstate variation in how they are designed and implemented. Further, large corporations with 5,000 or more employees, including Taft-Hartley plans formed pursuant to collective bargaining and rural electric and telephone cooperatives, can form their own alliances. These corporate alliances must offer plans that provide a nationally guaranteed level of benefits. They may also, however, be more likely to offer more generous supplemental coverage options than those available through the regional alliances.

The core benefits provided under the basic package are relatively comprehensive, emphasizing preventive care and expanded coverage for skilled nursing home and home health care, and phasing in mental health and substance abuse coverage. The act also provides for expanded home and community-based services for individuals with severe disabilities and improved institutional care for the mentally retarded through amendments to the Social Security Act. These provisions do not, however, adequately encompass coverage of the custodial care required by many elderly individuals in nursing homes currently covered largely through Medicaid or family out-of-pocket outlays.

Overall, the proposal reflects a commitment to a comprehensive decent basic minimum set of services, based on considerations of probable effectiveness (particularly in the expanded coverage of primary prevention-oriented benefits). It does not, however, incorporate an explicit consideration of an underlying continuum of prevention-oriented, treatment-oriented, and long-term care services and the extent to which such a continuum might be supported by investments in public health and associated community and social support, as well as medical care, services. Nor does it explicitly consider the impact of a focus on paying for medically oriented services on these and related public or nonprofit entities and agencies that might constitute such a continuum.

The Patients

The features to consider in minimizing financial barriers to access from the patient's point of view include (a) minimizing constraints on consumers' choice of provider, (b) the use of progressive (rather than regressive) methods for determining their contributions, and (c) limiting the amount that patients have to pay out of pocket. These are quite intimately linked, rather than discrete, criteria.

The main discretion that consumers have over the care they ultimately receive is a function of the choices they have of the providers that they can see in the first place. The more doors closed to them as a result of the unavailability of providers in an area or their unwillingness to see patients with certain types of coverage; the fact that only a limited number of preferred provider, health plan, or self-insurance options are offered to employees or Medicaid recipients; and/or the lack of an informed knowledge basis for choosing among providers, the fewer the de facto choices available to consumers. Universal health insurance options, even those that claim to maximize "consumer choice," should be scrutinized carefully with respect to the extent to which enrollees' *effective* choice of providers is, in reality, maximized.

Health insurance premiums are relatively regressive methods of paying for medical care in that they do not take into account the varying incomes or resources available to enrollees. Progressive taxation or related means of financing tied to ability to pay provide a more equitable basis for distributing the cost of coverage. The burden of out-of-pocket costs for medical care has traditionally fallen most heavily on those in the low-income bracket, for whom even a relatively small dollar outlay constitutes a substantial proportion of their financial resources. Evidence from the RAND Health Insurance Experiment suggests that increased cost sharing does reduce consumers' use of services (Brook et al., 1983). The findings also suggest that increased cost sharing may serve to ration more effective (preventive-related) rather than less effective (hospitalized) care and also differentially affect the access of those who either need it most or can least afford it, as a result.

Although choice is represented as being a tenet of the Clinton proposal, consumer choices of providers will be limited, as they are now, by the array of provider groups available in an area or a participating plan and whether they are offered as options to consumers during open enrollment. The availability of providers may continue to be especially problematic in rural and inner-city communities, particularly given the lack of specificity regarding how organizational and access enhancement program initiatives (such as the National Health Service Corps and "community-based" provider groups) will be affected and/or integrated with the expanded financing of largely medical-care-oriented programs and services.

Sliding scales and premium subsidies would be available for individuals near or below the poverty level. In general, however, the principal methods for financing the proposal tend to be more regressive than progressive (premiums, employer contributions, tobacco taxes). These approaches are likely to have a disproportionate financial impact on lower-income individuals due to accompanying wage or benefit reductions or by increased costs being passed on to consumers. Another principal source of projected revenues would be through reductions in expenditures under the Medicaid and Medicare programs. Some of the proposed sources of savings under these programs (e.g., phasing out disproportionate share payments to hospitals and increased consumer cost sharing under Medicare) may, however, have a greater access impact on low-income and indigent individuals.

The proposal places limits on the out-of-pocket costs that consumers must pay, which vary in low- versus high-cost option plans. The latter permit consumers more flexibility in choosing providers on either a fee-for-service or point-of-service basis, whereas the lower-cost option provides for coverage in health maintenance organization (HMO) or preferred provider organization (PPO) arrangements.

Overall, the proposal reflects limited de facto attention to the similar treatment norms from the patient's point of view, because the poor are likely to continue to bear a disproportionate share of the burden of the direct and indirect costs of expanded coverage.

The Providers

Plan features that diminish the incentives for providers to treat certain categories of patients, but not others, include using the same reimbursement rate regardless of who pays for the care (e.g., private vs. public insurer) and limiting or capping reimbursement across all providers.

One of the major dilemmas that has emerged with the current multitiered system of financing care is the widely varying rates of reimbursement to providers by different payers. The rates of Medicaid reimbursement in some states are much lower than those of private insurers, which has resulted in a dramatic reduction in the number of providers who are willing to see Medicaid-eligible clients (Mitchell, 1991).

The maintenance of the usual and customary fee arrangements under Medicare and Medicaid have contributed significantly to the spiraling costs of medical care in the decades that followed. Diagnosis-related groups (DRGs) and physician relative value-based reimbursement under Medicare are the major policy instruments that have been developed to deal with this issue in the public sector. medical care systems in other countries, such as Canada, use more macro- than micro-oriented approaches to limiting reimbursement through negotiating global budgets and fee schedules with providers (Saltman, 1992).

The assumption underlying these or other methods of capping provider reimbursement, however, is that providers, not patients, are the main generators of demand for costly medical care services (hospitalizations, high-technology procedures, tests, pharmaceuticals, and so on). Cost-containment incentives need to be developed for these important medical care "consumers" as well. However, if these incentives are to be implemented fairly, they must be applied across all the payers (or players) that reimburse providers for care. Otherwise, the incentives remain, as they do now, for providers to serve those who can pay their full asking price and to refuse to provide care for the rest, many of whom are the sickest *and* most vulnerable.

An important principle underlying the formulation of contractual arrangements with participating providers is that they offer competitive options to alliance members in providing basic or expanded benefits. An elaborate system of setting global budgets and monitoring premium increases in the state and corporate alliances is intended to contain increases in the overall amount and rate of growth of health care expenditures. Incentives are also provided to consumers to enroll in lower-cost HMO or PPO options, which ostensibly provide stronger incentives for containing the use of inappropriate or unnecessary services.

The single-payer model, in which all providers face comparable capitation rates or fee schedules, based on large-scale, pooled risk-sharing arrangements, is offered as an option for states in setting up their alliances. Related all-payer options have proven successful in containing the growth in the costs of care in states in the United States in which they have been implemented (Maryland, Massachusetts, and New York, for example). However, health services research to date provides little evidence of the likely success of other alternatives proposed by the administration (particularly PPO and global budgets and regional monitoring of price increases) in constraining the growth in health care costs. Health planning and price controls have similarly demonstrated limited utility in containing investments in or expenditures for health care services in the United States (Shortell & Reinhardt, 1992).

In summary, the proposal evidences limited attention to addressing substantial variations in reimbursement rates across providers and in constraining or capping provider reimbursement. The proposed methods for doing so have either limited or undocumented evidence of success in containing the growth of health care costs.

Conclusions

The arguments presented throughout this chapter pose the question of what *allocation* of medical *and* nonmedical investments may be most beneficial for enhancing Americans' health.

The answer provided here is that human and social capital and the families and communities in which these resources are both generated and consumed should be a primary focus of public and private investments in Americans' individual and collective well-being. This perspective considers the universal investments to facilitate this developmental process as well as the specific entitlements required to open more windows of opportunity for the most vulnerable. It calls for an evaluation of needed preventive medical care and public health investments and scrutinizes the incentives *and* disincentives built into existing and proposed systems of organizing and financing medical care in the United States for reducing the risk of poor physical, psychological, and social health.

The American Health Security Act proposed by the Clinton administration attempts to enhance equity of access to medical care through expanded financial coverage of a core set of covered services. However, it falls short of offering a framework for identifying and integrating the array of investments and resulting trade-offs in the medical care, public health, and social and economic infrastructure that may be required to enhance the equity, efficiency, and effectiveness of public investments in U.S. citizens' health and well-being.

Ultimately, this chapter argues that the current policy debate regarding how best to *reform U.S. health care* fails to adequately address the question of how best to *improve the nation's health.*

References

Aaron, H. (1991). *Serious and unstable condition: Financing America's health care.* Washington, DC: Brookings Institution.

Aday, L. A. (1993). *At risk in America: The health and health care needs of vulnerable populations in the United States.* San Francisco: Jossey-Bass.

Aday, L. A., Begley, C., Lairson, D., & Slater, C. (1993). *Evaluating the medical care system: Effectiveness, efficiency, and equity.* Ann Arbor, MI: Health Administration Press.

Anderson, O. W. (1989). *The health services continuum in democratic states: An inquiry into solvable problems.* Ann Arbor, MI: Health Administration Press.

Barber, B. R. (1984). *Strong democracy: Participatory politics for a new age.* Berkeley: University of California Press.

Beauchamp, D. E. (1988). *The health of the republic: Epidemics, medicine, and moralism as challenges to democracy.* Philadelphia: Temple University Press.

Bellah, R. N., Madsen, R., Sullivan, W. M., Swidler, A., & Tipton, S. M. (1985). *Habits of the heart: Individualism and commitment in American life.* Berkeley: University of California Press.

Bellah, R. N., Madsen, R., Sullivan, W. M., Swidler, A., & Tipton, S. M. (1991). *The good society.* New York: Alfred A. Knopf.

Brook, R. H., Ware, J. E., Jr., Rogers, W. H., Keeler, E. B., Davies, A. R., Donald, C. A., Goldberg, G. A., Lohr, K. N., Masthay, P. C., & Newhouse, J. P. (1983). Does free care improve adults' health? Results from a randomized controlled trial. *New England Journal of Medicine, 309,* 1426-1434.

Carlson, R. (1975). *The end of medicine.* New York: John Wiley.

Coleman, J. S. (1990). *Foundations of social theory.* Cambridge, MA: Harvard University Press.

Culyer, A. J. (1992). The morality of efficiency in health care—Some uncomfortable implications. *Health Economics, 1,* 7-18.

Daniels, N. (1985). *Just health care.* Cambridge, UK: Cambridge University Press.

Dougherty, C. (1988). *American health care: Realities, rights, and reforms.* New York: Oxford University Press.

Evans, R., & Stoddart, G. (1990). Producing health, consuming health care. *Social Science and Medicine, 31,* 1347-1363.

Fuchs, V. R. (1991). National health insurance revisited. *Health Affairs, 10*(4), 7-17.

Glaser, W. A. (1991). *Health insurance in practice: International variations in financing, benefits, and problems.* San Francisco: Jossey-Bass.

Glendon, M. A. (1991). *Rights talk: The impoverishment of political discourse.* New York: Free Press.

Gore, S. (1989). Social networks and social supports in health care. In H. E. Freeman & S. Levine (Eds.), *Handbook of medical sociology* (4th ed., pp. 306-331). Englewood Cliffs, NJ: Prentice Hall.

Gray, A. M. (1982). Inequalities in health: The Black Report. A summary and comment. *International Journal of Health Services, 12,* 349-380.

Hornbeck, D. W., & Salamon, L. M. (Eds.). (1991). *Human capital and America's future: An economic strategy for the nineties.* Baltimore, MD: Johns Hopkins University Press.

Illich, I. (1975). *Medical nemesis.* London: M. Boyars.

Kaplan, H. B. (1989). Health, disease, and the social structure. In H. E. Freeman & S. Levine (Eds.), *Handbook of medical sociology* (4th ed., pp. 46-68). Englewood Cliffs, NJ: Prentice Hall.

Knowles, J. (1977). Doing better and feeling worse: Health in the United States. *Daedalus, 106,* 1-278.

Kymlicka, W. (1989). *Liberalism, community, and culture.* New York: Oxford University Press.

Lalonde, M. (1975). *A new perspective on the health of Canadians.* Ottawa: Information Canada.

Last, J. (Ed.). (1983). *A dictionary of epidemiology.* New York: Oxford University Press.

McBeath, W. H. (1991). Health for all: A public health vision. *American Journal of Public Health, 81,* 1560-1565.

McGinnis, J. M., Richmond, J. B., Brandt, E. N., Jr., Windom, R. E., & Mason, J. O. (1992). Health progress in the United States: Results of the 1990 Objectives for the Nation. *Journal of the American Medical Association, 268,* 2545-2552.

Milio, N. (1983). *Primary care and the public's health.* Lexington, MA: Lexington Books.

Mitchell, J. B. (1991). Physician participation in Medicaid revisited. *Medical Care, 29,* 645-653.

Mulhall, S., & Swift, A. (1992). *Liberals and communitarians.* Cambridge, MA: Blackwell.

National Center for Health Statistics. (1992). *Health, United States, 1991* (DHHS Publication No. PHS 92-1232). Washington, DC: U.S. Government Printing Office.

Nozick, R. (1974). *Anarchy, state, and utopia.* New York: Basic Books.

Priester, R. (1992). A values framework for health system reform. *Health Affairs, 11*(1), 84-107.

Rawls, J. (1971). *A theory of justice.* Cambridge, MA: Harvard University Press.

Saltman, R. B. (1992). Single-source financing systems: A solution for the United States? *Journal of the American Medical Association, 268,* 774-779.

Shortell, S. M., & Reinhardt, U. E. (Eds.). (1992). *Improving health policy and management: Nine critical issues for the 1990s.* Ann Arbor, MI: Health Administration Press.

Task Force on National Health Care Reform. (1993). *Proposal: The American Health Security Act of 1993.* Washington, DC: Author.

Tesh, S. (1988). *Hidden arguments: Political ideology and disease prevention policy.* New Brunswick, NJ: Rutgers University Press.

Veatch, R. (1981). *A theory of medical ethics.* New York: Basic Books.

9

Federalism and Health Care Reform

COLLEEN M. GROGAN

At the heart of the health care reform debate are philosophical differences concerning the appropriate degree of government involvement in (or centralization of) the financing and administration of health care policy. The debate focuses, first, on the role of government in health care and, second, on the degree of power or authority that should be granted to each level of government—federal, state, and local. Interestingly, resolving the first part of the debate does not move us closer to resolving the second part of the debate: a single-payer system, where the government is the sole financier of care, could be run by state- (or provincial-) level governments, as in Canada, or by a central federal (or parliamentary) government, as in Britain. Therefore, in addressing Part 2 of the health care reform

AUTHOR'S NOTE: I gratefully acknowledge Deborah Stone's helpful suggestions for revision of an earlier draft, as well as challenging and insightful feedback from a talk I gave at Duke University, especially comments from Robert Sprinkle and Steven Rathgeb Smith.

104

debate we are forced to confront the larger, long, and enduring debate in this country about the division of power and the appropriateness of federal versus state control. In popular public policy discourse, the "federalist" question with regard to social programs is usually couched as having to do with the appropriate degree of centralization. In social policy, the United States has traditionally favored a decentralized system based on the belief that state-controlled approaches are more innovative, decrease administrative costs, and increase democratic responsiveness. The purpose of this chapter is to challenge these assumptions.

The terms *decentralization* and *democratic responsiveness* remain poorly defined, the relationship between them inadequately explained. Decentralization remains poorly defined because the term is relative and elusive. To illustrate this point, I explore the degree of program centralization in three different comparative contexts: a cross-national comparison, a comparison of existing health care programs in the United States, and a comparison of the four major health care reform proposals. The cross-national comparison is very brief; my main intent is simply to illustrate the great extent to which the United States has a decentralized system relative to other Western, industrialized countries. The second comparison is in some ways a qualification of the first: The U.S. *system* is highly decentralized; however, individual programs within the system span the centralization/decentralization continuum. I analyze four major health care programs in the United States—employer-sponsored health insurance, Medicaid, Medicare, and the Veterans Affairs health plan. The third comparison reveals where the major health care reform proposals fit into the existing system on the centralization continuum. From this analysis, I argue that states will have significant power under U.S. health care reform, based primarily on the belief that they will be more responsive to local needs.

I next challenge the assumptions underlying the push for state control. First, I consider what is meant by democratic responsiveness by discussing how the term takes on different meanings whether used for a public or private system. As the basis for my challenge, I present a literature review of the state-controlled Medicaid program to consider what we know about the relationship between decentralization (or state control) and democratic responsiveness, innovation, and administrative costs.

I conclude by offering some reasons why the United States continues to favor a decentralized approach and discuss how such an

Decentralized		Centralized
United States	Canada	Britain
	Germany	

Figure 9.1. Centralization continuum—cross-national comparison.

approach is unique (compared to other countries) because we advocate the use of "centralizing policies" to standardize the way medical care is provided.

Program Comparisons

Cross-National Comparisons

Although the terms *centralized* and *decentralized* are apt for describing the differences between Great Britain and the United States, they become less useful when describing the systems in Canada or Germany. For example, the health care systems in Canada and Germany are usually described as decentralized in relation to Great Britain; however, when compared to the United States, their high degree of central control is emphasized. Of course, the terms are imperfect descriptors because they imply discreteness—either a system is centralized or it is not. Clearly, there are varying degrees of centralization. Yet even the term *centralization* is ill defined. My working definition depends on, first, the degree to which any level of government is involved in financing health care and, second, the degree to which the national or central government is involved. More specifically (although the administration of the system is fairly decentralized), centralization depends on the number of payers, administrative agencies, and policy decision points in the system. For example, a single-payer system administered by a single federal agency where policy program changes come only from the federal legislature or parliamentary body is considered highly centralized. Figure 9.1 is an attempt to illustrate this notion of a centralization continuum and to show where the United States lies on the continuum relative to three other countries: Canada, Germany, and Great Britain.

Great Britain is at the far end of the centralization continuum because not only does it meet the above definition for being highly centralized, but it also has a high degree of public ownership—most hospitals are government owned, and the vast majority of general practitioners and specialists work for the government. There is a private health care system in Great Britain, but it is still quite small (10% of the population have private insurance, and only 5% of total hospital and physician expenditures are paid by the private sector) (Potter & Porter, 1989).

As mentioned, attempts to place Canada and Germany on the centralization continuum illustrate the elusiveness of the centralization concept. For example, my working definition becomes difficult to apply in this case because although I specify three dimensions (the number of payers, administrative units, and policy decision points in the system) that determine the degree of centralization, I do not discuss varying levels of importance among the dimensions. Therefore, Canada and Germany share the same location on the continuum because they have different centralizing and decentralizing components that prove difficult to determine if one country is leaning more toward one direction on the continuum than toward the other. They are, however, both clearly less centralized than Great Britain: Canada's system is administered and primarily financed by its 10 provincial governments (Terris, 1990); Germany's has multiple payers and administrative units varying by the type and locality of its 1,100 sickness funds (Kirkman-Liff, 1991). Their federal governments, however, have formidable regulatory and policy-making roles that serve as strong centralizing forces: They mandate broad coverage policies, restrict double billing (providers accepting participation in the system must accept the payment in full; that is, providers cannot levy an additional charge on the patient); mandate specific reimbursement policies, such as the use of expenditure targets for physician groups in Germany and capitation for hospitals in Canada (although each paying unit—provincial governments in Canada and sickness funds in Germany—actually determines the reimbursement levels by negotiating with provider groups); and regulate supply, such as hospital beds and technological acquisitions (Grogan, 1992).

Great Britain has the most centralized system of the three and is the most equitable in terms of benefits *covered*—all services are covered regardless of age, income, or geographic location (see Table 9.1). As a system moves down toward the decentralized end of the continuum, differences in coverage usually emerge. For example, coverage for some services differ by geographic location in Canada; copayment levels and certain amenity services, such as spas, differ by

Table 9.1   Services Provided in Britain, Canada, and Germany

Services	Britain	Canada	Germany
Inpatient care	X	X	X (copay)
Ambulatory care	X	X	X
Health education and promotion	X	X	X
Long-term care for chronically disabled elderly	X	X	Means tested
Dental care	X	Some provinces	X (copay)
Prescription drugs	X (copay)	Some provinces	X (copay)
Chiropractic care	X	Some provinces	X
Optometric care	X	Some provinces	X
Freedom to choose			
General practitioner	Limited	X	X
Specialist		X	X

SOURCES: U.S. Department of Health, Education, and Welfare (1980); Henke (1989); Potter and Porter (1989).

sickness funds in Germany. Note that the American system is so decentralized that it is impossible to include in Table 9.1; we must analyze each program separately to get a picture of the whole.

U.S. Health Care Programs

Employer-sponsored health insurance is the primary way by which Americans finance their medical care (see Table 9.2). About 75% of American workers have access to employer-sponsored group health insurance (Sullivan, Miller, Feldman, & Dowd, 1992). The three other major public programs in the United States are considered supplements to the private sector. Medicaid is a federal-state program that protects selected groups of low-income individuals and families who meet state-specific eligibility standards (Grogan, in press). It finances care for 42% of persons with incomes below the federal poverty level (Iglehart, 1992a). Medicare is a federal program primarily for the elderly, defined as persons over 65 years of age; however, it also covers persons who are permanently disabled or have end-stage renal disease. The medical care program for veterans is financed by an annual congressional appropriation; it is a highly centralized program on a par with Great Britain's National Health Service. Below, I compare the degree of centralization apparent in each program.

Table 9.2   Type of Health Insurance in the United States in 1990

Type of Coverage	Percentage
Private	
Employment based	59
Individual	6
Prepaid, HMO	14
Public	
Medicare	13
Medicaid	9
Uninsured	13

SOURCE: Iglehart (1992b).
NOTE: Percentages add to more than 100 because some people have more than one type of coverage.

Employer-Sponsored Health Insurance. Employer-sponsored health insurance is highly decentralized: There is minimal government involvement and thousands of payers, administrative units, and policy-making units (see Figure 9.2). Such health plans vary dramatically: They offer varying benefits—different usage review mechanisms, modes of delivery, funding sources, and reimbursement methods (Iglehart, 1992a). Some firms offer coverage for family members; others extend coverage only to the employee. In addition, most plans use experience rating methods that often eliminate persons with preexisting medical conditions (Stone, 1993).

There is very little government control over employer-sponsored health insurance plans and, despite signs of progress toward major health care reform, recent policies suggest that the government is moving toward a more limited role. For example, under the federal Employee Retirement Income Security Act (ERISA), self-insured companies are exempt from providing state-mandated benefits that private insurance plans must cover. The U.S. Supreme Court recently upheld the appeals court ruling that under ERISA self-insured companies are "free to create, modify and terminate the terms and conditions of employee benefit plans without governmental interference" (Iglehart, 1992c, p. 1719). Moreover, a growing number of states are exempting small businesses (fewer than 25 employees) from state-mandated benefit restrictions (Grogan, 1992). The federal government encourages employer-sponsored health plans by providing tax exemptions for the amount that firms spend on health insurance.

Decentralized			Centralized
Employer sponsored	Medicaid	Medicare	Veterans

Figure 9.2. Centralization continuum—U.S. health care programs.

Medicaid. Especially for a government-run program, Medicaid represents a fairly high degree of decentralization: It is financed by 50 different state governments and the federal government through general tax revenues; administered by 50 different state health departments (some states use more than one agency to administer the program—for instance, in some states, outpatient mental health services covered under Medicaid are administered by state mental health authorities), the federal Health Care Financing Administration, and some county governments; and all 50 state governments and the federal government can impose policy changes on the Medicaid program.

The states exercise significant control over Medicaid eligibility and benefit packages. The federal Medicaid requirements imposed on the states are only minimally restrictive. Especially in comparison to federal regulations in Germany or Canada, the U.S. federal government is a weak centralizing force under Medicaid. For instance, although states are required to provide Medicaid coverage to all Aid to Families with Dependent Children (AFDC) recipients (the majority of Medicaid eligibles), states are in effect allowed to define who is eligible. AFDC eligibility standards depend on income and asset limitations and specific categorical definitions set by each state. The federal government mandates a basic set of services under Medicaid; however, states are allowed to select from among 32 optional services (Ruther, Reilly, Silverman, & Abbott, 1990). Not surprisingly, the adoption of optional services varies significantly—from 9 in Wyoming to 30 in Massachusetts—as do income eligibility levels—from $144 per month in Mississippi to $866 in Alaska for a family of four.

Medicare. A key difference between Medicare and Medicaid is the level of government control. Medicare represents a fairly high degree of centralization on the continuum: It is financed by the federal government as the single payer, and all policy program changes are instituted by the federal government. The administration of the program, however, is decentralized: Payments for Medicare claims are administered by 82 different private health insurers under contract with the Health Care Financing Administration (HCFA), a federal agency. Because Medicare eligibility is determined at the federal level, all Medicare beneficiaries, regardless of location or income, have access to the same set of covered services (Iglehart, 1992a).

Veterans Affairs Medical Plan. At the opposite end of the continuum from employer-sponsored health plans is the program for veterans. It meets most of the conditions for being highly centralized: The federal government is the single payer, the Department of Veterans Affairs is the sole administrator, and major program policy changes are instituted by the federal government (although specific Veterans Administration hospital policies are granted by the regional authorities). In addition, most of the facilities used in the program are owned by the federal government: It owns and operates 171 hospitals, 127 nursing homes, and 93 clinics (Iglehart, 1992a). It also employs its own medical staff: 12,241 full-time physicians, 990 dentists, and 33,898 nurses were paid on salary in 1990 (Iglehart, 1992a). The eligibility criteria for this program is veteran status; among veterans, the program is highly equitable—everyone has the same coverage regardless of age or income. Of course, there are differences in the quality of various facilities; in this way, persons do not have access to the same level of care. However, this logic applies to all the programs: An insurance plan alone cannot equalize the quality of services provided in different locations.

This comparison also illustrates the elusiveness of the decentralization concept. For example, although characterizing the U.S. health system as a whole as very decentralized is accurate, that characterization can be misleading. Clearly, some programs, namely, Medicare and the Veterans Affairs health plan, are highly centralized. In this light, it is not surprising that current health care reform proposals span the centralization continuum. Yet it is perhaps equally predictable that the majority of proposals reside on the decentralized end of the continuum.

U.S. Health Care Reform Proposals

Health policy researchers often categorize the numerous reform proposals under various versions of the following four headings: expansion of existing programs, pay or play, managed competition, and single-payer model (Blendon & Edwards, 1991; Morone, 1992).

Proposals that fall under either pay or play, expansion of existing programs, or managed competition rely heavily on the existing system. Proposals that call for expansions usually do it in one of two ways: expand current government programs to include the uninsured (either expand Medicaid, Medicare, or both, or create a new federal-state program) or mandate that firms of a certain size (usually with 25 or more employees) offer health insurance and expand government programs as discussed to cover the remaining uninsured. Play-or-pay plans are similar to the second approach above except they offer employers a choice: Employers can either provide health insurance to their employees (play) or pay an equivalent tax to help fund a new or expanded public insurance program. The managed-competition approach calls for a set of regulatory policies to promote competition between health insurance plans. The intent of managed competition is to maintain the existing system but inject a dose of regulation to make the private sector more efficient. Indeed, proposals that fall under the rubric of play or pay or expansion also propose various managed-competition policies. "True" managed-competition plans, however, are unique in calling for new state-level public agencies—called public sponsors (Enthoven & Kronick, 1991) or health insurance purchasing cooperatives (HIPCs) (see Starr, 1993)—to act as the exclusive purchasing agent for small employers and individuals without access to employer-sponsored health insurance. In fact, the design of HIPCs is key to determining the degree of centralization in a managed-competition approach (Starr, 1993; Wicks, Curtis, & Haugh, 1993). If HIPCs are designed to be large, state-level entities where there is, for example, only one HIPC per state including large employers (as well as small businesses and individuals) and the policies governing HIPCs are determined at the federal level (although administered and run by state governments), the program would be fairly centralized relative to play or pay or simply expanding existing programs. Although the exact structure of these reform proposals is unclear, most explanations suggest that they would fall on the decentralized half of the continuum; however, the location could vary from the far left extreme to somewhere in the center (see Figure 9.3).

The vast majority of health care reform proposals fall under the three approaches discussed above. For example, of the 13 proposals presented in the *Journal of the American Medical Association*'s (*JAMA*'s) 1991 special issue on health care reform (Vol. 265, No. 19), 10 fell under the headings play or pay, expansion, or managed competition. The remaining 3 proposals advocated single-payer reform.

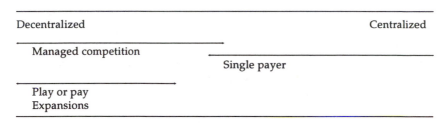

Figure 9.3. Centralization continuum—U.S. health care reform proposals.

Single-payer proposals would result in the most dramatic system change because the government would become the sole financier of health insurance (although most plans allow for private insurance). However, most single-payer models are only moderately centralized because they also advocate state-level control (Fein, 1991; Grumbach, Bodenheimer, Himmelstein, & Woolhandler, 1991). In addition, such plans usually provide a role for insurance companies, thereby decentralizing the administration of the program similar to Medicare (Grumbach et al., 1991; Roybal, 1991).

Not only do the proposals themselves indicate a decentralized approach, but several recent political signs point in that direction as well. For example, President Clinton's first health policy step was to grant states greater flexibility in running Medicaid programs by ordering the Department of Health and Human Services to streamline its process for granting federal waivers (McGinley & Stout, 1993). In particular, the HCFA is now limited to one request for further information from a state seeking a waiver, and the agency must grant automatic approval for states trying to adopt initiatives successfully introduced under waivers in other states (Gunnison, 1993). In addition, Health and Human Services recently granted Oregon its controversial Medicaid waiver. Second, after their January 1993 meeting in Washington, the National Governors' Association openly endorsed the managed-competition approach (McGinley & Stout, 1993). Finally, some of the key health care reform task force appointees (e.g., Ira Magaziner, Lynn Etheredge, and Paul Starr) favor managed competition.

All this adds up to a significant role for the states in almost any health care reform bill. The main argument for a decentralized, state-controlled approach is that it allows states to structure their system to meet local needs and demands (Fein, 1991; Kronick, 1993;

Starr & Zelman, 1993). Yet, because the premise for this argument is largely assumed, very little has been written about democratic responsiveness under state-controlled health care programs. When a decentralized approach is pursued, there is always a conflict over whom to empower—the federal government as regulator or state innovators (Morone, 1992). The granting of federal waivers to the states is an illustration of this conflict. In the next section, I explore what is known about innovation, efficiency, and democratic responsiveness under the largely state-controlled Medicaid program.

Lessons From Medicaid

Democratic Responsiveness

The term democratic responsiveness assumes a different meaning whether used for the private or the public sector. For example, in a competitive private market, individuals exercise their power by exiting the system: If they are dissatisfied, they can drop their health plan (or physician or hospital) and choose another to satisfy their needs or desires (Klein, 1979). Therefore, under private plans, democratic responsiveness usually means the extent to which individuals have the freedom to choose. Under a public health plan, democratic responsiveness usually means the extent to which the general citizenry's (or program recipients') views are represented in the program's policies (Klein, 1979). The United States is in the unique position of having to consider both types of democratic responsiveness under its health system. Although managed competition (HR 5936) is mainly concerned with how to improve democratic responsiveness in the private sector (create a private health plan market where consumers can exercise their power to choose), the need to consider public sector democratic responsiveness will still exist. For example, under a managed-competition model, everyone would receive a subsidy for the lowest-cost plan; those who want a more expensive plan (for more provider or facility choice or "higher" quality) must pay the difference. Persons with low incomes (below the poverty level) would receive this subsidy directly from the state. Although everyone has the option to pay additional money to upgrade their coverage, it would be very difficult for persons in poverty to exercise this option. Whereas some geographic areas might have several plans priced at the lowest cost, it is quite likely that other areas, such as rural or inner-city localities, will offer only one lowest-cost plan. The poor and many of the near poor will have no consumer power. Even advocates of managed competition admit that this would be a problem (Enthoven, 1993). A recent report from the task force to the nation's governors indicates that states will determine which incentives, mandates, and regulations are necessary to assure both coverage and cost containment, particularly in inner-city and rural areas ("Health Reform Secrets," 1993). In this situation, it is important to think about how the poor will be empowered or represented. Experiences under Medicaid may enlighten the debate.

The proposed advantage of a decentralized, state-administered Medicaid program is that states are more familiar with the financial requirements of health care providers and the health care needs of the poor in their state. "New federalists" (advocates for greater state control) argue that it is appropriate for states to determine the structure of their social policies through the state political process— states should have the right to decide what is best for themselves, including the degree to which they favor income redistribution or health care subsidies.

Several empirical studies have shown that Medicaid policy is very much influenced by state politics (Clauser, 1983; Grogan, in press; Peterson & Rom, 1990; Plotnick & Winters, 1985). The degree to which a poor person gains access to the Medicaid program and the types of medical services a person receives depends on state government party control (Democratic or Republican) and state political ideology, suggesting that state policy is responding to local political preferences as the "new federalists" would have it. However, other findings from these studies raise questions about who is actually represented in the states. This, in fact, is the key question when thinking about democratic responsiveness: To whom are states responsive? There are numerous constituency groups concerned about Medicaid, and their interests are usually not in harmony. Even when constituency interests are the same, politicians tend to make distinctions between groups perceiving their interests as conflicting rather than complementary. Constituency conflicts arise between providers and recipients and between recipients.

For example, there is some evidence that Medicaid provider interests tend to win out over the interests of recipients. Two studies document that states with below-average Medicaid spending per poor recipient are relatively generous to health providers (Cromwell,

Hurdle, & Schurman, 1987; Reutzel, 1989). Moreover, an empirical study of the factors influencing state Medicaid policy found a positive relationship between the strength of senior citizen, nursing home, and health provider interest groups and the provision of Medicaid benefits (Grogan, in press). Medicaid recipients are interested in Medicaid policy but are not politically powerful and have no discernible influence on state political decision making (Cook, Barrett, Popkin, Constantino, & Kaufman, 1988).

Several researchers have also suggested that the elderly and disabled (supplemental security income [SSI]) recipients are better represented under the Medicaid program than are AFDC recipients (Burwell & Rymer, 1987; Joe, Meltzer, & Yu, 1986). This view is usually based on the disproportionate amount of expenditures allotted to SSI recipients. For example, AFDC recipients represent 66% of Medicaid's case load but constitute only 25% of expenditures. In contrast, the aged and disabled represent only 29% of Medicaid cases but account for about 72% of total Medicaid expenditures. Institutional long-term-care costs for the elderly and the disabled have increased from 31% of total Medicaid payments in 1969 to 46% in 1982, whereas from 1973 to 1983 the share of Medicaid expenditures for AFDC families declined from 33.2% to 25.7%. Although total Medicaid spending has increased for all groups, spending for aged and disabled recipients has increased more than twice as fast as spending for AFDC families (National Study Group on State Medicaid Strategies, 1984). Some researchers use the above statistics to support the argument that attempting to serve all three of these population groups under Medicaid overburdens the system and has resulted in poor families and children receiving an increasingly smaller slice of the Medicaid expenditure pie (Burwell & Rymer, 1987; Joe et al., 1986). Although there is very little empirical evidence to support this claim, one study has found evidence of biased representation among Medicaid recipients (Grogan, in press). That study found that states with both senior citizen and nursing home interest group power tend to elicit categorical optional benefits (state adoption of "medically needy" programs) at the cost of more generous financial eligibility requirements for AFDC recipients.

There is also some evidence of biased representation by race. Three empirical studies have found that the race of AFDC recipients is associated with Medicaid policy decisions. In particular, controlling for other demographic factors, there is a significant negative relationship between the proportion of non-White AFDC recipients and AFDC income eligibility levels (Grogan, in press; Orr, 1976; Plotnick & Winters, 1985). In sum, the above findings suggest that public sector democratic responsiveness under Medicaid is skewed toward organized interest group representation and that the politically powerless voice of the poor tends to suffer.

State Medicaid policy is also affected by state economic capacity. Numerous studies have found that state income is an important factor in determining state AFDC payment levels and Medicaid benefit coverage (Grogan, in press; Orr, 1976; Peterson & Rom, 1990; Plotnick & Winters, 1985). Thus, although a significant proportion of state Medicaid inequity is explained by local political preferences, states' financial ability to provide services also plays a role. The federal government has attempted to correct for these differences in financial ability by using a federal matching rate ranging from 50% to 78% depending on state per capita income. Several policy analysts have argued that the matching rate is inadequate in its attempt to artificially equalize state economic resources (Cromwell et al., 1987; General Accounting Office, 1990; Gramlich, 1982) and suggest methods to reform such as using the percentage in poverty rather than per capita income (General Accounting Office, 1990). The failure of the federal matching rate to equalize Medicaid benefits among the states raises an important question about the federal-state financial relationship in health care reform: To what extent should there be income redistribution among the states so that poor states have the *opportunity* to meet the needs of their residents?

Innovation

Another part of the argument for a state-controlled health care system is that the states are more innovative than the federal government. Although there has been much discussion in state legislatures about proposals for universal coverage, only 9 of the 50 states have either proposed, implemented, or enhanced efforts to *both* increase health care access by the poor and increase or protect health insurance coverage for workers and dependents (Morrison & Schmid, 1992). These states have relatively high per capita incomes. The states with no access initiatives recently (1988-1991) implemented or proposed are relatively poor states—12 of the 17 were ranked 31 or higher for state per capita income (a ranking of 1 being the highest per capita income level) (Morrison & Schmid, 1992; U.S. Bureau of the Census, 1989). States with moderate to high per capita incomes and stable economies appear more likely to consider major health care reform. Hawaii, Vermont, and Minnesota fit this description and have enacted major health reform programs. Massachusetts passed landmark legislation in 1988 but recently delayed implementation until 1994 due to the state's poor economic situation (Morrison & Schmid, 1992). California, usually a front-runner in state policy innovation, is lagging behind in expanding access to the uninsured: In the face of a severe recession with high unemployment and a sizable budget deficit, the state is focusing on how to contain costs in its Medicaid program, rather than expanding access for the uninsured. Although some relatively wealthy states have and are able to pursue health reform policies, many states would face financial difficulties pursuing major delivery changes on their own (Kronick, 1993).

In addition, many of the reform efforts and innovative policies tested in the states received federal funding (Dobson, Moran, & Young, 1992; Stone, 1991). In many cases, such as Medicaid managed-care initiatives, the federal government promoted pilot testing in the states (Stone, 1991). Although many innovative health reform policies were implemented at the state level, they were really a federal-state partnership, and the reform idea did not originate solely in the states.

Administrative Costs

Many states argue that local administration assures a tighter, more efficient Medicaid program than one mandated by the federal government (Cromwell et al., 1987; Fein, 1991). Although there does appear to be a correlation between the degree of program centralization and administrative costs, simple cross-tabulations suggest the reverse of what decentralist proponents claim: Less centralized programs have higher administrative costs (see Table 9.3). Administrative costs include insurers' expenditures for claims processing (payment and review), marketing, sales, and resources spent to comply with regulations (Iglehart, 1992a). Of course, a major reason why administrative costs are lower in public systems is that no resources are needed for marketing or sales (although depending on the type of program, there could be community outreach and/or education costs). In addition, systems that use capitation to reimburse providers eliminate the need for claims processing (note that prepaid HMO plans have the lowest administrative costs among private plans).

Table 9.3 Administrative Costs, by Type of Health Insurance in the United States in 1990

Type of Coverage	Administrative Costs as % of Spending
Private	Average 14.2
Employment based	5.5 to 4.0
Individual	40.0
Self-insured	5.0 to 12.0
Prepaid, HMO	2.5 to 7.0
Public	
Medicare	2.1
Medicaid	3.2 to 11.8
Average	5.1
United States	5.8
Canada	1.3[a]

SOURCES: Data from Iglehart (1992b) and Thorpe (1992).
a. 1985 data from Terris (1990).

The average state Medicaid program has lower administrative costs than the average employer-sponsored health plan but has much higher administrative costs compared to the federally run Medicare program. Medicare is relatively efficient administratively in the American system; however, it has higher costs than Canada. One of the reasons why Medicare, a federally run program, has higher administrative costs than Canada (run by its provinces) may be that the one decentralizing force in Medicare is the relatively large number of administrative units. Medicare agents (called intermediaries if they reimburse for Part A claims or carriers if they administer Part B claims) are given a substantial degree of freedom in deciding what is a covered benefit and how much to pay for it. Medicare's 82 contractors use 14 different information systems to process and review claims (Iglehart, 1992b). In Canada, by contrast, each province has a centralized administrative unit.

Of course, this is a very cursory look at the relationship between levels of centralization and administrative costs. Clearly, there are numerous ways to measure administrative costs, and greater administrative costs do not necessarily mean that a program is inefficient (see Thorpe, 1992). My main intent here is simply to question the implication by decentralists that state-level-controlled programs are more efficient: The verdict is still out on the relationship between decentralization and efficiency.

Conclusion

In this chapter, I have attempted to illustrate the elusiveness of the decentralization concept by documenting the varying degrees of centralization among the major U.S. entitlement programs and the major reform proposals. I argue that U.S. health care reform will take a largely state-controlled approach emphasizing the assumed virtues of democratic responsiveness, innovation, and administrative efficiency. Yet claims of increased administrative efficiency are not well supported by the data. In addition, only relatively wealthy states have been innovative with respect to health care reform; most states would face financial difficulties in the absence of federal aid. Moreover, the democratic responsiveness argument is too simplistic. There are numerous constituency groups under state-controlled programs, and their interests cannot all be heard at once. Although states may be able to better understand and respond to local needs, they cannot respond to all local needs. Some constituents, namely, financially sound, organized interests, are better represented than others. Therefore, the assumption that state governments can respond effectively to local needs should be questioned on two fronts: First, whose needs do state governments respond to? Second, do states have the financial ability to respond to local needs? The second question is key to the federal-state funding relationship—to what extent and how should income be redistributed among the states? This has been a major issue in the Medicaid program that has yet to be resolved.

Despite these unanswered questions, Americans continue to favor a decentralized approach. Why? Many researchers, policymakers, and even politicians agree that the general public has a lack of faith in the federal government as an administrator (Morone, 1990; Tallon & Nathan, 1992). Ironically, although Americans scorn the thought of the federal government as administrator, they, at the same time, rely more and more on the federal government as a regulator of health care (Brown, 1992). This paradox produces a unique American situation: a decentralized system with centralized micromanagement.

Most other countries try to achieve efficiency (control costs) through systemwide mechanisms (global budgeting or fixed fees, controls on medical supplies, and/or restrictions on technological acquisitions) and promote clinical effectiveness (quality) by allowing a high degree of clinical autonomy. The United States, on the other hand, pursues effectiveness and efficiency jointly: In the absence of centralized political bodies to set budgets (or fees) or limit supply, Americans rely on bureaucratic entities to regulate the *way* medical services are provided (Morone, 1992). For example, the vast majority of health care reform proposals include provisions for the collection of outcomes research to develop clinical protocols (see *JAMA*'s 1991 special issue; Morone, 1992). To contain costs, the United States is in the process of trying to control the *behavior* of providers, not their budgets as other countries do. Indeed, "outcomes management" is hailed as the new cost control panacea (Blustein & Marmor, 1992). It is perceived as a panacea because proponents claim to achieve two principles with one policy: An outcomes management policy would control costs (increase efficiency) and improve quality (effectiveness).

The irony is that the degree to which the system is decentralized limits the degree to which these centralized policies can be instituted effectively. The federal government as regulator has been relatively more effective in containing Medicare costs than it has with Medicaid. Because the federal government is both the administrator and regulator of Medicare, it can implement a policy, such as the Prospective Payment System or the Resource-Based Relative Value Scale, with relative ease. However, when the federal government uses its power to control the formation of Medicaid policies, states balk. In light of significant state variations in service use (or practice style) (Zuckerman & Holahan, 1992), any effort by the federal government to impose standardized clinical protocols nationwide will likely meet state opposition. Therein lies the dilemma facing health care reformers: To what extent can the federal government impose centralizing cost control policies on a largely state-controlled system?

References

Blendon, R. J., & Edwards, J. N. (1991). Caring for the uninsured: Choices for reform. *Journal of the American Medical Association, 265*, 2563-2565.

Blustein, J., & Marmor, T. R. (1992). Cutting waste by making rules: Promises, pitfalls, and realistic prospects. *University of Pennsylvania Law Review, 5*, 1543-1572.

Brown, L. D. (1992). Political evolution of federal health care regulation. *Health Affairs, 11*(4), 17-37.

Burwell, B. O., & Rymer, M. P. (1987). Trends in Medicaid eligibility. *Health Affairs, 6*(4), 30-45.

Clauser, S. B. (1983). A comparative analysis of state discretionary Medicaid policies. *Dissertation Abstracts International, 44,* 9A. (University Microfilms No. 83-29503)

Cook, F. L., Barrett, E. J., Popkin, S. J., Constantino, E. A., & Kaufman, J. E. (1988). *Convergent perspectives on social welfare policy: The views from the general public, members of Congress, and AFDC recipients* (Research report). Evanston, IL: Center for Urban Affairs and Policy Research.

Cromwell, J., Hurdle, S., & Schurman, R. (1987). Defederalizing Medicaid: Fair to the poor, fair to taxpayers? *Journal of Health Politics, Policy and Law, 12*(1), 1-34.

Dobson, A., Moran, D., & Young, G. (1992). Role of federal waivers in the health policy process. *Health Affairs, 11*(4), 72-94.

Enthoven, A. C. (1993). The history and principles of managed competition. *Health Affairs, 12*(Suppl.), 24-48.

Enthoven, A. C., & Kronick, R. (1991). Universal health insurance through incentives reform. *Journal of the American Medical Association, 265,* 2532-2536.

Fein, R. (1991). The health security partnership: A federal-state universal insurance and cost-containment program. *Journal of the American Medical Association, 265,* 2555-2558.

General Accounting Office. (1990). *Medicaid formula: Fairness could be improved* (Testimony by Janet L. Shikles before Subcommittee on Human Resources and Intergovernmental Relations, Committee on Government Operations, House of Representatives, December 7). Washington, DC: Author.

Gramlich, E. M. (1982). An econometric examination of the new federalism. *Brookings Papers on Economic Activity, 2,* 327-360.

Grogan, C. M. (1992). Deciding on access and levels of care: A comparison of Canada, Britain, Germany, and the United States. *Journal of Health Politics, Policy and Law, 17*(2), 213-232.

Grogan, C. M. (in press). The political-economic factors influencing state Medicaid programs. *Political Research Quarterly.*

Grumbach, K., Bodenheimer, T., Himmelstein, D. U., & Woolhandler, S. (1991). Liberal benefits, conservative spending: The physicians for a national health program proposal. *Journal of the American Medical Association, 265,* 2549-2554.

Gunnison, R. B. (1993, February 2). Clinton eases rules for states on health care. *San Francisco Chronicle,* pp. A1, A9.

Health reform secrets. (1993, April 8). *Wall Street Journal,* p. A14.

Henke, K. (1989, December). Respondent to Johnson's article. *Health Care Financing Review, 10*(Suppl.), 93-96.

Iglehart, J. K. (1992a). The American health care system: Introduction. *New England Journal of Medicine, 326,* 962-967.

Iglehart, J. K. (1992b). The American health care system: Medicare. *New England Journal of Medicine, 327,* 1467-1472.

Iglehart, J. K. (1992c). The American health care system: Private insurance. *New England Journal of Medicine, 326,* 1715-1720.

Joe, T. C., Meltzer, J., & Yu, P. (1986). Arbitrary access to care: The case for reforming Medicaid. *Health Affairs, 5*(4), 59-74.

Kirkman-Liff, B. L. (1991). Health insurance values and implementation in the Netherlands and the Federal Republic of Germany: An alternative path to universal coverage. *Journal of the American Medical Association, 265,* 2496-2502.

Klein, R. (1979). Control, participation, and the British National Health Service. *Milbank Memorial Fund Quarterly, 57*(1), 70-94.

Kronick, R. (1993). Where should the buck stop? Federal and state responsibilities in health care financing reform. *Health Affairs, 12*(Suppl.), 87-98.

McGinley, L., & Stout, H. (1993, February 2). Clinton acts to give more flexibility on running Medicaid plans to states. *Wall Street Journal*, p. A14.

Morone, J. A. (1990). *The Democratic wish: Popular participation and the limits of American government*. New York: Basic Books.

Morone, J. A. (1992). Administrative agencies and the implementation of national health care reform. In C. Brecher (Ed.), *Implementation issues and national health care reform* (pp. 47-76). Washington, DC: Josiah Macy, Jr. Foundation.

Morrison, E. M., & Schmid, G. (1992). State initiatives in health care. In R. J. Blendon & T. S. Hyams (Eds.), *Reforming the system: Containing health care costs in an era of universal coverage* (pp. 103-124). New York: Faulkner & Gray.

National Study Group on State Medicaid Strategies. (1984). *Restructuring Medicaid: An agenda for change*. Washington, DC: Author.

Orr, L. (1976). Income transfers as a public good: An application to AFDC. *Economic Review, 66*, 359-371.

Peterson, P. E., & Rom, M. C. (1990). *Welfare magnets: A new case for a national standard*. Washington, DC: Brookings Institution.

Plotnick, R. D., & Winters, R. F. (1985). A politico-economic theory of income redistribution. *American Political Science Review, 79*(2), 458-473.

Potter, C., & Porter, J. (1989). American perceptions of the British National Health Service: Five myths. *Journal of Health Politics, Policy and Law, 14*(2), 341-365.

Reutzel, T. J. (1989). Medicaid eligibility, benefits, and provider payment: State preferences and implications for national goals. *Health Policy, 11*, 209-226.

Roybal, E. R. (1991). The "US Health Act": Comprehensive reform for a caring America. *Journal of the American Medical Association, 265*, 2545-2548.

Ruther, M., Reilly, T. W., Silverman, H. A., & Abbott, D. B. (1990). *The Medicare and Medicaid data book, 1990* (HCFA Publication No. 03314). Washington, DC: U.S. Government Printing Office.

Starr, P. (1993). Design of health insurance purchasing cooperatives. *Health Affairs, 12*(Suppl.), 58-64.

Starr, P., & Zelman, W. A. (1993). Bridge to compromise: Competition under a budget. *Health Affairs, 12*(Suppl.), 7-23.

Stone, D. A. (1991, May). *State innovation in health policy*. Paper presented at the Ford Foundation Conference on "The Fundamental Questions of Innovation," Duke University, Durham, NC.

Stone, D. A. (1993). The struggle for the soul of health insurance. *Journal of Health Politics, Policy and Law, 18*(2), 287-317.

Sullivan, C. B., Miller, M., Feldman, R., & Dowd, B. (1992). Employer-sponsored health insurance in 1991. *Health Affairs, 11*(4), 172-185.

Tallon, J. R., & Nathan, R. P. (1992). Federal/state partnership for health system reform. *Health Affairs, 11*(4), 7-16.

Terris, M. (1990). Lessons from Canada's health program. *Journal of Public Health Policy, 11*(2), 151-160.

Thorpe, K. E. (1992). Inside the black box of administrative costs. *Health Affairs, 11*(2), 41-55.

U.S. Bureau of the Census. (1989). *Statistical abstract of the United States: 1989* (109th ed.). Washington, DC: U.S. Government Printing Office.

U.S. Department of Health, Education and Welfare. (1980). *Responses of Canadian physicians to the introduction of universal medical care insurance: The first five years in Quebec* (DHEW Publication No. 80-3229). Hyattsville, MD: National Center for Health Services Research.

Wicks, E. K., Curtis, R. E., & Haugh, K. (1993). The ABCs of HIPCs. *Journal of American Health Policy, 3*(2), 29-34.

Zuckerman, S., & Holahan, J. (1992). Measuring growth in the volume and intensity of Medicare physician services. *Inquiry, 29,* 391-402.

10

Defining a Role for States in a Federal Health Care System

RUSSELL L. HANSON

*T*here is a health care crisis in the United States, and its dimensions are depressingly familiar. As many as 39 million people have little or no access to basic medical services because they lack any form of health insurance. Another 70 million have inadequate insurance, and although they can obtain routine services, these people and their families face financial ruin if they contract a catastrophic illness or disease. To make matters worse, the costs of medical care, hospitalization, and institutionalization are rising very rapidly. In 1970, Americans spent about 9% of their income on health; now they spend 14%.[1] That is nearly twice the rate paid by citizens in other industrialized democracies in the West (Mattoon, 1992). For many in the United

AUTHOR'S NOTE: I want to thank Pauline Vaillancourt Rosenau, who recruited me for this project, supplied valuable information, and provided editorial direction. Leroy Rieselbach also made several helpful suggestions.

States, health care is becoming prohibitively expensive, the technological wizardry of American medicine notwithstanding.

Politicians at the national level are beginning to respond to the health care crisis, especially now that voters have begun to demand some kind of action. Indeed, a wide variety of solutions is being debated in Washington, DC. Generally speaking, these solutions fall into three categories. Market-oriented reforms work within the existing system of private insurance, Medicare, and Medicaid to expand coverage. So-called play-or-pay proposals enlarge employer insurance plans and mesh them with expanded public insurance programs. National health insurance proposals envision universal, single-payer systems of the sort found in Germany or especially in Canada.

Market-oriented reforms, such as those proposed by the Bush administration, would solve the health care crisis by improving the current system of insurance. Coverage would be extended to the un- and underinsured by issuing vouchers (or tax credits) for purchasing private health insurance. This would alleviate the problem of access without creating another public bureaucracy, although critics fear that voucher payments might be too low to purchase adequate insurance. Medical costs would be controlled by "managed-care programs," or alternatively, by taxing health benefits to encourage restraint on the part of the consumers of health care.[2]

Play-or-pay proposals would expand coverage by requiring employers to provide minimal health insurance for their workers or be taxed for public insurance programs. Workers, their families, and many others who are now un- or underinsured could be covered by the new public insurance. Cost containment would be achieved through some form of rate setting, whereby public bodies establish fees for services, medications, and so on—a feature that is anathema to many conservatives. The effects of cost containment would be general, and both private and public insurance plans would benefit, according to proponents of play or pay.

National health insurance is the most radical proposal, for it would make the government the primary payer for all medical services.[3] Coverage would be universal, and health benefits would be standardized under this arrangement, although it might allow for secondary insurance plans to cover special costs, such as private hospital rooms. The single-payer system favors cost containment by allowing the government to use its concentrated purchasing power to negotiate charges and fees. It also reduces administrative overhead because providers deal with a single agency, instead of hundreds of private insurers. Questions about the efficiency of this single agency, as well as the cost of national health insurance, have been raised by proponents of the other two kinds of proposals for dealing with the health care crisis.

Congress is divided over these three strategies for improving access to affordable health care, and it is hard to predict which proposal will be adopted. In fact, the Clinton administration is exploring an alternative that combines elements of its three main rivals. Under the Clinton plan, all consumers would belong to health insurance cooperatives organized by state governments; these cooperatives would effectively function as single payers within regional spheres of influence. The cooperative would contract with a variety of private health plans, offering members a choice of alternatives at low rates for basic services, as devotees of market reform want. At taxpayers' expense, national, state, and local governments would subsidize coverage for poor individuals and families, achieving the same effect as the play-or-pay proposals for expanding access to health care. A cap on total spending would limit cost increases over time.

Obviously, the existing division of labor in health policy will be significantly altered no matter which plan ultimately wins approval from Congress. As things stand now, state governments have enormous responsibilities for health care. They bear the onus of protecting food and water supplies, disposing of waste, insuring public sanitation, and regulating a host of activities associated with disease prevention. States are also the primary regulators of the health industry; they license professional organizations, certify hospitals and institutions, and oversee private insurance companies. In addition, states help finance and administer Medicaid, the major public program of health care for the indigent.

States achieved their strategic importance in health care for many reasons, including the national government's historic reluctance to go beyond Medicare and the current list of public health activities. If Congress establishes new, and potentially much larger, responsibilities for the national government in health policy, the role of the states will change accordingly. However, it would be a mistake to think that states' influence over health policy will shrink once the national government becomes more involved. Their responsibilities might change, but states will continue to play a decisive role in providing health care to American citizens.

For example, if Congress enacts national health insurance, the states will probably administer the program. The single-payer systems of England, Germany, and Canada are administered by subnational agencies, and in the United States the most obvious (and experienced) candidates for subnational administration are the states. That was true in 1935 when the Social Security Act relied on states to implement public assistance and unemployment insurance, and it was true in 1965 when Medicaid was first established. It is still true today, when states are enjoying a political resurgence and a better reputation for administrative performance (Bowman & Kearney, 1986; Reeves, 1990). Thus it is quite likely that states would act as paying agents for services covered by a national plan (Graham, 1992). In addition, states might provide additional services at their own expense, as the Canadian provinces do.

The role of states would be even larger in play-or-pay programs. Again, states would probably act as paying agents of the national government, reimbursing health care providers according to predetermined rates. The rates would vary across regions, and state authorities would help set them. States would also take the lead in regulatory reform of the insurance industry, assuring a basic set of services in all employer plans and the new public (or at least publicly organized and subsidized) insurance program associated with the "pay" option. Cost containment efforts, too, would devolve to the states, who could take the lead in organizing managed competition between health care providers, for example.

Reforms built around a voucher system are political long shots, now that Democrats control the national government. However, Republicans and conservative Democrats could still join forces to improve current market arrangements for providing health care. Many of these reforms entail changes in federal tax laws; others involve new regulations on private insurance companies, which are governed primarily by state laws. States would still be at the center of public health care provision cost containment efforts, and so market-oriented reforms would actually expand state responsibilities.

Thus states will play a major role in implementing new approaches to health care, whatever Congress decides.[4] Consequently, states have a strong interest in defining their future responsibilities by participating in the debate over national policy. But states do not agree on what their role ought to be. Some prefer market-oriented reforms, which do not threaten existing programs, policies, and priorities of state government. Others favor a national play-or-pay system as a way of extracting them from the untenable position of imposing insurance costs on employers when other states do not. Still other states lean toward some version of universal insurance or even a single-payer system.

In short, the states are badly divided on health policy, and their division contributes to the current impasse in Washington, DC. To a significant degree, the alternatives being debated in Congress spring from the experiences and preferences of state policymakers. Elites from each state offer their programs as models for the nation, and their elected representatives and senators are happy to endorse models developed in their own state. At the same time, a state's congressional delegation opposes any legislation that would undermine the continuation of popular state programs or mandate locally unpopular actions. Thus congressional differences of opinion are themselves deeply rooted in the diversity of state innovations in health care policy. A brief review of these state experiences will show their relevance to, and impact on, the current debate in Congress and the proposal recently advanced by President Clinton's Task Force on Health Care.

Lessons From the States

While national officials discuss their policy options, states already have begun to implement different strategies for expanding access to health care and controlling its costs (Weissert, 1992). States have been driven to action by the soaring costs of health care. States help finance and administer Medicaid, the major public program of health care for the indigent in the United States. Largely because of Medicaid responsibilities, state and local governments supplied almost one third of the $283 billion spent by governments on health in 1990 (Health and Human Services, 1992). Although Medicaid expenditures represented a mere 4.2% of Alaska's total outlays in FY1990, on average they were almost 15% of a state's general expenditures in FY1990. Medicaid accounted for a whopping 19.1% of Rhode Island's outlays in that year. Moreover, Medicaid's share of state budgets is increasing; it is expected to average 17% in 1995, when it will absorb more than half of a typical state's annual increase in revenues (Dubin, 1992).[5]

State policymakers feel an urgent need to bring Medicaid under control so that other popular programs (e.g., education) can grow without requiring further tax increases (Gold, 1991). Governors from Florida to the state of Washington believe they cannot wait for a national response to the health care crisis (Gardner, 1992; Rohter, 1993b). Hence states are experimenting with measures designed to cope with the health care crisis in general and the explosive growth in Medicaid in particular. The experiments involve programs that resemble those being debated on the national level, and it is illuminating to discuss the experiments in those terms before turning to reforms favored by the Clinton administration.[6]

Market-Oriented Reforms and Regulatory Relief

As of this writing, no state has tried a voucher system, although several have recently adopted regulations that make private health insurance more widely available to workers and their dependents, the largest and fastest growing segment of the uninsured population.[7] In 1991 alone, 15 states moved to make insurance more affordable for small employers—California, Colorado, Delaware, Florida, Iowa, Kansas, Nebraska, New Mexico, North Carolina, Oregon, Rhode Island, South Carolina, Vermont, West Virginia, and Wisconsin (Government Accounting Office, 1992b). Another 26 established high-risk insurance pools for people whose "pre-existing illness or conditions" made them uninsurable in the eyes of private insurance companies (Biemesderfer, 1992; Rydell, 1991).[8]

Colorado's shared cost option for private employers, or SCOPE, exemplifies the effort to assist businesses in obtaining low-cost, comprehensive indemnity insurance for their employees (and very often their dependents). SCOPE is one of 15 pilot projects funded by the Robert Wood Johnson Foundation. It provides a wide range of primary and preventive services for which there are no deductibles or co-insurance. Small copayments are required for office visits and prescriptions, and catastrophic medical expenses are co-insured at a rate of 50% up to $5,000. Care is available only through a limited provider network, but premium rates are far below the national average for small business, especially for families (Begala, Kuehn, & Levine, 1991).[9]

Insurance premiums for small businesses can also be reduced by mandating community rating systems.[10] This spreads the risk from a single company's employees to a broader group or community of small businesses, making insurance affordable for firms whose employees have unusual health problems. Establishment of a reinsurance pool for all insurance companies operating in the small-group market would also help, equalizing the risk of large claims for catastrophic illnesses or chronic health problems (Begala et al., 1991).

Regulatory reform of private insurance has been combined with modest efforts to include people who cannot afford private insurance even when they qualify for it. Washington's basic health plan subsidizes health insurance for the working poor but enrolls fewer than 20,000 of the estimated 450,000 people who are eligible. (A plan for universal coverage was just approved by the Washington state legislature, however.) Similarly, Maine's health program expands Medicaid eligibility but reaches only 11,400 of the state's 113,000 uninsured people (Government Accounting Office, 1992a).

A more ambitious expansion of Medicaid was proposed by Oregon in 1989. The Oregon Basic Health Services Act (OBHSA) and related legislation guarantees health care for all persons whose income falls below the federal poverty line. Tax credits are given to small-business employers who begin offering insurance to workers and their dependents. If the credits do not induce enough new coverage, a tax on employers is scheduled to take effect in 1994. Persons without insurance would receive care under Medicaid, although services would be rationed. Treatments would be ranked according to a list of health care priorities, and the state's appropriation for Medicaid would then determine how many items on the list would be funded in any given year. "Essential" and "very important" services ordinarily would be financed, but the availability of other treatments would depend on the state's financial condition (Leichter, 1992a).

Oregon's plan aims to reverse the current situation in which some people have access to an extensive array of medical assistance, but many have no access at all. OBHSA would insure that all Oregonians can obtain minimal care, but there is a price: With increased access come reductions in services to clients of the state's existing Medicaid program. This trade-off has generated fierce opposition to the idea of rationing, which primarily affects the poor.[11] Rationing also harms the disabled, who frequently need expensive treatments and rehabilitation that do not have a high priority on Oregon's list. In 1992, the U.S. Department of Health and Human Services declined to issue the necessary waiver for rationing Medicaid services on the grounds that it was inconsistent with the recently enacted Americans with Disabilities Act. However, a revised application for waiver was submitted and approved in 1993; when implemented, the change will add about 120,000 to Oregon's Medicaid program (Pear, 1993b).

Some states are also moving aggressively to contain health care costs. Since 1971, Maryland's Health Services Cost Review Commission has set payment rates for all hospital-based inpatient and outpatient care. Discounts are provided to Medicare and Medicaid, and the rates are adjusted annually for inflation. As a result, hospital admission costs in Maryland are consistently lower than average. So are the profit margins of hospitals, despite an across-the-board rate increase in 1988 that was granted to offset a comparative decline in solvency (see article in the August 19, 1991 issue of *Medicine & Health Perspectives*, pp. 1-4).

Neighboring Virginia has begun to use its certificate of need program to limit costly expansions and unnecessary investments in medical technology. The certificate of need program was initiated by the federal government in 1974 but was largely abandoned by the states in 1986 when federal funding was eliminated. However, it may be revived as states seek to reduce the oversupply of hospital beds, duplication of services, and overinvestment in expensive technology that often occurs in the absence of state regulation (Mattoon, 1992).[12]

Play-or-Pay Experiments

A number of states have explored play-or-pay policies that require employers to provide insurance for their workers or pay into a public insurance fund. Perhaps the leading example is Hawaii, where Medicare, Medicaid, and veterans' health care programs are complemented by two additional forms of insurance. The first was created in 1974, after the adoption of Hawaii's Prepaid Health Care Act (PHCA). It requires all Hawaiian employers to provide health insurance for full-time workers, who contribute no more than 1.5% of their gross wages toward premiums.[13] The law does not mandate coverage of dependents, but many employers include them because unemployment is low and they must compete for workers (Dukakis, 1992).

The second form of insurance, the State Health Insurance Program (SHIP), was created in 1989 to provide coverage for 30,000 to 35,000 Hawaiians not covered under existing laws, generally because they are unemployed or part-time workers who do not qualify for Medicaid (Neubauer, 1992). General state revenues are used to finance SHIP, which is managed by the Hawaii Medical Services Association (a Blue Cross/Blue Shield affiliate) and Kaiser Permanente, the two dominant providers in the state. By October 1992, some 18,000 Hawaiians were insured under SHIP, and the state was approaching its goal of universal coverage.

Following Hawaii's lead, Massachusetts adopted a universal health care law in 1988. A number of previously uninsured groups have benefited from the extension of public insurance programs, including unemployed workers, students, and severely disabled adults and children. However, the play-or-pay program under which employers pay into a state-brokered insurance fund has been delayed until 1995 because of opposition from businesses. Small businesses in particular complain about the costs of playing or paying, which may decrease their ability to compete with firms in neighboring states that do not impose financial responsibility for health care on employers (Berger, 1991).

Iowa may have more success with a proposed play-or-pay plan, which was designed by a consortium of hospitals, businesses, labor unions, and insurers. Under the plan, employers must either provide insurance for their workers or pay a 5% payroll tax, which would subsidize health insurance premiums on a sliding scale up to 250% of the federal poverty line. In addition to extending insurance coverage, overall costs would be controlled by relying on managed care-methods, setting standardized reimbursement rates for private insurers, and limiting the percentage of insurance premiums claimed as profit and overhead by insurance companies. This would affect everyone, not just those included under the pay-or-play plan.

Governor Lawton Chiles has just proposed the Florida Health Plan, which would insure all 13.5 million residents of the state under nonprofit, state-chartered organizations called "community health purchasing alliances." The voluntary alliances would form a state-wide network and collect health care premiums from individuals, businesses, and governments, thus spreading out risks and increasing access. The alliances would sign contracts with health care providers, choosing those with the best services and lowest costs (Rohter, 1993b). This would help control costs and keep premiums low. (The poor would be entitled to premium subsidies, which would vary according to income.)

If the voluntary system does not produce widespread health coverage by 1994, Florida law authorizes the imposition of a play-or-pay program and the expansion of Medicaid to achieve the long-term goal of universal access (Biemesderfer, 1992). The mandatory program would take effect in 1995, making Florida the largest state with universal access to health care.

Insurance

Hawaii, Massachusetts, and Florida are working toward universal access to health care, but all of them rely heavily on employers' contributions toward insurance to achieve that objective. Two other states are experimenting with public insurance programs that might eventually cover all citizens, regardless of their work status.[14] Minnesota recently established HealthRight, now rechristened MinnesotaCare, a voluntary health insurance package with a sliding scale of premiums based on income. In October 1992, low-income families with children began to enroll; other families with children became eligible in January 1993, and adults could apply for subsidized insurance beginning in 1994.

MinnesotaCare is financed by taxes on cigarettes and hospitals; additional taxes will be levied in the future on health care providers. The plan restricts inpatient care and limits growth in spending to 10% a year for 5 years. Regional and state boards will advise the legislature on cost containment measures (Solomon, 1992a). A wide choice of health maintenance organizations (HMOs) should also help, but even so, the monthly premium is expected to be $250 to $300 for a family of four with an annual income of $30,000. Unless MinnesotaCare is given a wider revenue base, universal coverage will prove elusive.

Only one state is now considering a single-payer system. Vermont has established the Health Care Authority, which by 1994 will develop a plan for insuring universal access to health care by means of a Canadian-style system in which the state would pay all medical bills or through a multipayer system of private insurance regulated heavily by the state (Solomon, 1992b). In either case, the state would set all prices, thereby achieving control over costs. Vermont has already approved laws aimed at establishing a standard set of benefits, subsidizing primary care for pregnant women and teenagers in families with incomes lower than 225% of the federal poverty line, and setting cost targets for hospitals, clinics, and physicians (Mattoon, 1992).

Minnesota and Vermont are unusual among the states; most eschew radical reforms of the sort that might lead to a single-payer system. Primarily, this reflects fear over the costs of the program and the need to raise taxes to pay for it. Concern over taxes is particularly important at the state level because some states rely on low taxes to encourage business investment and relocation. This places "high-tax" states at a comparative disadvantage, making policymakers reluctant to adopt expensive new programs. National insurance plans are attractive to state policymakers in this predicament because such plans promise to create a level playing field by mandating uniform coverage in all states. Out of such concerns are born divisions in Congress.

Lobbying Congress

Health care experiments proliferate as policymakers in different states adopt policies suited to the specific needs of their constituents. This diversity of state innovations is a boon to national policymakers. Instead of discussing alternatives in the abstract or with reference to nations with different cultures and political traditions, policymakers can compare the effects of home remedies concocted by the states. The most effective reforms might then serve as a model for national health policy, as the states perform their historic function as "laboratories of democracy."

Ironically, optimism about the results of policy experimentation at the state level trades on Americans' confidence in medical science. Many people believe that a cure for some dreaded disease, say, cancer or AIDS, will result from increased experimentation in medical laboratories across the country. In the same way, reformers hope that discoveries made at the state level will settle the national debate and produce a satisfying solution to the health care crisis in this country. In both cases, the presumed solution to a problem is finding a cure or obtaining knowledge about what works—and what does not.

Subnational politicians promote this idea, suggesting that knowledge gained via experimentation at the state level might point the way for Congress. Booth Gardner, the chief executive of Washington, recently suggested that states could best influence the national debate "by demonstrating in the states that health care reform is viable" (Gardner, 1992, p. 27). Toward that end, the National Governors' Association has asked Congress to support experimentation at the state level, arguing that "by moving six to eight States forward to demonstrate comprehensive solutions, we may be able to break the impasse in terms of building a national consensus" (Schweppach, 1991, p. 1220).

Such optimism about the results of experimentation ignores an important political reality. As states make substantial political and fiscal investments in health programs, they develop strong preferences about the best or most desirable solutions to the health care crisis. More to the point, state policymakers acquire a proprietary interest in reforms they adopt. This leads policymakers to advance their own state's programs as models for the nation. It also makes them reluctant to cede leadership to other states with different, and potentially incompatible, ideas about solving the health care problem.[15]

Telling evidence of this rivalry among states can be seen in the inability of the National Governors' Association to agree on a single plan of national action. In 1991, the Governors' Task Force on Health Care spent more than a year studying reforms but failed to endorse a specific plan for addressing the nation's crisis in health care. The governors were too divided over which plan was best, and so they settled on a demand for greater freedom to experiment, even though they admitted that states cannot possibly solve the crisis on their own and that a national solution was desperately needed.

The same thing happened in January 1993 when the governors declared universal access to health care both a moral imperative and an invaluable tool for cost containment (Pear, 1993a). Yet the governors refused to say how Congress should act to provide universal access to health care. Although the governors expressed support for a policy that permits states to explore play-or-pay options, they opposed a national law mandating such a requirement. Once again, they concluded with a call for state experimentation in health policy and a demand that national officials make it easier to get exemptions to the Employment Retirement Income Security Act (ERISA) and waivers for innovations in Medicaid.[16] The demand was quickly met by newly elected President Bill Clinton, who as governor led the charge for more experimentation at the governors' meeting in 1991 (Friedman, 1993).

The paralysis of the National Governors' Association reveals much about health care politics. As a group, the governors are unable to enter, and perhaps settle, the national debate on health care reform because they are as badly divided as Congress. On the other hand, individual governors and their allies are free to express their preferences to national policymakers, hoping to shape congressional reforms in their own policies' image and likeness. Indeed, different state models are already being touted in Congress. A Community Health Care Act has been suggested by Harry Johnston (D-FL). It clearly anticipates a national policy that would both protect and propagate the Florida health plan suggested by Governor Lawton Chiles.[17]

Similarly, Fred Grandy (R-IA) has submitted health empowerment and access legislation (HEAL) (HR 1230).[18] HEAL is based on the idea of "using the best of what states have to offer" (Grandy, 1991, p. 319). In this case, the best of what states have to offer bears an uncanny resemblance to Iowa's own play-or-pay experiment, with an interesting twist. Grandy would require employers to offer insurance to employees, without requiring any employer contribution toward premiums. It is play or pay without the pay, so to speak.

Other models from the states have potent support in Congress (Peterson, 1992). S 1227, the so-called HealthAmerica bill, contains many elements championed in Massachusetts by Governor Michael Dukakis, including play-or-pay requirements. Senate Majority Leader George Mitchell of Maine is the first author of S 1227, but the coauthor is Edward Kennedy, the Democratic senator from Massachusetts.[19] In the House of Representatives, play or pay is the centerpiece of HR 2535, a bill submitted by Henry Waxman (D-CA).[20] Cosponsoring HR 2535 is another Democratic representative from Massachusetts, Joseph P. Kennedy II. Thus the Massachusetts model is well represented in the current national debate over health policy reform.

Play or pay is only one kind of proposal being advanced by state delegations in Congress. Universal health insurance under a single-payer system is advocated by Senator Paul Wellstone, a Democrat from Minnesota.[21] Likewise, Vermont's Bernard Sanders (D-VT) has introduced HR 2530, which would establish a Canadian-style system of health insurance. Both states, it will be remembered, are currently experimenting with comprehensive public insurance plans. Marty Russo (D-IL) is also advocating a single-payer system in HR 1300, although in his case there is no state precedent informing the bill.

Champions of market-oriented reforms are not to be outdone. Among the representatives from the South are the members of the Conservative Democratic Forum, a group of about 60 "Boll Weevils" organized by Charles Stenholm (D-TX). The forum has endorsed a plan to establish a nationwide system of HMOs. Competition between HMOs would keep premiums low and eliminate the need for government limits on health care spending, physicians' fees, hospital rates, and so on, according to the forum (Rich, 1992). The market orientation of the plan clearly suits the rural, conservative districts of the Boll Weevils, constituencies that are highly influential in Southern state legislatures not known for extensive Medicaid or other public health care programs.

Thus, instead of forging a political consensus on health policy, state experiments help fuel the controversy in Congress. Representatives put forth examples from their home states as models for the nation, making what are in effect "favorite son" policy recommendations. Partly, this is a matter of conviction, and partly it is a matter of pride in authorship and a corresponding desire to blaze a trail that others, including Congress, will follow.[22]

Another reason for the multiplication of favorite son policy recommendations is that state policymakers are not convinced that solutions developed elsewhere will work in their state. What is effective in California, New York, or Florida is not necessarily a viable solution to health care problems in North or South Dakota. Recognizing this, state politicians advance proposals tailored to the specific needs of their citizens—and incidentally the needs of citizens in similar states. The result is a profusion of state models for Congress to consider, not consensus on a single course of action.

A concern for protecting sovereign prerogatives also animates the lobbying efforts of governors, legislatures, and other state officials. Models developed in other states are not simply irrelevant to a state's problems. They may be incompatible with ongoing programs and innovations in a state pursuing other kinds of solutions. If Congress adopts a play-or-pay system modeled after Hawaii's PHCA/SHIP, the market-oriented reforms being tested in other states would be superseded. Policymakers from the affected states would then face resistance from the lineup of interests whose fate is linked to the continuation of market-oriented reforms: insurance companies, small businesses, and many health providers.[23] Rather than alienate these interests, state policymakers lobby Congress for friendlier legislation and against hostile proposals.

Politically speaking, the situation resembles the notorious problem of closing obsolete military installations. The members of Congress agree that it is both necessary and desirable to close bases, but each and every list of candidates for closure is vociferously opposed by representatives and senators from areas where the affected bases are located. In the end, little or nothing is done. Elected officials refrain from closing bases in others' districts in exchange for continuing operations in their own. The imperatives of coalition building and maintenance overwhelm the problem-solving aims of policy (Arnold, 1979, 1981).

Experiments in health policy reform are like military bases. State officials do not want their policy experiments ended any more than they want their bases closed. They exert pressure on the state's delegation in Congress, which opposes legislation based on principles antithetical to those governing reform at home. The pattern is repeated in state after state, where reforms have proliferated in the past decade. As a result, patterns of opposition in Congress are complex and paralyzing; in the end, perpetuation of the experiments in all states is the only point on which the majority can agree.[24]

For all these reasons, then, states are intimately involved in the congressional debate over health policy. They must be involved if they hope to shape their role in the health care system of the future. But states come to Congress with diverse policy preferences, reflecting their own experiences in health policy reform. Congress allows, and even encourages, this diversity, hoping it will isolate the best policy for the nation. It does no such thing. If anything, Congress's stance makes it harder to achieve a national consensus on health policy. By giving states free rein to experiment with possible solutions to the health care crisis, Congress assures its own continuing division of opinion.

Future Role of the States

What policy will emerge from the national debate on health policy? It is impossible to know for certain, and it is difficult to hazard predictions with any degree of confidence. However, it is safe to say that the debate will not end soon. Democrats control Congress, but they are deeply divided on the issue. Party leaders failed to overcome these differences in 1992, in spite of their desire to make health policy an issue for Democrats. Harris Wofford showed his party how to use the issue effectively in an upset victory over Richard Thornburgh in the Pennsylvania election to replace Senator John Heinz. Democrats wanted to do the same against George Bush and vowed to enact legislation that would force the President to veto a politically appealing bill. But the leaders failed to bring a bill to a floor vote; even Congressman Pete Stark's (D-CA) so-called first step bill, a modest reform proposal, died along the way.

The chance to embarrass George Bush and the prospect of a Democratic victory in November were not enough to unite congressional Democrats in 1992; it is therefore unlikely that Democrats will rally around President Clinton's proposals in 1993 or 1994. Clinton's plans include "global budgeting," managed competition, and a version of play or pay in which those who are not insured by employers are covered by private insurance subsidized by the national government. Global budgeting operates by setting national and state targets for spending on health care and assumes that premiums and fees can be controlled and outlays limited. It is opposed not only by Republicans but also by conservative Democrats who distrust government solutions and bureaucratic procedures.[25]

On the other hand, some influential Democrats are skeptical of managed competition, another element of Clinton's plan.[26] Managed competition assumes that there is, or can be, competition between health care providers, but competition is minimal or nonexistent in many areas of the country. How will managed competition work in sparsely populated areas with only a single regional hospital, or in urban slums where there are no physicians or clinics? Unless President Clinton can address these concerns, his program is unlikely to win a broad base of support among the Democratic party.

If the proponents of new health care policies are divided, their opponents are not. Small businesses have organized against any proposal that imposes increased costs on employers. Hospitals, clinics, and other health care institutions are opposed to limitations on charges or regulations on expansion and investment in new technology. Many, although not all, physicians and health care professionals are against limitations on fees or restrictions on services that are expensive but useful in diagnosis and treatment.[27] Insurance companies resist mandates that increase risks and oblige them to make larger payouts, thereby jeopardizing profits. Seniors oppose policies that would be financed by savings from restricting Medicare (Marmor, 1993). And middle-class citizens everywhere object to policies likely to increase their taxes. So far, the combined opposition has blocked reform legislation in spite of massive popular support for policies that promise expanded access to affordable health care (Wolfe, 1992).

The prospects for action in the immediate future are not good. Joseph A. Califano, Jr. (Secretary of Health, Education and Welfare under President Jimmy Carter) thinks it would be a "legislative miracle" if President Clinton is able to secure health care reform within 2 years of his inauguration ("Clinton Has Rx," 1992, p. 3716). Charlene Rydell, chair of the Health Committee of the National Conference of State Legislatures, suspects that a national consensus will not emerge for 3 or 4 years (Rydell, 1991, pp. 1225-1226).[28] And Raymond C. Schweppach, executive director of the National Governors' Association, predicts that it will take another 4 to 6 years before the impasse in Congress is broken (Schweppach, 1991, p. 1225).

Meanwhile, state governments will continue to explore alternatives. Some experts worry that state experiments will produce 50 different systems of health care. Access to care and standards of service already vary considerably from state to state, and the differences are likely to become larger over time. Some states may follow Minnesota in subsidizing universal health care insurance. Others will adopt play-or-pay plans modeled after Hawaii's PHCA. Still others may explore regulatory solutions or even voucher systems (as several states are already doing in public school systems). The inevitable result will be a "patchwork" of health care strategies, each state having a unique mixture of public programs and private insurance arrangements (Barrilleaux, 1989).[29]

A patchwork of health policies raises serious questions of equity, unless Congress begins to restrict experimentation at the state level.[30] For example, there is considerable sentiment in favor of establishing national standards of basic care and coverage, such that no matter where a person lives in the United States there would be access to essential services. Congress could set these standards and leave states free to improve on them and decide how the standards should be met.

Congress took this tack in combating air and water pollution, giving states the authority to impose tougher restrictions than required under national legislation. Extending this approach to health care is an obvious solution to the political conflict that now paralyzes the national legislature. The minimum standards will insure access to care, and from a political point of view, they create a level playing field across the states. No state will be placed at a competitive disadvantage because its neighbors do less in providing health care, as happens now. Hence minimum standards will attract support from governors and state legislatures—it may be the one thing they can agree on when it comes to national policy.

Progress toward national standards might be accelerated by the spiraling costs of Medicaid. If the states are unable to control public expenditures on health, they will turn to Congress for relief. (Indeed, states are already suggesting that Congress take full financial responsibility for long-term care, the most expensive portion of Medicaid.) Any increase in the subsidy for Medicaid would probably be made contingent on states' meeting new mandates for coverage, services, and standards of care. That has certainly been the trend in

Congress where Medicaid is concerned, and it might produce a de facto set of standards in public health care.

Of course, any standards that emerge from Congress are likely to be quite modest, particularly if states play a significant role in financing health care reform. The need for compromise will produce standards that represent the lowest common denominator of many different plans, and so the logic of the political situation works against ambitious health care requirements (Arnold, 1979). So do economic considerations: Poorer states will resist expensive mandates, unless they are subsidized. Because such subsidies come at the expense of richer states or their citizens, they will be resisted in Congress by representatives of wealthier states. Hence the drift is clearly toward basic, inexpensive standards in a decade of fiscal austerity at the state level (Gold, 1991).[31]

The desire to preserve states' flexibility will be equally strong in the log-rolling process.[32] Permissive arrangements will protect each state's ongoing experiments and allow policymakers to provide as little, or as much, health care as their citizens demand. Citizens who expect no more than what is guaranteed by minimum standards can be assured that elected officials will accommodate their demand; some states will continue to lag in health care. Others will continue to lead, as citizens press officials for more generous or expansive health care, which can be given only if national policies are open-ended. The gap between leaders and laggards will remain and may even grow larger over time.

All of this has happened before: Public assistance and unemployment insurance programs developed this way during the New Deal as Congress deferred to state initiatives and granted numerous exceptions to standard rules and practices. The creation of Medicaid during the Great Society years recapitulated this experience, proving that patchworks are not eliminated by the intervention of the national government in areas long dominated by state policymakers. Quite the opposite is true: Patchworks are protected and even promoted by Congress as it seeks compromises between political forces that sustain, and are sustained by, divergent state experiences.

Thus it would be very surprising if the current crisis in health care produced massive structural changes in American health care provision. Adaptation of the current system is far more likely, if the past is any guide (Tallon & Nathan, 1992). And if the past is a guide, the future of health politics is also clear: Access to affordable health care will vary greatly from state to state. The range of variation will be constrained only by whatever national standards are approved in

Congress and enforced by responsible agencies. Above these minima, states will devise programs consistent with the needs of citizens, demands of health care providers, and available resources. Because all three differ enormously from state to state, programmatic differences will persist and perhaps grow more pronounced with the passage of time.

That will set the stage for future debates on health policy. Equity will be an issue, because some will demand greater uniformity in access to health care. Others will defend the patchwork, saying it corresponds to local and regional differences in opinion and need. That is an old debate in American politics, and health care policy will be discussed in familiar terms for a long time to come.

Notes

1. By the decade's end, as much as 18% of the nation's income could be consumed by health care, according to estimates by the Congressional Budget Office (Starr, 1993, p. 45).

2. Because individuals pay only about one fourth of the costs of medical care, some economists say the system encourages overuse of services and treatments. Demand for health care, and hence its price, could be reduced by making individuals bear a higher proportion of the expense (i.e., by including the employer's contribution to health insurance in the report of an employee's income). The Heritage Foundation touts this strategy of cost containment.

3. The national government would not be the provider of services, as it is in Great Britain. Proposals being discussed in Congress all rely on the existing network of private, not-for-profit, and public health care providers.

4. States' prominence is assured for another reason as well. Policies will be needed for problems that fall outside the ambit of national policy (e.g., preventive health care). At the national level, preventive care has been overshadowed by concern over access to basic treatments for illnesses and disease. By contrast, states have been mandating seat belt use, raising the minimum drinking age, restricting the sale and advertising of tobacco products, distributing condoms and hypodermic needles, and coping with serious environmental hazards (Leichter, 1992b). These actions and many more are designed to reduce people's need for health care services, a strategy that has become increasingly prominent, and in the case of Hawaii—"the health state"—has become an explicit goal of state government (Neubauer, 1992).

5. Nationally mandated extensions of Medicaid are an important cause of spiraling increases: The National Association of State Budget Officers estimates that the cumulative cost of mandates taking effect between 1990 and 1994 will be more than $16 billion. That is two thirds of the total annual outlays by states in FY1990 (Hutchison, 1991). The states are protesting vigorously, and Senator LeRay McAllister of Utah is even advocating an end to that state's participation in Medicaid (Harden, 1991). Governor Ned McWherter of Tennessee has also discussed the possibility of withdrawing his state from Medicaid (Ayres, 1993).

6. Demkovich (1990) and Regan (1990) offer general surveys of recent initiatives in the 50 states.

7. Two thirds of the uninsured have ties to the workforce. Most are employed by small businesses that do not provide insurance (Harden, 1991).

8. Every state but Vermont and Rhode Island now limits insurance premium increases, and all except Vermont, Rhode Island, and Kansas guarantee policy renewal (Rydell, 1991, p. 1216).

9. MaineCare is another example of state-subsidized health insurance and managed care for small businesses and self-employed individuals. It, too, is supported by a grant from the Robert Wood Johnson Foundation. Other beneficiaries are Arkansas, Florida, Iowa, Minnesota, New Mexico, New York, North Dakota, Oklahoma, Oregon, Vermont, and Washington (Freudenheim, 1992).

10. In 1991, Vermont was the only state to enact legislation to require community rating (Rydell, 1991, p. 1216).

11. Defenders of the Oregon plan insist that rationing is already in place: Markets allocate health care according to income. For them, the question is one of fairness: Which system of allocation is more just?

12. See Rabe (1992) for a description of the Canadian system for siting medical facilities.

13. According to the law, employee insurance plans "must provide health care benefits equal to or medically substitutable for benefits provided by plans having the largest number of subscribers in the state" (Neubauer, 1992, p. 155).

14. Another universal plan has been proposed in Indiana but has no chance of approval (Perras, 1992). The same is true for the Missouri universal health assurance plan, proposed by Missouri legislator Gail L. Chatfield (Harden, 1991).

15. This explains Governor Mario Cuomo's eleventh-hour proposal for sweeping changes in New York's regulation of doctors' fees, which may be seen as an effort to influence Congressional action in the field of health care. No other state has created the regulatory powers that Cuomo is seeking, and if the legislature endorses his plan, national policymakers will be forced to accommodate the policies of such an important state (Sack, 1993).

16. The difficulty of obtaining exemptions and waivers, combined with a sharp increase in mandated services in federal programs, has reduced state policymakers' room for maneuvering. Increased flexibility is needed if states are to perform their historic function, say governors and many other state officials.

17. After the Florida legislature adopted his plan for comprehensive reform, Governor Lawton Chiles expressed the hope that Florida's reform would provide a model for the federal government (see Rohter, 1993a).

18. This and all subsequent bill numbers refer to the 102nd Congress.

19. Kennedy has long favored national health insurance, and I do not mean to suggest that his actions are inspired by Dukakis's plan. I am simply pointing to the sense in which a state's political culture shapes the positions of politicians at all levels of government, connecting the policy preferences of state officials and their representatives in Congress (so long as they are members of the same party).

20. Waxman specialized in health policy while serving in the California assembly before his election to the U.S. House of Representatives in 1974.

21. Another Minnesota model has been proposed in the House of Representatives, where Tim Penny (D-MN) has submitted a bill to enact a national children's health program. Schneider (1992) provides a general review of states' leadership in child and maternal health and their influence over national laws and regulations.

22. Skocpol and Ikenberry (1983) analyze the battle between the proponents of the Ohio and Wisconsin plans for unemployment insurance during the New Deal, an interesting precedent for the current debate.

23. Neither can these policymakers expect much from play-or-pay advocates in their state. That group's weakness is evident in the established preference for market reforms. Given this weakness, it will be hard to implement play-or-pay proposals, if that is what Congress enacts.

24. If Arnold (1981) is right, a large majority can agree on this point, particularly if the members of Congress are convinced that pressure on federal bureaucracies will generally "exempt" their states from meeting onerous mandates.

25. Members of the Conservative Democratic Forum will probably oppose Clinton's health care plan, and his leverage over them is reduced because of his support for policies that are anathema to the forum (e.g., the acceptance of homosexuals in the military).

26. Toner (1993) attributes the current impetus for managed competition to the Jackson Hole Group, a loose collection of economists, policy analysts, politicians, and advocates. One of its members, Paul Starr (1993), sketches the main outlines of managed competition, for which there are no current examples at the state or national level. Perhaps the closest approximation is the California Public Employees Retirement System (CALPERS), which buys $1.3 billion of health care annually. Last year CALPERS used its market leverage to keep average premium increases for 20 insurers at 3.1%, far below the state industry average of 13.2%. CALPERS also froze enrollments for Kaiser Permanente because it did not restrain its rate increases (Reinhold, 1993).

27. Worries about malpractice suits cause some physicians to use tests as a form of insurance against legal action; therefore, capping malpractice claims may reduce costs of treatment (Gronfein, 1991).

28. Rydell testified in favor of policies adopted by the National Conference of State Legislature's State-Federal Assembly, a body that guides NCSL's advocacy activities with Congress, the courts, and administrative agencies at the national level.

29. "In the end, national health care reform is likely to be comprised on many separate components arising from successful State models" (Rydell, 1991, p. 1211).

30. Questions of adequacy may also arise. Demkovich (1990) suggests that "the 'access problem' may not have been eradicated by the turn of the century. But thanks to the hard work and creativity of state policymakers, it will be considerably less serious than it is today" (p. 29). Gold (1991) demurs, citing financial constraints that limit states' ability to maintain (let alone expand) health policy reforms.

31. Some states, such as Indiana, may limit access to Medicaid so as to contain the growth of expenditures. This and similar actions in other states would reverse the process of "creeping national insurance" identified by Barrilleaux (1989). On the general problem of access to Medicaid in an era of experimentation, see Melden (1992).

32. For example, see the demands of the National Conference of State Legislatures (Rydell, 1991, p. 1218), and the National Governors' Association (Pear, 1993a).

References

Arnold, R. D. (1979). *Congress and the bureaucracy: A theory of influence.* New Haven, CT: Yale University Press.

Arnold, R. D. (1981). The local roots of domestic policy. In T. E. Mann & N. J. Ornstein (Eds.), *The new Congress* (pp. 250-287). Washington, DC: American Enterprise Institute.

Ayres, B. D., Jr. (1993, April 25). States hustle to adopt health-care overhauls. *The New York Times*, p. A17.

Barrilleaux, C. J. (1989). Uninsurance and creeping national health insurance: Recent developments and policy strategies. *Journal of Health and Human Resources Administration, 11*(3), 273-284.

Begala, J., Kuehn, S., & Levine, C. (1991). Options for state health policy: Alternative benefit designs. *Journal of State Government, 64*(3), 75-79.

Berger, J. (1991, June). Prognosis poor for universal health care. *State Legislatures*, pp. 35-37.

Biemesderfer, S. C. (1992, July). Running for coverage. *State Legislatures*, pp. 54-59.

Bowman, A. O'M., & Kearney, R. C. (1986). *The resurgence of the states*. Englewood Cliffs, NJ: Prentice Hall.

Clinton has Rx for reform: Will Congress take the cure? (1992, November 28). *Congressional Quarterly Weekly*, pp. 3714-3716.

Demkovich, L. (1990). *The states and the uninsured: Slowly but surely, filling the gaps*. Washington, DC: National Health Policy Forum.

Dubin, E. J. (1992). Medicaid reform: Major trends and issues. *Intergovernmental Perspective, 18*(2), 5-9.

Dukakis, M. (1992). The states and health care reform. *New England Journal of Medicine, 327,* 1090-1092.

Freudenheim, M. (1992, August 4). States weighing cost-control ideas. *The New York Times*, p. C2.

Friedman, T. L. (1993, February 2). Clinton allowing states flexibility on Medicaid funds. *The New York Times*, pp. A1, A8.

Gardner, B. (1992). Health care reform: The state perspective. *Intergovernmental Perspective, 18*(2), 27-29.

Gold, S. D. (1991, April 17). *The outlook for state government efforts to improve access to health care for the medically uninsured in the 1990s* (Testimony and statement on long-term strategies for health care, pp. 333-339). Hearings before the Committee on Ways and Means, House of Representatives, 102nd Congress, First Session.

Government Accounting Office. (1992a). *Access to health care: States respond to growing crisis* (Report to congressional requesters, GAO/HRD-92-70, pp. 1-6). Washington, DC: Author.

Government Accounting Office. (1992b). *Access to health insurance: State efforts to assist small businesses* (Report to congressional requesters, GAO/HRD-92-90, pp. 1-6). Washington, DC: Author.

Graham, D. W. (1992). Long-term health care reform: Three approaches. *Intergovernmental Perspective, 18*(2), 22-26.

Grandy, F. (1991, April 17). *Testimony and statement on long-term strategies for health care*. Hearings before the Committee on Ways and Means, House of Representatives, 102nd Congress, First Session.

Gronfein, W. (1991). Controlling large malpractice claims: The unexpected impact of damage claims. *Journal of Health Politics, Policy and Law, 16*(3), 441-453.

Harden, S. (1991). Confronting the health care crisis. *State Legislatures, 17*(6), 33-34.

Health and Human Services. (1992). National health expenditures. *Health Care Financing Review, 13*(1), 46.

Hutchison, T. (1991, June). The Medicaid budget bust. *State Legislatures*, pp. 10-15.

Leichter, H. M. (1992a). Rationing of health care: Oregon comes out of the closet. In H. M. Leichter (Ed.), *Health policy reform in America: Innovations from the states* (pp. 117-146). Armonk, NY: M. E. Sharpe.

Leichter, H. M. (1992b). The states and health care policy. In H. M. Leichter (Ed.), *Health policy reform in America: Innovations from the states* (pp. 3-23). Armonk, NY: M. E. Sharpe.

Marmor, T. (1993). Coalition or collision: Medicare and health reform. *American Prospect, 12,* 53-59.

Mattoon, R. H. (1992). Can the states solve the health care crisis? *Economic Perspectives, 16*(6), 15-27.

Melden, M. (1992). Medicaid recipients: The forgotten element in Medicaid reform. *Intergovernmental Perspective, 18*(2), 15-17.

Neubauer, D. (1992). Hawaii: The health state. In H. M. Leichter (Ed.), *Health policy reform in America: Innovations from the states* (pp. 147-172). Armonk, NY: M. E. Sharpe.

Pear, R. (1993a, February 1). Governors ask U.S. to set standards on health care. *The New York Times,* p. A10.

Pear, R. (1993b, March 19). U.S. backs Oregon's health plan for covering all poor people. *The New York Times,* p. A8.

Perras, J. (1992, November 17). Health reform plan unveiled. *Bloomington Herald-Times,* pp. A1, A8.

Peterson, M. A. (1992). Momentum toward health care reform in the U.S. Senate. *Journal of Health Politics, Policy and Law, 17*(3), 553-573.

Rabe, B. G. (1992). When siting works, Canada-style. *Journal of Health Politics, Policy and Law, 17*(1), 119-142.

Reeves, M. M. (1990). The states as polities: Reformed, reinvigorated, resourceful. *Annals of the American Academy of Political and Social Sciences, 509,* 83-93.

Regan, C. (1990). *Health insurance: The state initiatives.* Washington, DC: American Federation of State, County and Municipal Employees, Public Policy Department.

Reinhold, R. (1993, February 10). Wrestling health-care costs to the mat. *The New York Times,* pp. A1, A12.

Rich, S. (1992, September 17). Conservative Democrats back super-HMOs. *Washington Post,* p. A5.

Rohter, L. (1993a, April 4). Florida blazes trail to a new health-care system. *The New York Times,* pp. A1, A14.

Rohter, L. (1993b, January 5). Sweeping health plan is proposed in Florida. *The New York Times,* p. A7.

Rydell, C. (1991, October 23). *Testimony and statement on comprehensive health insurance legislation, including H.R. 3205, the "Health Insurance Coverage and Cost Containment Act of 1991."* Hearings before the Committee on Ways and Means, House of Representatives, 102nd Congress, First Session.

Sack, K. (1993, March 28). Cuomo wants cap on doctors' fees, private and public. *The New York Times,* pp. A1, A18.

Schneider, S. K. (1992). Improving the quality of maternal and child health in the United States: State-level initiatives and leadership. In H. M. Leichter (Ed.), *Health policy reform in America: Innovations from the states* (pp. 49-72). Armonk, NY: M. E. Sharpe.

Schweppach, R. C. (1991, October 23). *Testimony and statement on comprehensive health insurance legislation, including H.R. 3205, the "Health Insurance Coverage and Cost Containment Act of 1991."* Hearings before the Committee on Ways and Means, House of Representatives, 102nd Congress, First Session.

Skocpol, T., & Ikenberry, J. (1983). The political formation of the American welfare state in historical and comparative perspective. *Comparative Social Research, 6,* 87-148.

Solomon, C. M. (1992a). Minnesota health reform law draws national attention. *Health Systems Review, 25*(5), 15-16.

Solomon, C. M. (1992b). Vermont health reform law features global budget, heavy regulation. *Health Systems Review, 25*(5), 14.

Starr, P. (1993). Healthy compromise: Universal coverage and managed competition under a cap. *American Prospect, 12*, 44-52.

Tallon, J. R., Jr., & Nathan, R. P. (1992). Federal/state partnership for health system reform. *Health Affairs, 11*(4), 7-16.

Toner, R. (1993, February 28). Hillary Clinton's potent brain trust on health reform. *The New York Times*, Sect. 3, pp. 1, 8.

Weissert, C. S. (1992). Medicaid in the 1990s: Trends, innovations, and the future of the "PAC-Man" of state budgets. *Publius: The Journal of Federalism, 22*(3), 93-110.

Wolfe, B. L. (1992). Changing the U.S. health care system: How difficult will it be? *Focus, 14*(2), 16-20.

11

Institutional Change and
the Health Politics of the Nineties

MARK A. PETERSON

*I*nstitutions matter. Institutions change, and that also matters. These are simple declarative statements. No doubt they both are universally obvious. For all of their transparency, however, it is sometimes remarkable how steadfastly observers of the political process—indeed, even participants in government itself—either hold to erroneous conclusions about the impact of institutions or fail to appreciate

AUTHOR'S NOTE: This chapter derives from a health care policy-making project made possible by the generous support of many institutions and individuals. My appreciation is extended to the American Political Science Association Congressional Fellowship Program; Senator Tom Daschle, as well as Rima Cohen and Peter Rouse on his staff; Thomas Mann and the Governmental Studies Program at the Brookings Institution where I was a guest scholar; the Faculty Aide Program, Milton Fund, and Center for American Political Studies at Harvard University; and Susan Carls, Hanley Chew, Roger Kitterman, Adi Krause, Bryan Matthey, Judy Shih, David Wang, Will West, and Leon Yen for their assistance on the project.

the ways in which institutional change can dramatically alter the dynamics of political relationships. In the 1990s, for anyone interested in the prospects of comprehensive health care reform in the United States, this kind of interpretive inertia has far greater moment than simply frustrating the isolated political scientist seeking an enhanced understanding of state and society. It has practical consequences for how health policy reformers of every stripe approach one another, assess the intersection of substantive policy and political reality, and set the course for restructuring one of the largest economies in the world: the American health care financing and delivery system.[1]

My argument is quite direct. Too much of the contemporary health care reform debate has been conducted—even by Democratic leaders in the U.S. House and Senate, as well as by President Clinton, Hillary Clinton, and other members of the President's health policy team—on the at least implicit assumption that there are unyielding institutional characteristics of American government and politics that simultaneously make the reform enterprise itself extraordinarily precarious and constrict sharply the domain of viable policy options even if reform in some sense moves forward. This assumption follows, it is reasoned, from the failure of any of the competing reform plans to be enacted during the 1970s, when the hopes and opportunities for revamping health care financing were at their then 20th-century zenith. But the 1990s are not the 1970s: Not only have the problems of diminished access, rising cost, and threatened quality been aggravated since then (Aaron, 1991; Marmor, Mashaw, & Harvey, 1990, chap. 6; Reagan, 1992). Not only is the general public more ready than ever to ratify, even promote, significant intervention by the government as either the designer or steward of a new system, whatever its final characteristics (Blendon & Donelan, 1991). Not only is the middle class, suffering for the first time setbacks in its health care security, a fresh entrant in the clamor for change (Brown, 1992; Priest & Goldstein, 1992; Starr, 1991). The very institutional setting in which health care reform must be deliberated, crafted, enacted, and implemented has witnessed unprecedented changes since the era of Nixon, Ford, and Carter, when last the reform movement enjoyed such political currency. Change has reoriented both the private institutions—the array of organized interests that coalesce and collide on this issue—and the public institutions—particularly the national legislature—from whose interactions the rules for the nation's 21st-century health care system will emerge

(Peterson, 1993). In this new institutional environment, effecting fundamental policy change remains a decidedly challenging proposition, but the presumed lessons of the 1970s are likely to be self-defeating rather than enlightening. The current circumstances, including the return of unified government under the leadership of an activist president committed to reform, suggest that federal policy-makers could be poised—if they choose to be—for bold action, rather than primed for "déjà vu all over again," to quote Yogi Berra.

I offer here an institutionalist assessment of the health care reform politics of the 1990s. I begin with a reinterpretation of the lessons of the 1970s (as well as 1960s), using a brief comparison of the U.S. and Canadian experiences to examine the central role of divergent institutional arrangements in explaining differing policy responses to similar substantive situations (there was a serious struggle over reform in both countries, but Canada acted, whereas the United States did not—institutions, perhaps more than anything else, mattered). Given these cross-national institutional differences, however, I ask how the United States could now nonetheless proceed successfully with the reform agenda. The answer is to be found in major shifts in the interest group community and in the organization of Congress (institutions change and that matters).

What Should We Learn From the 1960s and 1970s?

After several years of cumulative policy enactments and implementation, Canada consolidated its disparate streams of health care financing reform in 1971, establishing a national "single-payer," provincially administered, publicly financed system with partial subsidy from the federal government (Taylor, 1987). By the end of the same decade, in the United States the heated debate over a similar national health insurance scheme and an employment-based alternative ended with reform advocates soundly defeated and the status quo firmly in place. From these contrary outcomes many drew the conclusion that nations such as Canada—portrayed as smaller and less diverse than the United States, more enamored with the communitarian spirit, and constituted under the Westminster parliamentary rules of responsible party government—could adopt such sweeping interjections of the public sector in what had been a significant part of the private economy. The United States, on the other hand—with a population that values individualism and private enterprise and with fragmented governing institutions highly permeable to the influence of concentrated private interests—cannot enact any policy reform predicated on major public sector involvement, be it regulatory or fiscal. The origins, terms, means, and context of the debate were simply different in the two societies.

Scholars attuned to the nuances of both country's health care experiences, populations, and political systems, however, have found that many of these distinctions are more myth than fact (Evans, 1984; Kudrle & Marmor, 1981; Marmor et al., 1990, chap. 6). The U.S. and Canadian health care systems—from financing to delivery—were remarkably similar prior to the implementation of Canada's new financing system. Although the population of Canada is indeed smaller (one tenth of its southern neighbor's), the values and perspectives of its citizens are not all that different (Taylor & Reinhardt, 1991). What pushed Canada over the reform threshold, however, was greater previous experience with meaningful subnational experimentation in financing health care (something the United States has now begun), and, perhaps most important, a parliamentary system's capacity to enact controversial legislation once it has been adopted by the majority party in government (Kudrle & Marmor, 1981).

Where does this disparity leave the United States? Lowering the institutional threshold for reform could theoretically occur in one of three ways. First, the achievement of comprehensive reform could await the substantial restructuring of governing institutions. Quite a few scholars and practitioners have sounded a general alarm about the propensity of the American constitutional system, with its separation of powers born of an earlier age, to generate stalemate rather than action in any number of policy areas. Some of these critics have promoted the cause of constitutional revisions that would engender more coordinated executive-legislative functions along the lines of parliamentary democracy (Cutler, 1980; Mezey, 1989; Sundquist, 1986). Few individuals in the academy, government, or politics, however, grant that such wholesale changes represent a plausible course of action (see Peterson, 1990, chap. 8).

A second option is to wait for a pressing crisis to envelop the health care system. Even as sluggish a policy-making apparatus as the United States political system can and has responded to the threat or actual advent of disaster. There are those who may wish to argue that the health care system is well on its way to such a calamity.

If current trends in medical care inflation should continue, for example, in the lifetimes of the youngest Americans, health care expenditures will absorb 100% of the nation's gross domestic product (GDP) and all of its federal budget! But that nightmare is still some time off. As disconcerting as it may be to have witnessed a near doubling of health care costs as a percentage of national income from 1970 to 1992 (7.5% to 14.2%; see Pear, 1993), while perhaps 70 million citizens either possess no or insufficient insurance coverage, a foreboding sense of crisis is not yet so pronounced as to overcome the kind of institutional rigidities that proved so frustrating by the end of the 1970s.

A third possibility, however, is that U.S. politics and government writ large are not static phenomena, even in the essential character of the institutions by which we are represented and governed. Access, influence, and decision making depend not only on the constitutional outlines of the political system but also on the evolving details of how private power and public authority are manifest in each policy domain. In these respects, there have been some profound institutional changes over the past 20 to 30 years of considerable relevance to health care—in the way in which private groups are mobilized and allied, in the nature of their relationships with elected officials, and even in the structure of Congress itself. The exact institutional rigidities of the 1970s simply no longer exist.

There is little question that a valuable opportunity to secure substantial employment-based reform of the U.S. health care system was lost in the 1970s, when lead activists pressed for a Canadian-style policy that could not survive the political and institutional gauntlet that existed in the United States at that time (see Starr, 1982). Today's policymakers, one hopes, are better readers of the tea leaves. But they have to be the right leaves. The real comparative lessons of the 1960s and 1970s, I would suggest, are twofold. First, the divergence in policy outcomes between Canada and the United States derived more from differences in state than society—in the prevailing structure of governance, not medical experience or social values. Second, although the core character of post-World War II American constitutional government has not been directly assaulted, there have been institutional changes in the ensuing years that make for a qualitatively different setting in which to consider comprehensive health care reform in the 1990s. These transformations in private power and public authority and their potential consequences invite closer examination.

Whither the Antireform Alliance

Writing about the health care reform conflicts of the 1940s, Monte Poen (1979) entitled his book, *Harry S. Truman Versus the Medical Lobby*. It is an apt title. Truman, with his plan for compulsory medical insurance, was the first president to put health care reform formally on the nation's agenda. Although the effort had the support of organized labor and allied associations, Truman found himself relatively alone among elected officials challenging the central precepts of American medicine. The American Medical Association (AMA), which invested vast organizational and financial resources, took the lead in deflecting the President's initiative by working with a receptive Congress (particularly when under Republican control from 1947 to 1948) and playing to the public's neo-Cold War fears of "socialism" (Campion, 1984). The medical interests were so effective at thwarting comprehensive reform efforts that reform proponents shifted the strategy to one of first enacting a considerably more limited program of coverage for the elderly, finally achieved after much delay in 1965 (Marmor, 1973). As Franklin Roosevelt had always feared, the AMA and its allies demonstrated that they could dominate this aspect of U.S. policy-making.

The 1970s may originally have seemed to present a different situation. Medical inflation had changed the dynamics of the debate so much that even a Republican president, Richard Nixon, was promoting a version of national health care financing, albeit more dependent on a mix of private and public insurance mechanisms. The organized advocates of reform also had developed so much political presence that they were cocky enough to reject Nixon's employment-based plan and later compel President Carter to adopt, although reluctantly, the mantle of national health insurance. What they lacked, however, was the capacity to win (see Starr, 1982).

Organized medicine had not lost much political influence since the 1940s. Its alliance with private insurance carriers and the business community had been strengthened. Since the last full-scale reform debate, the U.S. had experienced a dramatic increase in the percentage of the population covered by private health insurance. This expansion of protection derived largely from businesses picking up the health care bill. World War II wage and price controls and recent government protection of labor organizing made nonwage compensation, such as health benefits, appealing to both employers and employees. They became a focus of collective bargaining. The protection that health benefits received in the tax code continued their attractiveness once regulations restricting cash wages were lifted and as long as health care costs remained relatively stable. Although the rising costs of medical care in the 1970s worried most business leaders, they shared the desire of the medical providers and insurance companies to find private solutions and to prevent the government from imposing alternatives. Together, they had the clout to forestall any major public sector interventions, especially when reform proponents grew more confident about their own influence than wisdom may have dictated.

To borrow from a medical technology firm's recent series of television commercials, "That was then, this is now." The reform coalition may be weakened somewhat by the decline of organized labor over the last 20 years (Goldfield, 1987), but the previous antireform alliance of medicine, insurance, and business faces a far more significant internal threat. Even physicians alone are no longer speaking with a unified voice. Both the American College of Physicians and the American Academy of Family Physicians, not to mention more activist organizations such as Physicians for a National Health Plan, have outpaced the AMA in their willingness to accept restructuring of the health care system (see Ginsburg & Prout, 1990). The AMA itself no longer can nor wishes to sustain the status quo and has joined the call for reform, albeit with the hopes of defining policy changes that serve its own interests. Doctors in particular have also suffered under recent insurance practices, including intrusive case-by-case utilization review that interferes in their clinical decision making. The burdens of collecting fees from patients, processing the variegated paperwork of hundreds of insurance companies, and undergoing utilization review have transformed physicians into business managers and pulled them increasingly away from the practice of medicine. Given the past policy positions of the AMA opposing government programs, it is ironic that doctors in Canada and Germany, countries with universal social insurance systems of health care financing, enjoy the very clinical autonomy that American doctors desire but find rapidly disappearing in our predominantly private system. Despite incomes that remain the highest among providers in the world, the life of the U.S. physician has lost much of its luster. It is little wonder that doctors in Canada and Germany are far more likely than their U.S. counterparts to encourage students to enter the field of medicine. Under these circumstances, it will be hard for doctors to marshall the will or the resources to stand unified in the way of policy change.

The approach of insurance carriers to cost containment erodes the cooperation they previously enjoyed with health care providers. The insurance industry itself, however, is also deeply divided, a schism that has festered under the surface between members of the Health Insurance Association of America (HIAA), the industry's primary trade association. In the past year, the rifts have become more pronounced and public. Whereas the business of small insurance companies is seriously threatened by anything but the most incremental reforms of the health insurance market, larger carriers can adapt more readily to significant market restructuring (assuming they are not cast entirely from the health insurance domain). Larger companies that have moved primarily into managed care, however, have quite different views about acceptable reform strategies than do the companies still concentrating on indemnity plans, which led them to dissent sharply from the HIAA's recent unprecedented acceptance of reform proposals that would standardize reimbursement rates (Pear, 1992).

Despite the over 20 years of unmitigated medical care inflation, many businesses large and small remain philosophically opposed to government intervention in the health care economy. But quite a few others, watching their competitive position in domestic and international markets weaken as a result of untamed health care costs, no longer fear, and in some cases actually invite, government efforts of some kind to rationalize health care financing and contain costs. Even a few CEOs of *Fortune* 500 companies, such as now retired Lee Iacocca of Chrysler Corporation, have either accepted or promoted the idea of a publicly financed system, in part or in total. During the 1970s, it would have been inconceivable for the leaders of major business enterprises to stride so boldly into the domain of what was so pejoratively (and erroneously) called "socialized" medicine. Business at the time maintained a commitment to private, competitive solutions to control provider costs, only to find them wanting. In the meantime, the heightened use by private insurance carriers of experiential instead of community rating of premiums, preexisting condition exclusions and medical underwriting, and the "skimming" of business clients with the youngest and healthiest employees left many businesses that were previously dedicated to private health coverage unable to provide for their own employees (see Stone, 1990). Given the economics of the 1990s, it is increasingly difficult for business to argue that it should play the primary role of organizing and paying for the health care of U.S. workers, or, through cost shifting, the costs of care for the uninsured (see Bergthold, 1990; Martin, 1993).

The 1990s have also seen the culmination of a process of institutional change that has transformed the ways in which all kinds of interests are mobilized and represented in the national policy-making process. Mancur Olson (1965), examining the issue of collective action, provides the theoretical groundwork for understanding why occupationally based, particularly profit-sector interests—such as trade associations—have had an enormous advantage when it comes to organizing for political purposes (see also Walker, 1991). They have fewer potential "members," and the political economics of organizing—the benefits over costs—provide a rational basis for even one member to subsidize substantially the organizational effort.

Other groups, with large potential memberships, confront the "free rider" problem. They have difficulty organizing, especially if their political objectives are to secure policy outcomes (e.g., consumer protection, environmental quality, and universal health care) that can be enjoyed by all individuals even if they have not contributed to the collective action. Medical, insurance, and business interests previously had this edge in organizing collectively. Only labor unions, with the assistance of "closed-shop" laws that compel membership or contributions, could maintain a sustained organizational presence as advocates of reform.

Since particularly the late 1960s, however, cause-oriented citizen groups, the type of membership associations most threatened by the Olsonian logic of organizing, have benefited from the emergence of new resources that aid in solving the collective action problem. First, the citizenry has become more educated, attuned to politics, and finds greater personal reward from the actual participation in political and social action, thus diminishing free rider inclinations (Walker, 1991; Wilson, 1973). Second, according to Jack Walker (1991), "patrons of political action"—including foundations, government agencies, unions, churches, and wealthy individuals—have become much more significant sources of revenue for citizen groups, permitting these organizations to form without having to depend so extensively on unpredictable membership dues and contributions. In 1985, for example, voluntary associations organized around occupations or industries in the profit-making sector of the economy received almost 90% of their revenues from routine membership contributions, whereas less than half of the citizen group budgets came from such sources (Walker, 1991, p. 82).

These trends in the interest group community have affected the health policy domain. Citizen groups, a substantial majority of which oppose the past positions of the medical, insurance, and business interests and favor expanded federal involvement in health and human services, now account for almost 38% of the national membership associations expressing intense interest in these issues. Four in 10 began operations between 1970 and 1985. Another 38% of the groups very interested in health and human services represent individuals and institutions in the nonprofit sector, a healthy majority of which also support greater government commitment in this area (Peterson, 1993).

The world of private power organized in the health care policy arena is markedly different today from what was experienced in the 1970s. Whereas once, medical providers, insurance carriers, and business leaders had compatible interests that nurtured their alliance against government-mandated comprehensive reform of the health care system, in the 1990s many of these interests are increasingly in conflict with one another and even prone to internal fissures. No one believes that they, in any numbers, will join a reform crusade, but they are hardly the concerted barrier to reform that they once represented, even as late as the 1970s. At the same time, those organizations within the old alliance that continue to adhere to the antireform theme are confronted by a much expanded collection of citizen groups assisted by the changed institutional dynamics of mobilizing and financing organized interests in America.[2]

Many of these changes would be easy to miss, if one were resident "inside the beltway" or one were well versed in the media coverage of how special interests apparently swagger through the halls of Congress. There is no question, for example, that campaign contributions from political action committees (PACs) are staggering in absolute terms and increased in the 1992 election cycle. The efforts of PACs representing the interests of medical providers, medical equipment manufacturers, pharmaceutics, and insurance carriers are particularly impressive ("Campaign Contributions," 1992; Neuffer, 1993a, 1993b). From personal experience as a congressional fellow serving as a legislative assistant on health policy in the U.S. Senate, I can attest that the lobbyists for these interests appear to be as intelligent, informed, with as much previous Capitol Hill experience, and as handsomely compensated as ever.

These legitimate surface impressions, though, fail to recognize much of what has happened to transform group politics in general and health care politics in particular. First, with the increasing number and new diversity of interests resplendent in Washington, DC, it is more difficult for any one group or even block of groups to wield the kind of influence that they might have had in the past, unless an extraordinarily harmonious coalition can be held together (see Salisbury, 1990). I believe that the former medical, insurance, and business alliance is failing that test. Second, the social science research on the terribly complex question of whether campaign financing affects congressional behavior has produced somewhat ambiguous results, with little support for the conventional notion that these dollars translate into actions by legislators that they otherwise would not have taken. It does seem fairly certain, however, that PAC money has far less significance as a source of political influence on those high-visibility policy issues that are especially salient to the public (Grenzke, 1989). The debate over health care reform is anything but a backroom affair. Finally, the impact of organized interests depends to some extent on the nature of the institution they are attempting to manipulate. How public authority itself is organized affects the pathways of influence. With Congress at the center of these institutional concerns, it is the subject of the next section.

A New Congress?

Back when President Truman was fighting the American Medical Association, it did not help his cause that Congress had long since become an oligarchical institution, dominated by either a Republican majority or the conservative coalition of Republicans and southern Democrats. Even when the President's party nominally held most of the seats in the House and Senate, the three-decades old seniority system left many committee chairmanships—then the core of legislative power—in the hands of the southern Democrats who were opposed to federal policy interventions such as compulsory health insurance. The oligarchical nature of Congress in the 1940s and 1950s, in combination with closely allied, industry-based interest groups, lent empirical credence to the widely accepted model of policy-making captured by the term "iron triangle." Government action, from this perspective, was the product of (or held captive to) the relatively low visibility and commonly consensual decisions reached by bureau-level executive branch officials, congressional committee leaders, and like-minded representatives of organized interests (see Gais, Peterson, & Walker, 1984). Given the way public authority was organized at the time, it was fairly easy for the medical lobby to control the outcome of any health care reform debate.

When Richard Nixon took the oath of office in 1969, little had changed in the structure of Congress, other than the elevated restiveness of less senior members frustrated by the oligarchy of committee chairmen. Any major reform initiative, for example, would have to pass through the House Committee on Ways and Means, whose legislative domain included all revenue issues, social security, and the new Medicare and Medicaid programs. Ways and Means was still chaired by Representative Wilbur Mills (D-AR), one of the most influential members of Congress in the 20th century. He ran his committee without subcommittees, so that all legislature work had to be accomplished under his direct guidance and with all staff resources firmly in his command. The Democrats on the committee also functioned as the party's "committee-on-committees," responsible for making all Democratic committee assignments. This duty gave these senior Democrats, and their chairman, tremendous influence over the rank and file of their party in the House. If Wilbur Mills did not want something, and it was within the jurisdiction of Ways and Means, it is fair to say that it did not happen (Manley, 1970).

By the mid-1970s, however, Congress had become quite a different institution after the implementation of a long series of structural reforms. The restive rank and file had finally accumulated enough strength in the House Democratic caucus to challenge that chamber's committee "barons." Three particularly intractable committee chairmen were actually deposed, but the major strategy employed for overcoming the dominance of committee chairs was to redistribute *institutional*, not personal, power. Ultimately all committees were required to have subcommittees of standing jurisdiction; no member could chair more than a single subcommittee, and they would be selected by the Democratic members of the committee (usually according to seniority as a norm, not a rule); each of the subcommittees was to have its own independent professional staff; at the full- and subcommittee levels, staff resources would have to be shared with the minority party; and the committee chair could no longer single-handedly dominate the meeting times and agendas of the committee. Ways and Means was also stripped of its committee-on-committee responsibilities, and Chairman Mills soon stepped down from his post in the wake of a personal scandal. Although the Senate was already a more decentralized body, somewhat similar changes took place on that side of the Capitol as well (Smith & Deering, 1984).

Enter the health care reform debate of the 1970s. It started with a Congress organizationally hostile to comprehensive reform proponents and ended with a chaotic Congress largely institutionally unsettled after its major internal battles over the distribution of power and its intense clashes with President Nixon over the Vietnam war, the President's impoundments of congressionally appropriated funds, and the Watergate scandal. Wilbur Mills had possessed the power to block, but also to broker, as he did with Medicare and Medicaid in 1965. No one in the new Congress remained, or no one any longer had the position, to broker a legislative solution, if one was to be achieved. The Ways and Means Committee itself was under the new and less experienced leadership of Oregon's Al Ullman, who would be defeated in the 1980 election. The Health Subcommittee had just been organized. The full committee also was increased from 25 members to a more cumbersome 37. A decentralized Congress remaining in a state of flux was far more beneficial to the still relatively cohesive antireform alliance of medicine, insurance, and business than to the maturing reform coalition, if only because in this type of setting stymieing action is easier than guiding it through multiple veto points. In addition, having just overwhelmed the old guard, and having acquired some institutional authority of their own, the congressional advocates of policy reform may have been blinded to just how precarious, ironically, their policy agendas would be. President Carter, the health care reform movement's next best hope, also ended up partially a victim of the changed institutional ways of Congress (Jones, 1988; Peterson, 1990). By the end of the 1970s, Washington had become a far less predictable arena for the game of politics, including in the realm of health policy (Peterson, 1993).

On first appraisal, the current situation in Congress may appear no better than the chaos of the late 1970s. The legislature remains a decidedly decentralized, if not fragmented, institution. Reelection incentives tend to direct members all too frequently toward parochial (constituency-specific) considerations and short-term policy fixes (Fiorina, 1989; see Arnold, 1990). The laws passed in the 1970s intended to reform campaign finance have instead institutionalized "special" interest giving by promoting the creation of thousands of PACs (Sabato, 1985). There has been a hue and cry from all quarters about the problems of stalemate and gridlock, a charge laid mostly at the door of Congress. Various think tanks, such as the Brookings Institution, are pondering possible reforms for making the legislative process more responsive and efficient, and even leaders in

Congress have organized an internal review of House and Senate procedures and committee systems (see Hook, 1992). Few, therefore, would anticipate a sudden ability on the part of Congress to set course and take bold action. Nevertheless, it is worth repeating that the Congress of the 1990s is interacting with a universe of organized interests that is quite different from 20 years ago, and that fact, in and of itself, is significant. Providers, insurance companies, and business have lost much of their organizational advantage, and by 1985, groups of all kinds, including citizens association, were reporting equivalent levels of cooperative interactions with congressional committees and subcommittees (Peterson, 1993).

There is more to the story of institutional change, however, some elements of which may even inspire restrained optimism. First, during the 1980s, more of the legislative action in the House was moving from the committees to the floor, and the House leadership demonstrated greater effectiveness at managing the floor agenda (Smith, 1989). Some power has actually flowed back to the formal leadership (Davidson, 1988). Second, never before have so many party, committee, and subcommittee leaders been as committed to health care reform, and been as experienced in developing the necessary legislation (Peterson, 1993). Third, a significant number of rank-and-file members of both the House and Senate have become health care reform policy entrepreneurs in their own right, crafting and promoting their own comprehensive plans for restructuring the financing of medical services (Kosterlitz, 1991; Peterson, 1992c). A few, such as Senator Robert Kerrey of Nebraska, do not even serve on committees of jurisdiction. Although there is the danger that such expansive entrepreneurship could fragment the reform effort, if members become overly dedicated to their own plans with their individual nuances, the activities of these policy entrepreneurs to date has elevated the overall knowledge base in Congress about the intricacies of the health care system. Never before have so many members of Congress been as well versed in the problems and the possible policy alternatives (Peterson, 1992b, 1992c, 1993). Fourth, although it is too early to judge their impact, the 1992 election cycle has brought 110 new representatives and a dozen first-time senators to the 103rd Congress, reflecting the largest change in the membership of Congress since 1948. They are younger and more diverse than their more senior colleagues, and they all directly or indirectly ran on the campaign theme of breaking the gridlock—with health care reform as one of the central issues of concern.

Finally, Congress now has a capacity for sophisticated policy analysis that may even surpass that of the president of the United States (Peterson, 1992a). As part of the institutional reforms of the 1970s, Congress established the Congressional Budget Office (CBO) and the Office of Technology Assessment (OTA), as well as enhanced the program analysis capabilities of the General Accounting Office (GAO) and the Congressional Research Service (CRS). In conjunction with reforms of Medicare's procedures for reimbursing doctors and hospitals, it created the Physician Payment Review Commission (PPRC) and the Prospective Payment Assessment Commission (ProPAC). These agencies, required to satisfy a bipartisan, multicommittee environment, have in the past two decades fully established their empirical and analytical credibility, with only scattered charges of partisanship (Peterson, 1992a; see Bimber, 1992). Together with the significantly expanded professional committee, subcommittee, and personal office staffs, and the information available from executive branch officials and the diverse community of interest group lobbyists, Congress has an unprecedented potential to evaluate rather complex social policy initiatives (Peterson, 1992a). It was not just savvy interbranch politics that motivated the administration to include scores of congressional staffers among the over 500 individuals who participated in the working groups of the President's Task Force on Health Care Reform. In addition to knowing the political terrain of Capitol Hill, these legislative aides also had long and detailed professional experience with the nuances of health policy.

Judging the Opportunities for Policy Change

Social scientists have long been interested in understanding the processes by which issues draw the attention of both electorates and political leaders, and, in some cases, initiate particularly striking shifts in the status quo. Recent research has shown that policy changes can be rapid and that these processes may have little to do with simplistic notions about the emergence of problems and identification of solutions. Instead, policy change depends on fairly momentary "policy windows" engendered by a confluence of problem awareness, events, public mood, electoral outcomes, and policy entrepreneurship (Baumgartner & Jones, 1993; Kingdon, 1984).

What happens once these windows of opportunity open, however tentatively? Major shifts in policy probably depend on the

results of what John Campbell (1992) calls "political" decision making, when ideas and people with influence are both energetically in
contention: "Participants have different goals or preferences; the
process is some sort of fight or bargaining; the result is determined
by each participant's relative power, or by the amount of energy each
is able and willing to expend on that issue and how skillfully resources are deployed" (p. 30). The ideas, participants, their resources,
and the institutional setting in which they "fight" or "bargain,"
however, are not static phenomena. They are all influenced, to some
extent, by what has been wrought before—what policies have been
deliberated, enacted, or rejected; how previous programs and the
government authorities established to administer them have transformed substantive understanding as well as the political resources
of groups; and the degree to which forces either endogenous or
exogenous to the immediate issue at hand have reshaped the institutions through which power is applied and by which decisions are
made. These attributes define the character of a "polity" at the time
of any given policy discourse and set the parameters of what is
possible and what is done (see Skocpol, 1992).

From this perspective, policymakers, reform advocates, and scholars watching the current health care reform debate must strike a
careful balance in assessing the reform opportunities of the 1990s.
On the one hand, for reformers to assume that the circumstances are
the same as the 1970s, and thus a time to accept the very compromise
that they perhaps carelessly rejected at the time, is to both misinter-
pret the comparative U.S. and Canadian experiences of that era and
ignore a sea change that has occurred in U.S. national institutions
(not to mention in the dimensions of the health care problem itself).
With the advent of an activist president, the first in more than a
generation genuinely committed by principle and campaign promise to serious health care reform, the current institutional setting
affords the best chance in this century for fulfilling the most ambitious reform objectives. On the other hand, while avoiding the propensity to seek too little, reformers are also cautioned by the 1970s
episode to assess carefully the fluctuating politics of medical care
reform and know when to strike a deal—when to fight and when to
bargain—rather than seek too much and once again watch the opportunity slip away.

Experience has taught us that the costs of timidity are great.
President Johnson and the designers of the Medicare program were
convinced that the medical lobby retained so much clout that pas-

sage of the program required accommodating their interests. As a result, Medicare began by paying doctors fee-for-service reimbursements based on "customary, prevailing, and reasonable" (CPR) rates and hospitals on the principle of cost-based reimbursements (Califano, 1993). In effect, doctors and hospitals set their own incomes, courtesy of the U.S. Treasury, and in the process helped fuel the subsequent inflation in medical costs. Theodore Marmor (1973) and others suggest that Johnson underestimated the leverage he had gained from the prevailing public mood, his own electoral landslide in 1964, and the extraordinary influx of liberal Democrats into the 89th Congress. With health care costs out of control, the access problem worsening, and the quality of services under threat, a similar miscalculation today—giving away too much to the interests with a stake in the status quo—could have devastating consequences. For the same reasons, however, failure to enact any kind of reasonable plan for restructuring the financing of U.S. health care by missing the opportune bargain would leave the economy vulnerable and seriously impair any effort to bring fiscal discipline to federal and state government budgets. As then-President-elect Clinton stated with some exasperation at the economic conference in Little Rock: "We are kidding each other . . . if we think we can fiddle around with the entitlements and all this other stuff and get control of this budget, if you don't do something on health care. . . . It's going to bankrupt the country" (quoted in Rovner, 1993, p. 28).

Throughout this chapter my argument has been about the prospects, given the institutional setting of the 1990s, of achieving the kind of comprehensive reform that would tackle the problems and fulfill the principles articulated by President Clinton initially in Little Rock, later in his first State of the Union address, and most forcefully in his September 22, 1993, speech to a joint session of Congress announcing his reform plan. Although there are many, like the President, who sincerely advocate employment-based managed-competition initiatives predicated on the perceived substantive merits of this approach, much of the support that it has received—from health policy specialists, the Democratic leadership in the House and Senate, some of organized labor, and the Clinton administration—undoubtedly derives from the belief that it represents the most politically viable, even if not the best, way in which to reform American health care (see Peterson, 1992c). The Jackson Hole Group (JHG), the originators of the most "free market" version of managed competition, tout the political sensibility of their plan: "For many years in this country we have had an employment-based system of health care coverage. Seeking politically feasible incremental change, the JHG proposes to build on that system and correct its deficiencies rather than to replace it radically" (Ellwood, Enthoven, & Etheredge, 1992, p. 160). Political viability demands constant reassessment, however, as the character of the polity changes. I would suggest that these arguments in favor of employment-based approaches alone are suited more to the distribution of private power and structure of public authority present in the 1970s than what we find today.

That is not to say that the U.S. political system and its governing institutions are now primed to adopt a single-payer Canadian model or its conceptual equivalent with sudden ease and happy flourish. Rather, if the U.S.-Canadian comparison of the 1960s and 1970s has been misinterpreted, if the institutional changes in the United States since the 1970s have been as pronounced as I have suggested, and if presidential commitment and unified party government can make a difference, then reform plans that involve extensive government involvement and public financing are not as politically vulnerable as some experienced participants and pundits would have us believe (see Feder, 1993).

Given the problems facing the U.S. health care system, and the remarkable changes in the institutional setting in which reform is being debated, all issues and approaches should be on the table, including the single-payer model, which the media have cavalierly stopped covering, despite the nearly 90 cosponsors that a single-payer bill has received in the House (see Marmor & Boyum, 1992). The 1990s are so different from the 1970s—indeed, 1993 is so different from 1990-1992—that we should all relinquish the particular reform labels to which we have become attached and think anew about how to craft effective and politically sustainable restructuring of the system for financing, and delivering, health care services. Labels such as "pay or play," "managed competition," and "single payer" standing alone do not get us very far in the current climate. Conceptual fusion may be the key. What is important about single-payer approaches is not the explicit channeling of funds through public coffers but, rather, the commitment to ensuring universal access to a comprehensive package of benefits, the linkage between access and cost control, portability of coverage, clinical autonomy for providers, efficiency of financing, and budgetary control over health care expenditures. From employment-based designs we are reminded of the effective role that employers have and can play in directing information to beneficiaries and acting as collection agents for health care premiums. Managed competition, whatever its form, highlights the importance of finding ways to rationalize the delivery of health care services.

The trick of the 1990s is to identify the sensible way to weave the themes together (see Marmor & Boyum, 1992; Starr, 1992). Because in some senses everything is possible today in a way that was never before true, we should regard anything as possible and strive to construct a new health care system that serves both the policy and political interests of the current American polity. President Clinton and his wife have raised the debate to a new plateau and given us one vision of what is desirable and doable. In the process, they have established principles—such as security, simplicity, savings, and choice—that all serious reformers can share. The formal introduction of their reform plan moved the U.S. policy-making system from the realm of pure rhetoric to the exigencies of actual legislative drafting. With health care reform now in the hands of Congress, it becomes more important than ever to get the politics of the 1990s right, to solve the trick and realize its treat.

Notes

1. At $838 billion in 1992, the U.S. health care system is about the size of Great Britain's entire economy, and with annual increases on the order of 10% to 12%, it is growing quite a bit faster (Pear, 1993).

2. The ramifications of these changes are possibly susceptible to sophisticated procedures for estimating the likelihoods of different policy outcomes. Stanley Feder, in a draft paper (1993), illustrates how an empirical analytic technique developed for predicting policy outcomes in foreign nations can be adapted to the domestic debate over health care reform. Called "Factions," this model forces the analyst to consider the full range of participants, their policy positions and the salience of the issue to them, and their political clout.

References

Aaron, H. J. (1991). *Serious and unstable condition: Financing America's health care.* Washington, DC: Brookings Institution.

Arnold, R. D. (1990). *The logic of congressional action.* New Haven, CT: Yale University Press.

Baumgartner, F. R., & Jones, B. D. (1993). *Agendas and instability in American politics.* Chicago: University of Chicago Press.

Bergthold, L. A. (1990). *Purchasing power in health: Business, the state, and health care politics.* New Brunswick, NJ: Rutgers University Press.

Bimber, B. (1992). *Institutions and ideas: The politics of expertise in Congress*. Unpublished Ph.D. dissertation, MIT.

Blendon, R. J., & Donelan, K. (1991, Fall). Public opinion and efforts to reform the U.S. health care system: Continuing issues of cost-containment and access to care. *Stanford Law & Policy Review*, pp. 146-154.

Brown, L. D. (1992). Getting there: The political context for implementing health care reform. In C. Brecher (Eds.), *Implementation issues and national health care reform* (pp. 13-46). Washington, DC: Josiah Macy, Jr. Foundation.

Califano, J. A., Jr. (1993, January 28). Break the billion-dollar Congress. *The New York Times*, p. A21.

Campaign contributions to those making health policy: Big givers and big takers. (1992, November 15). *The New York Times*, p. E5.

Campbell, J. C. (1992). *How policies change: The Japanese government and the aging society*. Princeton, NJ: Princeton University Press.

Campion, F. D. (1984). *The AMA and U.S. health policy since 1940*. Chicago: Chicago Review Press.

Cutler, L. N. (1980). To form a government. *Foreign Affairs*, *59*(4), 126-143.

Davidson, R. H. (1988, Summer). The new centralization on Capitol Hill. *Review of Politics*, pp. 345-364.

Ellwood, P. M., Enthoven, A. C., & Etheredge, L. (1992). The Jackson Hole initiatives for a twenty-first century American health care system. *Health Economics*, *1*, 149-168.

Evans, R. G. (1984). *Strained mercy: The economics of Canadian health care*. Toronto: Butterworths.

Feder, S. A. (1993). *Forecasting health policy decisions*. Paper presented at the Health Policy Workshop, School of Organization and Management, Yale University, New Haven, CT.

Fiorina, M. P. (1989). *Congress: Keystone of the Washington establishment* (2nd ed.). New Haven, CT: Yale University Press.

Gais, T. L., Peterson, M. A., & Walker, J. L. (1984). Interest groups, iron triangles, and representatives institutions in American government. *British Journal of Political Science*, *14*(2), 161-185.

Ginsburg, J. A., & Prout, D. M. (1990). Access to health care. *Annals of Internal Medicine*, 112, 641-661.

Goldfield, M. (1987). *The decline of organized labor in the United States*. Chicago: University of Chicago Press.

Grenzke, J. M. (1989). Shopping in the congressional supermarket: The currency is complex. *American Journal of Political Science*, *33*(1), 1-24.

Hook, J. (1992, June 6). Extensive reform proposals cook on the front burner. *Congressional Quarterly Weekly Report*, pp. 1579-1585.

Jones, C. O. (1988). *The trusteeship presidency: Jimmy Carter and the United States Congress*. Baton Rouge: Louisiana State Press.

Kingdon, J. W. (1984). *Agendas, alternatives, and public policy*. Boston: Little, Brown.

Kosterlitz, J. (1991, April 27). Radical surgeons. *National Journal*, pp. 993-997.

Kudrle, R. T., & Marmor, T. R. (1981). The development of welfare states in North America. In P. Flora & A. J. Heidenheimer (Eds.), *The Development of welfare states in Europe and America* (pp. 81-121). New Brunswick, NJ: Transaction Books.

Manley, J. (1970). *The politics of finance*. Boston: Little, Brown.

Marmor, T. R. (1973). *The politics of Medicare*. Chicago: Aldine.

Marmor, T. R., & Boyum, D. (1992, Fall). American medical care reform: Are we doomed to fail? *Daedalus*, pp. 175-194.

Marmor, T. R., Mashaw, J. L., & Harvey, P. L. (1990). *America's misunderstood welfare state: Persistent myths, enduring realities*. New York: Basic Books.

Martin, C. J. (1993). Together again: Business, government, and the quest for cost containment. *The Journal of Health Politics, Policy, and Law 18*(2), 359-393.

Mezey, M. L. (1989). *Congress, the president, and public policy*. Boulder, CO: Westview.

Neuffer, E. (1993a, February). Funds flowing to guide health reform's course. *The Boston Globe*, p. 1.

Neuffer, E. (1993b, February 14). Members of key health panels benefit from PAC largess. *The Boston Globe*, p. 24.

Olson, M. (1965). *The logic of collective action*. Cambridge, MA: Harvard University Press.

Pear, R. (1992, December 3). In shift, insurers ask U.S. to require coverage for all. *The New York Times*, pp. A1, A22.

Pear, R. (1993, January 5). Health-care costs up sharply again, posing new threat. *The New York Times*, pp. A1, A10.

Peterson, M. A. (1990). *Legislating together: The White House and Capitol Hill from Eisenhower to Reagan*. Cambridge, MA: Harvard University Press.

Peterson, M. A. (1992a, September). *Health policy making in the information age: Is Congress better informed than the president?* (Center for American Political Studies Occasional Paper 92-7). Paper presented at the conference on Governance in an Era of Skepticism: Administrators and Politicians, sponsored by the International Political Science Association Research Committee on the Structure and Organization of Government, Stockholm, Sweden.

Peterson, M. A. (1992b, September). *Leading our way to health: Entrepreneurship and leadership in the health care reform debate* (Center for American Political Studies Occasional Paper 97-6). Paper presented at the Annual Meeting of the American Political Science Association, Chicago.

Peterson, M. A. (1992c). Report from Congress: Momentum toward health care reform in the U.S. Senate. *Journal of Health Politics, Policy and Law, 17*(3), 553-573.

Peterson, M. A. (1993). Political influence in the 1990s: From iron triangles to policy networks. *Journal of Health Policy, Politics and Law, 18*(2), 395-438.

Poen, M. M. (1979). *Harry S. Truman versus the medical lobby*. Columbia: University of Missouri Press.

Priest, D., & Goldstein, A. (1992, December 22). Middle-class uninsured up by 1 million. *The Washington Post*, pp. A1, A4.

Reagan, M. D. (1992). *Curing the crisis: Options for America's health care*. Boulder, CO: Westview.

Rovner, J. (1993, January 2). A job for the deficit bomb squad . . .: Defusing exploding health-care costs. *Congressional Quarterly Weekly Report*, pp. 28-29.

Sabato, L. J. (1985). *PAC power: Inside the world of political action committees*. New York: Norton.

Salisbury, R. H. (1990). The paradox of interest groups in Washington: More groups, less clout. In A. King (Ed.), *The new American political system* (2nd ed., pp. 203-230). Washington, DC: American Enterprise Institute.

Skocpol, T. (1992). *Protecting soldiers and mothers: The political origins of social policy in the United States*. Cambridge, MA: Harvard University Press.

Smith, S. S. (1989). *Call to order: Floor politics in the House and Senate*. Washington, DC: Brookings Institution.

American business sponsors 89% of privately financed insurance policies through employer-sponsored plans. But business also pays for health care in less visible ways, such as contributions to the Medicare Health Insurance Trust Fund, workers' compensation and temporary disability insurance, and direct provision of employee health programs in industrial plants. With the cost of health insurance premiums increasing at the rate of between 8% and 15% a year, and the impact of that cost being equivalent to 100% of after-tax profits, one would assume that business would take an active interest in controlling those costs (Darman & Williams, 1991).

Employers who provide health insurance to their employees have tried a variety of measures to control the increase in health expenditures. If they were large enough (1,000 or more employees), they have self-insured, thus exempting themselves from state mandates to provide specific levels of benefits. If they had a nonunionized workforce, they have increased cost sharing by employees by increasing deductibles, copayments, and out-of-pocket expenditures. If they were bold enough, they have taken on the provider community by negotiating directly with hospitals and physicians for discounts and performance standards, have hired third-party firms to monitor use and quality of medical care being delivered to their employees, and in some cases have begun to provide services directly to employees through the hiring of physicians and nurses by the corporation.

None of these measures has substantially slowed the increase in health care expenditures by region or for the country as a whole. The trend toward self-insurance may have eliminated some administrative costs, but the benefit packages offered by self-insured employers have mirrored the packages mandated by the states. Although deductibles have increased, the overall growth in deductibles has been small in comparison to the growth in medical care costs (Levit & Cowan, 1990, p. 135). And for every innovative measure taken by a large corporation with a large and well-educated benefits staff, the providers have responded by finding another way to increase their revenue by doing more or doing it in locations where the profits flow directly back to the provider.

Despite the success of some payers in reducing overall expenditures without decreasing quality, most American businesses have failed in the prudent purchasing of medical and insurance services for their employees over the past 20 years (Bergthold, 1990). Why is American business, then, not at the forefront of the reform movement? Why aren't businesses demanding that the Clinton administration pass the most comprehensive reform possible and even take the responsibility for providing health insurance coverage out of the workplace entirely? Before these questions can be answered, we need to review the way in which American business participates in the policy process and review the activities that business leaders have actually taken to support or oppose various health care reform proposals in the past several years.

Business and the Policy Process

For the purposes of this chapter, I choose to use the term *business* instead of *corporate* to reflect the range of business organizations involved in health care policy-making; I also refer to the role of business as *purchaser* or *payer* of health insurance coverage, not provider of medical services or supplies; and finally, *business leaders* refers mainly to senior vice presidents of benefits and compensation within an organization, not generally the chief executive officer (CEO). Although CEOs have become increasingly aware of the health care cost crisis, it is usually the benefits and compensation staff who make decisions about how to control costs or recommend what positions to take externally (Bergthold, 1990, p. 7).

Some would argue that business power is such that the participation of business leaders in the policy debate is not necessary. Paul Starr (1982) contends that there is a difference between the market or structural power of business and the power of interest groups in the policy process. Business confidence acts as a constraint on policy without business leaders even having to lobby their specific interests. As long as government is acting in ways that consistently protect business interests in a given situation, there is no need for business leaders to intervene in the policy process. Therefore, some regard the active entry of business into the health policy process as an indicator of the fundamental threat to business that the uncontrolled growth of the health sector has posed. Business is participating in the health policy process precisely because it can no longer rely on government to consistently protect private sector interests.

Regardless of the motivation for business participation, there are clear indicators that business participation has increased. Business leaders have become involved in three types of interventions: the organization of institutional mechanisms for change, such as coalitions, associations, and lobbying groups; participation in an advisory role to state and federal governments; and direct legislative participation through membership on state or federal commissions (Bergthold, 1990, p. 5).

The first year that top business leaders began to be quoted in the national press about the health care cost "crisis" was 1970, when *Fortune* magazine declared, "American medicine now stands on the brink of chaos. The time has come for radical change" ("It's Time," 1970, p. 79). In the past 23 years, business leaders have done an enormous amount of participating, complaining, speaking, and intervening. New associations, such as the Washington Business Group on Health (WBGH), have been formed to address specifically the interests of America's largest corporations in health care policy; dozens of state-level commissions have been formed to investigate ways to solve the health care cost crisis, and business leaders have been the first invitees to the table; business leaders have helped to write legislation at both the state and national level; and business has become a partner with the public sector in exerting their purchasing power at the state level, such as in Florida, California, and Massachusetts. In 1973, when the HMO Act was being written, business was absent from the table; in 1993, when Congressman Jim Cooper's managed-competition bill was being redrafted by congressional staff, present at each weekly meeting were representatives of the WBGH, the National Forum of Business Coalitions, and one or two individual business representatives.

Although it is logical that business should now be an active, if not dominant, participant in the debate over health care reform, some are puzzled that *there has been no unified voice speaking for business interests.* Businesses are split in their policy preferences by their size, by whether or not the business has substantial supplier or provider interests or is mainly a purchaser of coverage, and by region of the country in which they are located. Big business is tired of paying cost shifts perpetuated by small businesses who do not cover their employees. Manufacturers feel differently about reform than do companies that produce medical supplies. Business headquartered in California or Minnesota, where managed care is prevalent and acceptable, have different views about reform possibilities than do businesses located in the East or South. Larry Brown (1990) indicts private purchasers for their lack of action and ambivalence: "The federal government has played the prudent purchaser. Business remains the imprudent purchaser and proud of it. No regulations or public-private partnerships for corporate America—only the pristine garden paths of volunteerism, competition, and coalition" (p. 795).

This ambivalence is reflected in the organizations that represent business views on health care reform. The U.S. Chamber of Commerce that includes many small-business members and has been strongly influenced in the past by insurance interests has not yet supported any reform proposal, although they have been generally positive about the broad concepts of managed competition. The Business Roundtable, representing *Fortune* 100 companies, and also influenced by insurance interests, is tentatively supporting managed competition proposals. The WBGH, on the other hand, has taken very specific positions on the need for organized systems of care, high-quality care, and adequate data. It is more ambivalent on issues such as taxation of benefits and employer mandates. There have been a few exceptions to inaction. The National Leadership Coalition, composed of large corporations, unions, and academics came out in support of play-or-pay reform in 1991.

Business Opinion on Health Care Reform

Even before the election of Bill Clinton in November 1992, some consensus about reform had begun to emerge among business leaders. In half a dozen surveys taken in 1991 and 1992, more companies began to express interest in health care reform (e.g., Metropolitan Life Insurance Company, 1991).[1] If a company's health care costs were more than 10% of a company's payroll, health care reform was that company's top priority (Cantor, Barrand, Desonia, Cohen, & Merrill, 1991, p. 99). Several threads of agreement ran through these surveys:

- The American health care system doesn't work; significant and fundamental reform is needed.
- Universal access to care should be a top priority of reform.
- The current system with its public-private mix of financing and delivery should be continued.
- Cost sharing by consumers, in the form of copayments, deductibles, and other incentives to purchase prudently, is appropriate and necessary.
- Uniform data collection and reporting is critical to the effective management of care.
- Cost management and standard setting in medical care are essential strategies, perhaps implemented on a national basis.

- Compromise will be essential, especially for one's own interest group; everyone must share the pain.
- Physician, insurer, and hospital interests are viewed as the biggest barriers to reform; no interest group reports business as a barrier.

There have been, of course, significant areas of disagreement between business leaders in the past few years; whether change should be radical or incremental, how the system should be financed—through a payroll tax, premiums, provider taxes, and so on—and what role government should play.

A survey conducted by William M. Mercer Incorporated in mid-1992 asked approximately 1,500 medium and large employers to respond to a survey called *In the Cards: Health Policy Trade-Offs* (Mercer, 1992). Although not a representative sample, over 400 human resource executives responded. The survey consisted of two parts: a short questionnaire and a pack of eight cards to sort. The cards contained alternative scenarios for the future of the U.S. health care system. Each scenario was based on five factors:

1. Major system financing—what should be its source?
2. Out-of-pocket financing—whether there should be point-of-purchase cost sharing in the form of patient copayments.
3. Access to care—whether it should be controlled, and if so, how?
4. Management and quality assurance—who should be responsible for administration, budgeting, and quality of care?
5. Compensation—how health care providers should be paid.

Respondents were asked to sort the cards and rank them in order of preference.

The results showed strong differences between respondents who were characterized as "Revampers," the 77% who believed that significant change is needed in some areas but not others, and "Overhaulers," the 23% who believed that the health care system should be completely overhauled. Revampers believed that the current system of financing should continue, that out-of-pocket payments should include patient copayments, that access should be universal with some form of rationing of high cost services, that the current system of management and quality assurance should be privately provided, and that the fee-for-service system of compensating providers should be rejected and other forms of reimbursement such as paying salaries or on a per-person per-month basis should be implemented. The Overhaulers differed in their approach to financing, selecting income or employer taxes over the current system, and in their preference for federal or state government to assist in the administration and quality oversight of care. The survey did not determine the relationship between the opinions of the respondents and the type of business that they represented.

As the election approached, interest in health care reform increased as business leaders realized that a Clinton win could produce comprehensive change in health care. In a fax poll of national corporate clients the week before the 1992 election, William M. Mercer Incorporated asked its corporate clients who would win, what the new President's health priorities might be, and what their own priorities were. Eighty percent predicted a Clinton win. Although 87% believed that mandated family leave benefits would be a top priority of the new administration, only 13% believed it should be a priority for their companies. Two thirds expected a "play-or-pay" health reform proposal (a way to finance health care by requiring employers to provide health insurance for their employees or pay a tax to help the government provide it), but only 21% thought it would be their own priority. Over half of these same respondents believed that "managed competition" (see description below) should be a national priority, but they were less confident that it would be Clinton's priority. Although they were correct about family leave, they missed the message delivered by Clinton midway through the campaign that he favored managed competition over a play-or-pay approach.

Business and Managed Competition

Although there have been no major national surveys on business opinion on health care reform since the election, there have been clear signals from Hillary Rodham Clinton, head of the administration's Inter-Agency Health Care Reform Task Force, that there will be no compromise on the principles of universal coverage, comprehensive benefits, and security for all Americans. Business leaders have been generally very supportive of these principles in the context of *managed competition*. But what does this term mean, and what would it mean for employers?

Managed competition is a purchasing strategy designed to group public and private purchasers together in coalitions called health insurance purchasing cooperatives or alliances. These health alliances

(HAs) would negotiate the best price and service from competing health plans. Along with the strengthened purchasing power of the buyers, the providers or sellers of service would be restructured into organized systems of care called accountable health plans (AHPs) that would sell their health plans in a newly restructured health care market characterized by a uniform set of plan benefits; access to all who wish to enroll, regardless of their previous illness history, age, sex, or other status; a limit on tax deductions for any plan that provides benefits in excess of a benchmark or low-cost plan; and mandatory participation of employers and/or individuals in these plans.

What this would mean for employers, large and small, is beginning to be clear. In the short term, if HAs for small business (less than 100 employees in a given region) were implemented it would mean access to insurance coverage for employees currently uncovered, even if their employers did not pay for it. If the HAs were effective in negotiating good prices for the plans they offered to small business, and if plans were allowed to charge differential rates, there is a strong potential for cost shifting to employers outside the HA to occur. They would then be forced to pay more, negotiate directly with providers in their areas, or combine with other employers to form their own alliances.

For the insurers and provider companies who currently operate and sell health maintenance organization (HMO) products to employers, the dominant sellers would be most likely to succeed in the new market. The Kaisers, U.S. Healthcare, and major insurance plans would have the market penetration, name recognition, and network management tools to successfully sell their plans in the new environment. Smaller plans or plans with weaker cost control incentives (i.e., plans that pay their providers on a fee-for-service basis and do not ask providers to bear risk) would be at a tremendous disadvantage and eventually disappear. Thus small employers who currently provide expensive coverage to their employees would undoubtedly find coverage through the HA more reasonable. Small employers who currently provide no coverage might not be able to continue in business if the costs of required coverage exceeded their margins. In Hawaii, when universal coverage was mandated, there was much talk of business failures, but in fact very few failures resulted. Some think that Hawaii's healthier population has made coverage cheaper, plus the reality is that businesses cannot easily relocate to another state to escape the mandates.

For medium and large employers, health care reform would have mixed consequences. The elimination of experience rating and some of the more costly aspects of the administration of health benefits might bring cost savings, as would the coverage of small employers who are major cost shifters to big business. If these larger employers wished or were able to join the HA, they would be likely to encounter more reasonable coverage, but there would be a loss of control over benefits and accountability for employees. In the HA, employees of many firms and public sector programs would be equal subscribers. To whom would employees complain if the plans did not deliver high-quality care? HAs are supposed to have mechanisms for ensuring consumer accountability but may not be as responsive as individual employers.

Another issue of responsiveness is the competition for the HA to provide high-quality service. If there is only one alliance per area, with whom would the HA compete to be the best purchaser? With monopsony power comes the potential for arrogance, bureaucratic density, and capture by special interests. For that reason, many larger employers wish to retain control over the delivery of health plan coverage to their employees, either through their own alliances or by constructing health plans of their own.

Business Disagreements Over Health Care Reform

As health reform is being debated, employers are speculating about what impact the final plan will have. There are areas of disagreement between business leaders even on issues they generally support. Employers support universal access and cost containment, but embedded within these debates are issues about which business is deeply divided. Universal access is of highest priority, stemming not only from issues of social justice but from the realities of cost shifting and cost increases that result from large numbers of Americans who are not covered by health insurance. To insure universal coverage requires mandatory participation. Voluntary coverage schemes have never succeeded in enrolling anything over a fraction of the target enrollees. Employers find themselves in a very difficult bind over this issue. They support universal coverage, but to get it they have to support the mandating of coverage, which many employers oppose vehemently on ideological grounds.

If universal coverage is the top priority, effective cost containment is a close second. Here again, employers find themselves in a

Mercer, W. M. (1992). *In the cards: A survey on the future of the U.S. health care system.* Unpublished report.
Metropolitan Life Insurance Company of New York. (1991). *Tradeoffs and choices: Health policy options for the 1990s.* Unpublished report.
Starr, P. (1982). *The social transformation of American medicine.* New York: Basic Books.

13

Managing National Health Reform

Business and the Politics
of Policy Innovation

CATHIE JO MARTIN

*F*rom Seattle to Jacksonville, New York City to Newton, Iowa, a common theme echoes through big-city skyscrapers and suburban industrial parks: health care is killing American business. Just as fast-food and motel chains create a seamless web of interstate culture, pervasive concerns about health costs defy regional distinctions. In a research project cum road trip, I visited corporate headquarters to find out what business managers think about national health reform and how they contribute to the policy debate.[1]

In the aftermath of the Clinton victory, I found an impressive level of support for reform. Many business managers embraced

AUTHOR'S NOTE: The author would like to thank the Robert Wood Johnson Foundation, Jim Milkey, Jim Morone, Mark Peterson, Marc Roberts, Theda Skocpol, and many business respondents.

government intervention as a necessary corrective to the failings of the market. This support was often uneasy. One vice president for human resources remarked, "Public policy is like a black hole, but you can't ignore it" (interview, May 1993). Support was not universal. Although the companies I visited were all quite large, they varied greatly in their experiences with national policy-making forums. Some were clearly at the core of the government-industrial complex; others remained rooted to the periphery. One midwestern businessman explained: "National politics has an East Coast bias" (interview, March 1993)

But despite big differences in companies, most of those I met with were eager for the newly elected President to fix the health care system. A large majority believed that employer mandates were necessary to ensure universal access. Over half of the companies had either developed a position on health reform or planned to do so when the President's proposal came out. Some employers have recently become disillusioned with Clinton's reform, but their earlier concern brought the issue to the public agenda.

Many of these human resource professionals had struggled with health care cost containment since the early 1980s: Their conversion to national reform was a product of much deliberation and considerable experimentation with market alternatives. These were men and women likely to oppose increased government intervention in other settings; yet they were caught in a bind between protecting their firms' profitability from the assault of health costs and maintaining commitments to their workforce. Driven by the irrepressible forward march of health costs, they considered radical alternatives to the status quo.

My respondents were not silent sufferers; indeed, many had aired their concerns publicly in national policy groups and regional coalitions such as the Washington Business Group on Health, the National Leadership Coalition, the Business Health Care Action Group in Minnesota, and the Health Action Council of Northeast Ohio. They talked about their struggles in the inspirational tones usually reserved for left-wing political activists and evangelical Christians. This was not mere interest group lobbying; this was a movement. Their activities had attracted media coverage, guided state-level commissions, and influenced national legislative proposals. In fact, my corporate respondents had contributed greatly to making national health reform a major issue for the American public.

I came away from this experience feeling impressed by the commitment and technical expertise of these private sector policy experts and hopeful that committed business managers could help to offset the traditional provider dominance of health policy (Bergthold, 1990). With many business supporters at their side, the Clintons might just be able to pull it off.

But I also felt a bit uneasy. Despite their knowledge and enthusiasm, corporate reformers, by definition, must be ever cognizant of their companies' bottom lines. They must balance a desire to solve a pressing collective problem with their essential mandate of protecting their firms' self-interests. Consensus often unravels at the level of detail, and health care is promising to be no exception. Companies with very different interests are already making very different demands for reform. The health reformers certainly cannot claim to speak for all of business, much less for the public good.

It seems, then, that business involvement in national health reform presents a paradox. On the one hand, changes in corporate America's ability to provide health care and attitudes toward the current system have contributed enormously to the emergence of health reform as a political issue. On the other, the interests and institutional legacies of the employer-based system put severe constraints on the range of possibilities for reform. The following pages present a story of how employers made health reform an important issue and how at the same time they circumscribed the range of alternatives available to policymakers. Understanding this paradox is essential to assessing the possibilities for true reform of the health care system.

Corporate America and National Health Reform

Business complaints about health costs go beyond hypochondriac whining: Health costs have hit companies in the solar plexus. In 1960, we managed to limit health spending to 5% of the gross national product. Certainly with the expansion of coverage in the 1960s to the Medicare and Medicaid populations, health costs were bound to rise. But by 1989, they were up to 12%, and are projected to hit 17% to 19% by the year 2000 (Reinhardt, 1993, p. A17). Health really was a fringe benefit when employers devoted 2.2% of salaries and wages to health in 1965, but when this figure increased 8.3% in 1989, health became a major drain on their bottom line (Levit, Lazenby, Letsch, & Cowan, 1991). Companies were also jolted into action by the passage of FASBI 106, a regulation that made firms account for future retiree health care liabilities in their financial reports.

"We have to spend our money somewhere," you might protest. "Why not on health care?" Indeed, if health care meant trips to the spa and massages three times a week, I'd sign on in a minute. But the recent increases in health care spending have not delivered vastly improved health outcomes. We rank number 11 in infant mortality; fundamental public health problems continue to plague pockets of poverty. Even for those of us lucky enough to get top-rate care, we get less health for more money every year. The buildup of the medical industrial complex, like the arms race, is frustrating in its lack of tangible benefits.

Even more threatening for employers is the impact of rising health costs on American competitiveness. Underlying the corporate pressures for national health reform has been a fundamental change in the trading context of American business. Fierce international competition over both export opportunities in foreign countries and our own domestic market share is driving U.S. firms to search for new ways to cut costs. Gone are the days when America could claim to make 30% of the products sold in all Western countries. Now American firms are lucky if they can claim 30% of domestic market share for some products. Health care supposedly adds $700 to the price of an American-made car, but only $200 to an auto made in Japan (Schneider, 1990). Health costs for an hourly Canadian steelworker are $3,200, whereas his or her American counterpart's coverage costs $7,600 (Williams, 1991).[2] This is a world where our companies are paying twice as much as their Canadian competitors for health care. Who's going to have an easier time selling cars?

As with every catastrophe, not everyone is equally victimized by hemorrhaging health costs. Rising medical prices frustrate many business people because the distribution of the health burden is so uneven. Firms have been touched by this financial disaster in varying fashion: Their pain is related to the amount of benefits they provide and their costs for these health services. Large companies are more likely than small ones to offer health care. Back in the 1940s, unionized companies started offering rich fringe benefits packages as alternatives to wage increases; their historical commitments to a given level of services are now well established. Company efforts to scale back these benefits have generated considerable workplace strife: health related strikes jumped from 18% of all disputes in 1986 to 78% in 1989 (Victor, 1990). Companies with older workers and many retirees tend to have higher costs for obvious reasons. Those small businesses that provide health care have also been devastated by the cost increases. This is because small companies with tiny risk pools must pay much higher rates for coverage. Different patterns of medical provision lead companies to disagree about mandating benefits, limiting the tax deductibility of health insurance, and regulating health prices.

Companies have responded to the health crunch in a variety of ways: through cost shifting, firm-level innovations, and/or political activism. First, firms with a limited commitment to their workforce have shifted costs or simply abandoned health care coverage altogether. For example, a large southern grocery manufacturer requires its full-time employees to pay at least 65% to 70% of the health tab, and provides no coverage for part-time employees. Although this company was attracted to managed-care networks, it rejected this option as unsuitable to its operations in rural towns with only one hospital and thus no possibility for competition. The vice president for human resources rather hilariously explained the hospitals' superior bargaining position to this scholarly, female interviewer: "If you're the only girl in town, you can charge what you want." Nor did this company consider national reform to be an appropriate option: "Kennedy is ridiculous, play or pay is ridiculous, paying into a kitty for someone who isn't part of the organization is ridiculous. The whole system needs to be improved. There are lots of people on welfare—that has to end" (interview, January 1993).

This employer's attitude toward its workforce may reinforce common negative perceptions about big business. But the majority of the large companies I interviewed were reluctant to shift costs, due to union promises or to feelings of responsibility for their employees' health needs. Thus a second group of firms addressed rising health costs through experimentation with benefits packages at the firm level. These benefits adjustments aimed at reducing unnecessary treatment through utilization review, improving the general health of the workforce through wellness projects, cutting the costs of services through contract purchasing, and improving the productivity of the health care system through managed-care networks.

Benefits innovations at one Northeastern firm grew out of a companywide concern for improving productivity through cooperative alliances. As part of significant changes in manufacturing processes in the early 1980s, the company greatly reduced component suppliers. The benefits department realized that it could make a parallel move by reducing the number of its health plans, moving the population into health maintenance (HMOs), and controlling for quality (interview, May 1993).

The most popular of the current innovations, managed-care networks, organizes physicians into groups and assigns patients to a primary care physician who must refer those under his or her care to specialists in the group. In some cases the medical group receives a fixed amount per patient prospectively; thus this type of practice has incentives both to avoid unnecessary care and to keep costs down. Managed-care networks have received mixed reviews to date. Although workers are often reluctant to enter into such arrangements in advance, satisfaction rates usually increase over time. For example in an Allied-Signal employee survey, 86% responded being satisfied with their quality of care (Block, 1991). The practice also seems to eliminate unnecessary care. But the down side is that the administration costs of managing these loosely organized HMO-type arrangements are quite high. Some of the early employer participants in managed-care arrangements are now finding annual health cost increases that resemble those under their old indemnity plans. Many employers fear that what they gain through reductions in unnecessary care they will lose in higher administrative costs.

A final response to skyrocketing health costs is a political one: Some companies have decided that the problems with the health system can be solved only with comprehensive national reform. Dedicated human resource professionals from these companies are by no means inclusive of the entire business community. But they have worked to put comprehensive health reform on the national agenda.

The Business Movement for Health Reform

Ours is a country where business usually prefers market interventions; so how were employers persuaded to consider a comprehensive government solution to the health problem? The growing awareness of the health care problem and support for a larger state role took place in groups, networks, and coalitions (Martin, 1993). With benefits managers at the helm, a gradual paradigm shift transformed business thinking. Specifically, three factors helped to move many in the business community on this issue.

First, the evolution of business thinking was assisted by the development of a stratum of policy experts within the firm consisting of human resource and government relations professionals. In response to the turbulent regulatory environment of the 1970s, large corporations began to develop government affairs departments (Post, Murray, Dickie, & Mahon, 1983). These internal political experts offered information about the regulatory setting and technical issues and dramatically changed business participation in politics (Harris, 1989). A similar professionalization of benefits within firms has brought companies closer into the community of policymakers and farther from a separate corporate consciousness. Companies that listen to their policy experts tend to have a more practical view of the state and to rely less on ideology and more on technical-rational criteria. Peterson (see his chapter in this volume) points out that Congress in the 1990s has greater staff capacity for producing technical health care analysis. A similar development of capacity has occurred in the business community.

The second factor facilitating a cognitive transformation among business about national health reform was a process of social learning. Benefits managers exhausted a range of firm-level interventions and ultimately determined that only a collective government solution could address the perverse incentives in the health system. Thus lessons learned from past failures pushed corporate America in new directions. Many firms were brought to the reform option by a series of frustrating experiments with ultimately futile, firm-level innovations. One benefits manager remembers the turning point when she realized that national reform was the only answer:

> I was sent a survey to fill out. In the course of filling it out, I came across a question: "What will be the solution to our crisis?" There were a number of multiple-choice answers, but the only one that I liked was to change to a national health reform. . . . Every other control that was put into place failed because people found a way around it. As hard as we tried, as innovative as we were, we couldn't stop the increases. (interview, January 1993)

The final factor contributing to the evolution of business thinking was the development of networks and coalitions that brought human resource professionals together collectively to consider the issues. Three types of forums were important settings for this process: national policy groups, regional coalitions, and labor-management committees.

First, national policy groups provided a setting where benefits managers could meet to discuss health-related issues. The Washington Business Group on Health (WBGH) was the earliest group and continues to be among the most important today. WBGH was developed by the Business Roundtable as a special forum to consider health questions, but its leader, Willis Goldbeck, quickly established the group as an independent body. Goldbeck wanted the group to include all the members of the roundtable but also felt that the group had to be independent to make big business "a credible participant in national health policy" (Bergthold, 1990, p. 42) instead of simply a lobbying force in the health arena.

WBGH primarily served an information and education function, exposing its members to new concepts of cost containment. In the 1970s, the group played an important role in helping local communities set up coalitions. But it also intervened in key political conflicts. In the early 1980s, WBGH opposed Reagan administration deregulatory efforts to phase out health planning and physician peer review. Goldbeck's controversial stands (often to the left of his members) made him an object of criticism; yet even his detractors admit that his enthusiasm for health reform helped to make it a national issue (Demkovich, 1983). Goldbeck (1989) emerged as an early supporter of national health insurance:

> When purchasers talk about the need for a national health system, they are not advocating nationalizing the health care industry, nor cutting needed benefits. On the contrary, they are . . . recognizing that the only way to preserve benefits will be a comprehensive system that unites all purchasers in a new social and economic compact with providers and patients. (p. 48)

The National Association of Manufacturers (NAM) also provided a setting for employer deliberation about health problems, although the broad scope of the association's constituency made it difficult to reach consensus. NAM members as a group are losers in the cost-shifting game because they tend to spend a lot on employee benefits. A 1989 NAM study found that 99.3% offered health benefits and that these health costs represented 37.2% of employer profits (DiBlase, 1989). The NAM board set up a health care task force in 1990 that eventually offered a proposal based on play or pay. This proposal was rejected by the board, due in part to the representation of provider interests. In October of 1993, the association urged the Clintons to scale back their proposal, improve the financing component of the bill, and think through the huge bureaucracy that will be created through the proposed purchasing cooperatives (Chandler,

1993). The Chamber of Commerce was quite visible in openly supporting reform but has moved away from this position.

Another national policy group devoted to health reform is the National Leadership Coalition (NLC). The coalition grew out of an earlier forum called the National Leadership Commission that was organized by Henry Simmons (current chair of the NLC) and funded by the PEW Foundation in 1986. The original commission produced a report in 1989 that urged systemic reform to cope with three health concerns: access, cost, and quality. The report was widely noted in the popular press, and the commission leadership began a speaking tour of corporate boardrooms, hospitals, state legislatures, and labor organizations. The media success combined with the enthusiasm generated from the speaking tour convinced the leadership that the commission should continue in new guise, and the group reconstituted itself as a business, labor, and consumer coalition.[3]

In 1991, the coalition offered a health reform plan based on play or pay, aiming to reduce the growth rate in health costs by 2% per year (Couch, 1992). It managed to avoid the policy stalemates that plague umbrella groups with an important organizational rule: To belong to the coalition, firms had to support the plan. The group deserves points for producing a specific proposal. But at the same time, many companies left the coalition because they did not believe that play or pay was the way to go. Ironically, some of these firms now accept or are at least neutral toward employer mandates.

A second forum for the evolution of business thinking about health reform was the regional coalition movement, intellectually based on the work of Alain Enthovan. Enthovan believed that the primary problems with health care delivery are related to faulty market incentives. Third-party payers disrupt the natural relationship between purchaser (demand) and provider (supply) so that individuals no longer evaluate treatment decisions from a cost perspective. To correct for these incentives, Enthovan suggested the development of community-based purchaser coalitions. These coalitions would negotiate cost and collect information about quality so that individuals could make better health decisions (Cronin, 1988; Jaeger, 1985).

Institutionally, the coalition movement received help from a number of sources. John Dunlop founded the Big Six to bring together providers and purchasers to study "the three legs of the health care stool": costs, access, and quality. Dunlop believed that true reform demanded a cooperate effort in which business, labor providers, and insurers would address local community problems (Dunlop, 1985). The WBGH helped to set up local coalitions in a number of regions, as did the Chamber of Commerce. The Robert Wood Johnson and Hartford Foundations also invested in the coalition movement (Craig, 1985).

Recently, much of the focus of local coalitions has been on quality and outcomes management. Coalitions in Cleveland, Minnesota, and other places have determined that cost controls alone will not produce a better health system. Too many health dollars are directed toward ends that fail to cure illness. We need to find out what works in health care and make sure that these treatments are used. If we can redirect the health dollar toward quality health care, the cost problem will follow. In Cleveland, the coalition has set out to evaluate the hospitals with the best outcomes. In Minnesota, the emphasis has been on developing good medical practices. A focus on quality is especially appealing because it suggests that the productivity of health care can be improved and costs lowered without sacrificing benefits levels. One benefits manager involved in the Cleveland movement recalls why chief executive officers (CEOs) liked the quality focus:

> The CEOs were in a very uncomfortable position. They were between three rocks: health care costs . . . significant employee relations problems, and the medical people or doctor problem. . . . The CEOs did nothing about the health problem because they got beaten up any way they went. Quality gave them a way out. First, it clearly had appeal and had a chance of actually working. Second, it didn't cost them anything financially. Third, it gave them a good-guy position in the community. People thought about how it would play in the papers. (interview, May 1993)

The purchaser coalitions organized around costs have been criticized for failing to contain costs, in part because voluntaristic, community-based efforts do not have the scope to address the structural sources of cost increases (Brown & McLaughlin, 1990). It is still too early to evaluate the benefits of the outcomes-oriented coalitions. But another contribution of the coalitions should not be neglected: These have been important forums in which local business leaders have learned about health issues.

A final strand of the movement for health reform consisted of industrial relations committees. Some firms and industries formed ongoing committees with their labor unions to address cost containment. Labor negotiations within the steel industry moved more employees into managed care and produced a commitment from both parties to participate in the national policy debate. One respondent from a large manufacturing firm remembers the labor-management wars of the late 1980s and the subsequent coalescing around reform:

> The strikes over the issue were very emotional; management and unions were polarized and the issue was very complex. So the company set up an informal process to educate people at each location, including union and management committees at each plant. . . . In this way, we began to peel back the onion. We began to realize that the problem wasn't a labor-management problem. The things that management had done were quite logical. Rather, we realized that it was a systemic problem and that the entire system needed to be changed. This took the emotion out of the issue and made us focus on what the best options were. (interview, April 1993)

These forums helped to transform the thinking of the participants. One participant reports that her participation on an association's health care task force radically altered her perspective:

> On most issues I am a hard-core Republican, but I'm radical on this issue. I generally don't believe in regulation, but regulation should be when the market breaks down, and it has in health care. I know that I sound like a bleeding liberal, but we need to know that each person will be accounted for. Maybe employers will have to pay more, but at least it will be explicit. . . . I like managed competition because it is basically a free market system. But we need managed competition within the context of a global budget. Business cannot afford to wait 5 years. (interview, March 1993)

Other respondents feel that the national groups are so eager to participate in the policy debate that they have committed themselves too quickly to the reform position. They worry that the desire to participate had made it harder for the business perspective to be represented:

> I am also concerned that the Chamber of Commerce, NAM, and APPWP [Associated Private Pension and Welfare Plans] are all trying to develop a strong position and to show the administration that they can be flexible. But it is too early to put stakes in the ground. . . . In

market incentives over government intervention. Managed competition made some of the regulatory aspects of play or pay more politically feasible. Tying mandates and global targets to a market approach enhanced their perceived legitimacy among business.

Second, the managed-competition part of the Clinton proposal is politically appealing because it is quite consistent with developments in the employer-based system. Managed competition's concept of health care alliances on the purchaser side grew directly out of the work of Alain Enthovan that also inspired the business coalition movement. Because many in the business community have become sensitized to the health issue through their participation in regional coalitions, the concept of health care alliances, at least theoretically, is an easy step.

Managed competition's concept of accountable health plans on the provider side also has much in common with current business practices. With the accountable health plans the government hopes to move health users away from fee-for-service arrangements and toward managed-care networks. These networks are likely to look a lot like the point of service plans already serving many corporate clients. A Foster Higgins study found 45% of its sample enrolled in managed care with three fourths of the firms offering this option (Foster Higgins, 1992, p. 5).

Third, the big insurers' vested interests in the system add to the political feasibility of managed competition. The big five insurers have been the primary organizers of managed-care networks for corporate purchasers and hope to administer the new Clinton system (interview, September 1992). Not surprisingly, small and medium-sized insurers, represented by the Health Insurance Association of America, have opposed managed competition even while supporting the more radical mandates and community-rating proposals. These small companies realize that managed competition could virtually put them out of business and allow the big insurers to develop an oligopoly (interviews, September 1992; Pear, 1992a).

Fourth, as the proposal currently stands large employers may form their own health care alliances. Thus most corporate supporters of health reform will be able to opt out of the system and continue to provide their current benefits package as long as it meets the minimum requirements. Available employer opt-out is critical to corporate support (interviews with several major industry groups, January 1994).

Fifth, the employer mandates are not an especially big leap for the large employers because many of them already provide health benefits. Some employers feel that mandates might actually improve their competitive advantage because they will force other firms in the industry to provide comparable levels of health benefits (interviews, 1992-1993). Employers also feel that a defined minimum-benefit package with tax caps on employee deductions might help the firms cut back their health commitments to their unions.

Sixth, the Clintons' efforts to devise a health reform that essentially preserves the current system also protects the jobs of the private sector health care professionals. An enormous private sector bureaucracy is now in place consisting of company benefits managers, consultants, and insurance administrators, none of whom is connected to the actual delivery of health care. Many of these individuals are drawn to support system rationalization but not at the expense of their own livelihood. One benefits manager explained:

> With significantly rapidly increasing costs, if someone said, "Turn the management of the benefits system over to us," I would have more of a willingness to say, "Be my guest." You now hear a lot of executives say, "We are not in the business of medical care".... But I'd also want to see what kind of job opportunities there are out there before phasing out the employer-based system. (interview, April 1993)

Thus, where a single-payer arrangement and the virtual end of the employer-based system would be a very big leap for business, managed competition is a much smaller step from the status quo. This is not to minimize the impressive cognitive leap that corporate reformers have made in endorsing a national health system. Also some kind of cross-subsidization scheme will make big companies contribute to the costs of providing coverage for the uninsured. But the actual impact of the new system on corporate provision of health benefits will be limited.

Implications for the Future

As we have seen, the current proposal for national health reform in many ways preserves the status quo. This is its political strength; yet this may also be its substantive weakness. If a major attraction of the current proposal is its ability not to disrupt the employer-based system and if the system itself is deeply flawed, the Clinton initiative will not accomplish its far-reaching goals. The institutional legacy of

Block, L. (1991, October 14). Unique health plans pose data comparison problem. *Business Insurance*, p. 10.

Brown, L., & McLaughlin, C. (1990). Constraining costs at the community level: A critique. *Health Affairs, 9*(4), 5-28.

Cantor, J., Barrand, N., Desonia, R., Cohen, A., & Merril, J. (1991). Business leaders' views on American health care. *Health Affairs,* (1), 99-101.

Chandler, C. (1993, October 20). Business group hits Clinton on health. *The Boston Globe*, p. 3.

Couch, R. (1992). A health care plan with no loopholes—Promises, promises? *Financial Executive, 8*(1), 5.

Craig, J., Jr. (1985). Private foundations' role in coalitions. In J. Jaeger (Ed.), *Private sector coalitions: A fourth party in health care* (pp. 66-76). Durham, NC: Duke University Press.

Cronin, C. (1988). Business wields its purchase power. *Business and Health, 6*(1), 4-7.

Demkovich, L. (1983, June 18). On health issues, this business group is a leader, but is anyone following? *National Journal*, pp. 1278-1280.

DiBlase, D. (1989, May 29). Group health bills equal a third of profits. *Business Insurance*, pp. 37-38.

Dunlop, J. (1985). Health care coalitions. In J. Jaeger (Ed.), *Private sector coalitions: A fourth party in health care* (pp. 7-14). Durham, NC: Duke University Press.

Foster Higgins. (1992). *Health care benefits survey: Managed care plans*. Princeton, NJ: Author.

Goldbeck, W. (1989, July). Health is not a free market commodity. *Business & Health*, p. 48.

Harris, R. (1989). Politicized management: The changing face of business in American politics. In R. Harris & S. Milkis (Eds.), *Remaking American politics* (pp. 261-268). Boulder, CO: Westview.

Jaeger, J. (1985). *Private sector coalitions: A fourth party in health care*. Durham, NC: Duke University Press.

Levit, K., Lazenby, H., Letsch, S., & Cowan, C. (1991). National health care spending, 1989. *Health Affairs, 10*(1), 117-130.

Maioni, A. (1993). *The failure of postwar national health insurance initiatives in Canada and the United States*. Unpublished manuscript.

Marmor, T., Feder, J., & Holahan, J. (1980). *National health insurance: Conflicting goals and policy choices*. Washington, DC: Urban Institute.

Martin, C. J. (1993). Together again: Business, government, and the quest for cost control. *Journal of Health Politics, Policy and Law, 18*(2), 359-393.

Pear, R. (1992a, December 3). Budget office sees no savings in Clinton's health care plans. *The New York Times*, p. A16.

Pear, R. (1992b, December 3). In shift, insurers ask U.S. to require coverage for all. *The New York Times*, pp. A1, 22.

Post, J., Murray, E., Jr., Dickie, R., & Mahon, J. (1983). Managing public affairs: The public affairs function. *California Management Review, 26*(1), 135-150.

Reinhardt, U. (1993, October 18). A billion here, a billion there. *The New York Times*, p. A17.

Roberts, M. (1993). *Your money or your life*. Garden City, NY: Doubleday.

Schneider, W. (1990, April 21). Is there a cure for America's medical inflation? *National Journal*, p. 983.

Starr, P. (1992). *The logic of health care reform*. Knoxville, TN: Whittle Direct Books.

Stone, D. (1993). The struggle for the soul of health insurance. *Journal of Health Politics, Policy and Law, 18*(2), 287-317.

Victor, K. (1990, March 24). Gut issue. *National Journal,* pp. 704, 706.

Williams, W. (1991). United States Senate Committee on Finance hearing on health care costs (April 16, 1991). *Healthwise, 2*(2).

14

Health Care Reform

A Labor Perspective

J. PETER NIXON

*I*t is no longer disputed that the health care system in the United States needs a major overhaul. The United States spends a greater percentage of its national income on health care than does any other industrialized nation—14% of gross domestic product, versus 9% in Canada and France, and close to 7% in Japan. Despite expenditures of more than $2 billion a day, 37 million Americans have no health insurance, and more than 50 million citizens are underinsured.

The rapid increase in health care costs is depleting the income necessary for working families to maintain their homes and educate their children. A recent study from the Families USA Foundation (1991) showed that the percentage of family income spent on health care increased from 9% in 1980 to 11.7% in 1991. By the year 2000, that figure is expected to increase to 16.4%.

One of the reasons for this is that employers are requiring employees to pay a greater share of the cost of their health insurance. Approximately 55% of employers require their employees to contribute to the cost of their health insurance premiums. These employees pay, on average, 20% of the premium cost for single coverage, and almost 30% for family coverage (Foster Higgins, 1991).

In addition to higher premium costs, workers are also facing increased cost-sharing requirements. Between 1990 and 1991, the median deductible for traditional indemnity plans rose from $150 to $200. More than half of employers now require deductibles of $200 or more, compared with only 25% in 1986. The median family plan deductible is now $400, and one third of employers require family deductibles of $500 or more. An increasing number of traditional indemnity plans also have co-insurance requirements in addition to the deductible. Copayments are usually 20% of the cost of service (Foster Higgins, 1991).

Rising health care costs have also contributed to decline in wages over the past decade. Adjusted for inflation, workers earned 4.4% less in 1992, on average, than they did in 1980. In each of the last 12 years, rising employer health insurance costs consumed dollars that would otherwise have gone to wage increases. If health care costs during that period had grown only as fast as the economy, hourly wages would have been about 46 cents higher in 1992, an average annual loss to workers of almost $1,000 (Service Employees International Union, 1992). The combination of falling wages and rising health care costs has proved too much for some families. Between 1981 and 1991, approximately 100,000 families filed for bankruptcy because of catastrophic health care costs.

Rising health care costs have led some employers to limit the scope of their health insurance coverage or eliminate it entirely. Employers who have tried to retain coverage have found that many health insurance companies refuse to allow workers with preexisting conditions to join their plans. The result has been a dramatic increase in the number of uninsured individuals.

In the fall of 1990, the American Federation of Labor and Congress of Industrial Organizations (AFL-CIO; a voluntary federation of 90 national and international labor unions in the United States) held a series of hearings around the United States that focused on the health care crisis and its impact on American families. Many of the witnesses were working Americans, union and nonunion, who had fallen through the cracks of the current system, unable to afford medical insurance for themselves and their children.

They included Louis Calderon, a single parent of two young boys, who was unable to afford health insurance even though he worked as a nurses' aide at a local hospital. Mr. Calderon made only $6.40 an hour. He had recently paid off a $500 hospital bill for taking one of his son's to the emergency room to treat an ear infection.

Another witness, machinist Kevin Sieczkiewicz, lost his job and his health insurance while facing a $1,400-a-month bill for maintenance medication for a transplanted kidney. His wife took a lesser paying job that provided health insurance coverage, but the policy contained a "preexisting condition" clause that denied him coverage for a full year.

Judith Maske, a member of the Communication Workers of America, had a 17-year-old son who required a liver transplant. Although Maske had insurance, the company wouldn't pay for the $250,000 operation because it considered it to be an "experimental" treatment. At a hearing in Louisville, Kentucky she told the audience, "If they were to tell me 'Judy, give us your house, and your car and everything else you own and Johnny can have a new liver.' I'd do it in a second. But I don't have enough money in my home and possessions to begin to cover all the expenses for the procedure. We're barely keeping our heads above water" (AFL-CIO Department of Information, 1990, p. 12).

The American Labor Movement and Health Care Reform

From the very beginnings of the trade union movement in this country, labor organizations have wrestled with the problem of how to secure health benefits for their members and for working people generally. In the early 18th century, local unions established mutual aid societies that provided benefits similar to those offered by immigrant fraternal orders. In 1877, the Granite Cutters established the first national sick benefit plan (Starr, 1982).

Early in the 20th century, the labor movement lent its support to a number of campaigns for national and state-based public health insurance. Ten of the largest state federations within the AFL, including New York, California, Massachusetts, Pennsylvania, and Wisconsin, supported public health insurance proposals in their states. Despite the support of many unions, the movement for national health insurance collapsed due to the pressures created by the United States' entry into World War I and the "red scare" that followed the Russian Revolution of 1917 (Starr, 1982).

World War II would prove to be the defining event in the construction of the United States' peculiar system of health insurance coverage. After the federal government froze wages at the outset of the war, the War Labor Board ruled in 1942 that moderate increases in fringe benefits were not inflationary and would be permitted. Unions began pressing for health benefits, and employers, facing wartime labor shortages, began offering them to attract workers.

After the war, a renewed effort to get Congress to add national health insurance to Social Security failed. In response, unions attempted to bargain for more generous health benefits for their members. Employers resisted and attempted to include a provision in the Taft-Hartley Act that would exclude benefit plans from collective bargaining. They failed in this, and soon after, the Supreme Court ruled that employers were required to bargain over benefits.

By 1950, more than 7 million workers were covered by union-negotiated health plans; by 1955, 12 million workers and 17 million dependents were covered. Unions had become the single most important source of health insurance for working Americans and their dependents.

As they worked to expand private health insurance for their members, labor unions did not ignore the plight of those without access to health insurance. Labor unions and union retirees were in the forefront of the fight for Medicare and Medicaid in the mid-1960s. United Auto Workers President Walter Reuther played a major role in putting national health insurance back on the agenda with a speech in November 1968 to the American Public Health Association. Reuther went on to help organize the Committee for National Health Insurance, which worked throughout the 1970s to build support for a national health insurance system in the United States. President Nixon, pressed for action on the issue, put forward a plan for an employer-based system of national health care, but it was rejected by congressional Democrats who were seeking more far-reaching changes.

With the election of President Carter in 1976, many believed that the nation would finally move toward comprehensive reform of the health care delivery system. Under pressure from the medical lobby, and plagued by divisions within his own party, Carter was unable to create a consensus behind any proposal. The President made an effort to move forward on a cost-containment strategy, but he ran into heavy opposition from conservative Democrats who were leading the campaign for "deregulation," and who were strongly against any plan that would regulate prices in the medical industry. In the end, Carter was able only to secure a promise from the nation's hospitals that they would engage in a "voluntary effort" to keep prices under control, a strategy whose failure would become clear over the next several years.

The Crisis of Employer-Provided Health Insurance

As the cost of health insurance has continued to rise at double the rate of inflation, the system of employer-provided health insurance has been under increasing strain. Virtually all employers have tried to shift more of the burden of health care costs onto their workers. As a result, health care has become one of the most contentious issues at the bargaining table.

Unions in manufacturing industries facing foreign competition have been particularly hard hit because the rising costs of health care have made those industries less competitive with firms in countries that have a national strategy for keeping costs under control. But unions in all sectors have faced employer demands for increased cost sharing or reductions in the scope of coverage. A survey of collective bargaining negotiations in 1990 by the Bureau of National Affairs found that health care was the major issue in 83% of contract negotiations and that a majority of employers intended to seek further cost shifting to employees in 1991 and beyond (AFL-CIO, 1991).

Employers are also trying to cut back health benefits for retirees because of the high cost of such benefits. The cost to employers for retiree health plans has been rising by 30% to 50% a year, more than twice the rate of increase for health plans for active workers. Retiree health care costs are particularly a problem for older firms in the manufacturing sector, such as Bethlehem Steel, which has two retirees for every active worker. The fallout from the leveraged buyout craze of the 1980s has also contributed to the problem, as debt-laden companies downsized by offering early retirement packages, swelling the ranks of their retirees. Navastar, the truck maker left after the breakup of International Harvester, now has 12 retirees for every active worker.

Partly as a result of these kind of practices, the Financial Accounting Standards Board (the accounting profession's rule-making body) voted to require all employers to reflect unfunded liabilities for future retiree health care in their balance sheets beginning last year. This accounting change will negatively effect the financial position of a number of large companies, giving them an incentive to reduce or eliminate retiree benefits. A 1992 survey by William Mercer, Inc., a major benefits consultant, showed that 83% of surveyed employers had made changes to their retiree benefits plans specifically because of the new regulations.

Although most disputes over health care costs have been settled without industrial action, health care costs have been the major issue in a number of strikes. A study conducted by the Service Employees International Union found that the percentage of workers striking over health care jumped from 18% in 1986 to 78% in 1989. Similar studies done by the AFL-CIO in 1990 and 1991 showed a similar trend, with a majority of strikers in both years going out over health benefits issues (AFL-CIO, 1991). Some of the more well publicized of these strikes include the walkout of the Communications Workers of America and the International Brotherhood of Electrical Workers at the regional Bell operating companies in 1989 and the strike of the United Mineworkers at Pittston Coal Company in 1990.

Even when bargaining disputes over health care did not result in strikes, the issue often brought tempers on both sides to the boiling point. In 1989, the Federal Mediation and Conciliation Service reported that in a majority of the cases that they serviced health care was the major issue. Union research also suggests that workers who strike over health care are often risking the loss of their jobs. In 1990, for example, of the 26,450 workers who were "permanently replaced" during strike actions, 18,300 (69%) were striking primarily over health care benefits (AFL-CIO, 1991).

What Are Labor's Goals for Reform?

The labor movement is committed to the fundamental reform of our health care system. Unions members will oppose incremental reforms and will be advocating a comprehensive solution to this multifaceted problem of declining coverage, rising costs, and uneven quality. Although individual unions have concerns specific to their membership, there is general agreement on the following four principles:

Universal Access. There should be a universal package of benefits to which all individuals are entitled. All employers must contribute to the cost of care, and a public program should be established for those not in the workforce.

A Global Budget. The only way that health care costs can be brought under control is through a global budgeting system that encourages a more equitable distribution of resources within the health care system and puts a cap on the annual rate of increase in health care spending. There is no compelling evidence that market forces alone will be sufficient to accomplish either of these objectives.

Protection for Retirees. Our nations' health care system must guarantee benefits to retired workers regardless of age. One solution would be to lower the eligibility age for Medicare to 60 and expand the program's benefit package to include prescription drugs. Retirees under the age of 60 could be covered through industrywide pools that would finance basic benefits. Whatever the ultimate design of the system, retired workers must be covered by a comprehensive package of benefits.

Fair Financing. Union members believe that the cost of health care reform should be distributed as broadly and equitably as possible. Organized labor opposes proposals, such as the taxation of employee health benefits, that place an unfair burden on workers who are already sacrificing income to maintain health care coverage.

Labor and the Clinton Health Care Reform Plan

The election of President Bill Clinton has significantly improved the chances for comprehensive health care reform. For the first time in over a decade, we have a President committed to ending the gridlock in Washington, DC, and seriously examining the range of policy options on this issue. The labor movement was a strong supporter of the President during the campaign, and union leaders have been consulted regularly as the President and Mrs. Clinton developed their proposal.

The labor movement is strongly supportive of President Clinton's proposed Health Security Act because it meets the four principles outlined above. The plan calls for all Americans to have access to a comprehensive range of health care services, regardless of health or employment status. The plan would significantly reduce the rate of growth in health care costs and would spread the cost of reform equitably without unfairly burdening any one sector of society. Taken as a whole, the President's plan is a significant step forward for the working people of the United States.

The most important part of the plan is its guarantee of universal access to a comprehensive range of benefits. Although the Clinton plan builds on the existing system of employer-provided insurance, it breaks the connection between employment and coverage that is at the core of the present crisis. The administration's plan would require all employers with fewer than 5,000 employees to belong to large purchasing cooperatives called *regional health alliances*. The alliances would pool the workers from hundreds of small and medium-sized businesses, to spread risk and cost more widely. Employers and workers would make premium payments to the alliances, which would then offer a menu of health plans that all workers in the alliance could choose from. (White House Domestic Policy Council [DPC], 1993).

Workers who change jobs, or lose their jobs, can remain with their health plans. In the case of a worker who changed jobs, the only thing that would change is that the new employer would take over payment of the employer share of the premium. Unemployed workers would also be able to remain with their health plans; they would be eligible for government subsidies to help pay their premiums, as would low-income workers generally (DPC, 1993).

The labor movement is also supportive of many of the financing mechanisms included in the Clinton plan, such as the requirement that all employers contribute to the cost of insurance for their workers. Under the administration's proposal, employers will be required to pay at least 80% of the cost of the average-priced plan in their region for each worker. Workers will then choose a health plan from those offered by their health alliance and will be required to pay the difference between the employer contribution and the total cost of the plan. This is meant to give individuals and families an incentive to choose lower-cost plans. Unions and employers will still be able to negotiate for 100% employer-paid benefits (DPC, 1993).

Unions are also strongly in favor of the President's proposal to lift the heavy burden on businesses competing in the global marketplace by subsidizing the cost of health insurance for early retirees. By the end of the decade, the federal government will pay 80% of the premium for early retirees. The remaining 20% will be paid by the retiree. Unions will be able to negotiate for employers to pay the retirees share of the premium (DPC, 1993).

The President also won praise from the labor movement for his decision not to make the taxation of benefits a major part of his proposal. Under the Clinton plan, the core package of benefits will not be subject to taxation. Trade unionists have argued that they have suffered real

Families USA Foundation. (1991). *Health spending: The growing threat to the family budget*. Washington, DC: Author.

Foster Higgins. (1991). *Indemnity plans: Cost, design, and funding in 1991*. Princeton, NJ: Author.

Mercer, W. M. (1992). *In the cards: A survey on the future of the U.S. health care system*. Unpublished report.

Service Employees International Union. (1992). *Out of control, into decline: The devastating 12-year impact of health care costs on worker wages, corporate profits and government budgets*. Washington, DC: Author.

Service Employees International Union. (1993). *The CalPERS experience and managed competition*. Washington, DC: Author.

Starr, P. (1982). *The social transformation of American medicine*. New York: Basic Books.

White House Domestic Policy Council. (1993). *Health security: The president's report to the American people*. Washington, DC: Author.

15

Older Americans and Health Care Reform in the Nineties

ROBERT H. BINSTOCK

*T*he importance of older people in the American health care scene is reflected in the simple facts that (a) a substantial amount of our health care dollars is currently spent on them, and (b) even larger amounts are projected for the future. Persons aged 65 and older, about 12% of our population, account for one third of the nation's annual health care expenditures, or about $300 billion of an estimated total of $900 billion in 1993. Because the older population is growing, absolutely and proportionally—from about 32 million persons today to an estimated 68 million (23% of our population) in the year 2040—health care costs for older persons have frequently been depicted as an unsustainable burden, or as one observer put it, "a great fiscal black hole" that will absorb an unlimited amount of national resources (Callahan, 1987).

Governments finance nearly two thirds of health care for older Americans. The Medicare program, which provides a basic package of health insurance for most Americans who are aged 65 and over, accounts for 45% of the total. Medicaid provides another 12%, principally for long-term care in nursing homes and residential environments. Care financed through the Department of Veterans Affairs, Department of Defense, Indian Health Service, and a variety of state and local government programs constitutes about 6% of the total. Older persons pay 28% of the costs of their care out-of-pocket. An additional 8% is funded through private insurance, and less than 1% comes from philanthropy (U.S. Senate, 1991).

Projections indicate that government expenditures on health care for older people will increase markedly during the next decade. The director of the Congressional Budget Office estimates that between 1992 and 2002 the proportion of our gross domestic product spent by the federal government on Medicare and Medicaid will increase from 3.4% to 6.1% (Reischauer, 1992). Accordingly—even as the President's Task Force on National Health Care Reform was just beginning its deliberations in February, 1993—President Bill Clinton proposed specific measures for limiting Medicare outlays and increasing the program's revenues, which Congress subsequently legislated in the Omnibus Budget Reconciliation Act (OBRA) of 1993.

Beyond the proximate challenges of financing the costs of existing programs, however, two major new policy issues concerning the health care of older people have emerged on the public agenda in recent years. One is the notion of old-age-based rationing—cutting back on or setting limits to acute health care interventions provided to old people. The other agenda item is an expansion of public financing for long-term care of older persons and others with chronic diseases and disabilities.

President Clinton's Health Security Plan (White House Domestic Policy Council, 1993), made public in the fall of 1993, would allow states to integrate Medicare beneficiaries into the "purchasing alliance" cooperatives that are pivotal to the "managed-competition" cost containment strategy in his reform efforts. An unintended consequence of this provision may be that the health care of older people will be covertly and informally rationed. In addition, the President's plan puts forward a serious, although initially limited, long-term care initiative. And it adds to the agenda of health care for older people two new items: coverage under Medicare for outpatient prescription drugs and federal subsidies for employer-sponsored health insurance plans for retirees aged 55 and older.

This discussion of older people and health care reform begins with a brief overview of the patterns through which older people use health care services. Particular attention will be paid to high use rates at advanced old ages, because the American older population is rapidly becoming older, within itself. Following this are analyses of (a) measures to reduce expenditures and increase revenues in the Medicare program, (b) proposals to ration the care of older people and the possibility that it may happen as a consequence of broader health care reform, and (c) issues involved in expanding public long-term care insurance. A concluding section considers what impact the politics of older persons and old-age interest groups may have as American health care reform efforts unfold in the next few years.

Utilization Patterns of Older People

Hospitals account for 42% of the expenditures on older people: 21% is on physician services; 20% on nursing homes; and 17% is distributed among a wide variety of other types of care including home health care, dental services, prescription drugs, vision and hearing aids, and medical equipment and supplies (U.S. Senate, 1991).

Persons 65 and older currently account for two thirds of the deaths in the United States (National Center for Health Statistics [NCHS], 1993) and have higher prevalence rates of diseases and disabilities than does the population at large. Consequently, older persons use most kinds of health care at much higher rates than do persons under 65 years of age. And at older ages within the elderly population, the rates of care use increase substantially.

About 35% of the elderly population is discharged from short-stay hospitals each year (NCHS, 1989). Persons 65 and older account for 42% of the days of care in such hospitals and about 31% of discharged patients. At ages 75 and older and 85 and older, each of the these dimensions of usage increases in rate. For example, the hospital discharge rate for those aged 85 and older is 90% higher than that for people 65 to 74 years old.

Some 1.5 million older people, or 5% of persons aged 65 and older, are in nursing homes. The rate of nursing home use increases sharply at older ages within the elderly population. About 1% of Americans aged 65 to 74 years are in nursing homes; this compares with 6% of persons ages 75 to 84 years of age, and 22% of persons aged 85 and older (Hing, 1987).

An additional 3.6 million older people receive some form of long-term care in their own homes or some other residential facility such as a congregate living community, an adult foster home, or a board and care facility (Leon & Lair, 1990). Some 80% to 85% of such "community-based" care to older patients is provided to them on an informal, unpaid basis by their spouses, siblings, adult children, and broader kin networks. About 74% of dependent community-based older persons receive all their care from family members or other unpaid sources; about 21% receive both formal and informal services; and only about 5% use just formal services (Liu, Manton, & Liu, 1985). As is the case with nursing home patients, the percentage of older persons residing in the community who need help with long-term care increases dramatically at advanced old ages. For instance, the proportion needing care rises from 7.7% in the 65 to 69 year old category to 26.6% among those aged 85 and over (Gornick, Greenberg, Eggers, & Dobson, 1985).

Although older persons are about 12% of the population, they account for 20% of all contacts with physicians (NCHS, 1990). Persons of all ages average 5.4 contacts per year; but persons 65 to 74 average 8.2 contacts, and persons aged 75 and older average 9.9 contacts. Similarly, the probability of seeing a physician increases by advancing age categories. Among persons 45 to 64 years old, 76.5% see a physician within a 12-month period; 85.1% of persons 65 to 74 years and 89.1% of people aged 75 and older have such a contact in the same time interval.

Dramatic estimates of staggering health care costs for older persons in the future are derived from projections that the population conventionally termed *old* is becoming markedly older, on average, within itself. In 1980, for example, persons 85 years of age and older were only 8.8% of the population aged 65 and older; in the year 2040 they will be 18% (Taeuber, 1990). As implied by comparatively higher rates of health care use among persons in their late 70s and 80s, the rates of disease and disability are much greater among persons in this age range than the rates for the total group aged 65 and over. Accordingly, sensational cost implications have been predicted, such as an estimate that over the next 50 years the national cost of nursing homes will rise from about $48 billion now to as much as $139 billion, as projected in constant, inflation-adjusted dollars (Schneider & Guralnik, 1990).

Medicare Reform: Containing Costs and Increasing Revenues

Up to now, neither increases in the number and proportions of older persons nor the aging of the older population have been major factors in the growth of health care expenditures. Demographic factors have been negligible contributors to spiraling health care costs. A recent study by Mendelson and Schwartz (1993), for instance, indicated that although population aging accounted for about one fifth of the annualized rise in real expenditures for long-term care from 1987 through 1990, it was a relatively negligible factor in the rise of spending on hospitals, physicians, and other forms of health care. Moreover, this analysis found a steady reduction in the contribution of population aging to health care costs between 1975 and 1990 and projected little impact of aging on costs through 2005. Earlier analyses (Arnett, McKusick, Sonnefeld, & Cowell, 1986; Sonnefeld, Waldo, Lemieux, & McKusick, 1991) yielded similar findings regarding the minimal impact of aging and other demographic changes on increases in health care expenditures through the end of this century. If population aging has a major impact on U.S. health care costs, it will not be felt strongly until after 2015 when the Baby Boom population cohort joins the ranks of persons aged 65 and older; and even this is not at all certain (see Binstock, 1993).

Nonetheless, most of the specific policy actions and proposals to contain health care costs in recent years—including those in the early months of the Clinton administration—have focused on Medicare. There are a number of fundamental reasons for this focus.

First, Medicare is the biggest single source of payment for health care in America. Its large aggregate national costs and its rapid inflation are easily determined and highly visible. In 1992, the program paid about $133 billion for personal health care services. Medicare expenditures are projected to nearly triple during this decade, from $121 billion in 1991 to $303 billion in 2000. Second, as implied by such projections, Medicare expenditures will contribute substantially to the federal deficit for years to come unless drastic changes in the program are effected. Third, because the federal government pays the bills for Medicare patients, Medicare costs are more directly responsive to government action than those paid for through private insurance and out-of-pocket. And fourth, changes in Medicare approaches to paying for care are a plausible strategy for implementing the more general goal of cost containment, because this nationwide governmental program affects the financial incentives of most American hospitals, nursing homes, physicians, and other health care providers and suppliers. In fact, the most far-reaching cost-containment measures undertaken to date have been changes in reimbursement procedures under Medicare, through prospective payment and other

measures designed to control expenditures on hospital and physician charges (see Coulam & Gaumer, 1991).

Moreover, the issue of how to pay for Medicare has been rather
immediate. Recent reports of the Trustees of the Social Security Trust
Funds have consistently estimated that Medicare's Part A Hospital Insurance (HI) costs will substantially exceed revenues by the mid 1990s and
that by the end of the decade, the HI trust fund reserves will be exhausted
and annual costs will exceed revenues by about two thirds of a billion
dollars (Ross, 1991; Social Security and Medicare Boards of Trustees,
1992). And the financing of Medicare's Part B (nonhospital) Supplementary Medical Insurance (SMI) has moved from being principally financed
by premiums from Medicare enrollees, in the early years of the program,
to being 75% financed from general revenues, today.

OBRA, the federal budget act of 1993, partially responded to these
immediate issues by enacting Medicare spending reductions and revenue increases that are estimated to total $85 billion over the 5-year
period 1994 to 1998 (Congress of the United States, 1993, pp. 28-33). On
the spending side, $48 billion has been cut by reducing Medicare
reimbursements to hospitals, physicians, and other health care providers. And an additional $8 billion will be saved from general revenues
expenditures on Medicare through the establishment of a higher than
scheduled rate of Part B (nonhospital) Supplementary Medical Insurance (SMI) premiums to be paid by Medicare enrollees from 1996
through 1998. On the revenue side, OBRA 1993 provided the Part A
trust fund with an estimated $29 billion increase over 5 years by
eliminating altogether the cap on payroll earnings subject to the Medicare portion of the Federal Insurance Contributions Act (FICA). In 1993,
this Medicare tax obligation ended when an employee's annual payroll
earnings reached $135,000.

President Clinton's Health Security Plan proposed to increase Part
B premiums even further for individuals with incomes above $100,000
and couples above $125,000. An additional two dozen relatively tech-
nical changes in Medicare—including the extension of the prospective
reimbursement method to hospital outpatient radiology, surgery, and
diagnostic services—are proposed for reducing Medicare expenditures
(see White House Domestic Policy Council, 1993, pp. 226-228).

Curbing Costs Through Old-Age-Based Rationing

Proposals to curb the costs of health care for older people have
extended well beyond the scope of the Medicare program to more

general propositions for limiting the care of elderly people. These proposals, which vary in specific content and in the age ranges they use to define "older persons," have been made with increasing frequency since the early 1980s. They appear to be an expression of a larger backlash against an artificially homogenized group labeled "the aged," which has become a scapegoat for a variety of societal problems that have been rhetorically unified as issues of intergenerational conflict and equity.

As expenditures on benefits to the aging have climbed to 30% of the annual federal budget, about $450 billion in 1992 (Congress of the United States, 1992), older people have become increasingly stereotyped in the media as prosperous, hedonistic, selfish, and politically controlling "greedy geezers." They have been blamed for problems of children, the declining strength of the U.S. economy, and the nation's general inability to free up resources for use in a variety of worthy causes (see Binstock, 1992c).

Especially prominent among the problems for which elderly people have been made scapegoat is health care costs. A number of academicians and public figures—including politicians—have urged vigorously that American society set limits to health care for older people.

The suggestion that health care should be rationed on the basis of old age began to develop, through implication, in 1983. In a speech to the Health Insurance Association of America, economist Alan Greenspan, now chairman of the Federal Reserve Board, pointedly asked "whether it is worth it" to spend 30% of Medicare funds annually on just 5% to 6% of Medicare insurees who die within the year (Schulte, 1983).

In 1984, Richard Lamm, then Governor of Colorado, was widely quoted as stating that older persons "have a duty to die and get out of the way" (Slater, 1984). Although Lamm subsequently stated that he had been misquoted on this specific statement, he has been delivering the same message repeatedly since leaving office, in only somewhat more delicately worded fashions (Lamm, 1987, 1989). In 1990, John Silber, the Democratic candidate for governor in Massachusetts, carried forth Lamm's torch by proclaiming that when people have lived a long life, it is time for them to die (Butterfield, 1990).

During the past few years, discussion of this notion has spread to a number of forums. Ethicists and philosophers have been generating principles of equity to undergird "justice between age groups" in the provision of health care, rather than, for instance, justice between rich and poor, or justice between ethnic and racial subgroups (Daniels, 1988; Menzel, 1990). Conferences and books have explicitly addressed the issue with titles such as "Should Health Care Be Rationed by Age?" (Smeeding, Battin, Francis, & Landesman, 1987).

Late in 1987, this theme received substantial popular attention with the publication of a book entitled *Setting Limits: Medical Goals in an Aging Society*, by ethicist Daniel Callahan. He depicted the elderly population as "a new social threat" and a "demographic, economic, and medical avalanche . . . one that could ultimately (and perhaps already) do [sic] great harm." Callahan's remedy for this threat was to use "age as a specific criterion for the allocation and limitation of health care" by denying life-extending health care—as a matter of public policy—to persons who are aged in their "late 70s or early 80s" and/or have "lived out a natural life span" (p. 171). Although Callahan described "the natural life span" as a matter of biography rather than biology, he used chronological age as an arbitrary marker to designate when, from a biographical standpoint, the individual should have reached the end of a natural life and be viewing life retrospectively rather than prospectively.

Setting Limits received a great deal of national attention. It was reviewed in national magazines, *The New York Times, Washington Post, The Wall Street Journal,* and just about every relevant professional and scholarly journal and newsletter. Callahan has continued to present and defend his point of view in a subsequent book and in a number of public forums throughout the country. His and other proposals for age-based rationing have come to be rather firmly embedded in public discourse concerning health care policies in the United States.

Putting aside the issues of the moral implications and political feasibility of such proposals, which are considerable (see Binstock & Post, 1991), what sorts of financial "savings" might be achieved through rationing measures such as categorically denying life-saving care to older persons? Would these savings be of economic significance?

Proponents of old-age-based rationing have not identified the magnitude of savings that their proposals might achieve. But, for illustrative purposes, we can construct an example.

For a number of years, about 28% of annual Medicare expenditures has been on those Medicare insurees who die within a year (Lubitz & Riley, 1993). Suppose we were to deny care to prospective high-cost decedents (although, clinically, it is rarely possible to make highly reliable prospective distinctions between high-cost survivors and decedents). Even if it were ethically and morally palatable to implement a policy that denied treatment to such high-cost Medicare patients, and thereby eliminate "wasteful" health care, the dollars saved would be insignificant in the larger context of national health care costs.

High-cost Medicare decedents annually account for 3.5% of Medicare expenditures (see Lubitz & Prihoda, 1984; Scitovsky, 1984, 1988). In 1993, when Medicare expenditures were estimated to be $143 billion (Congress of the United States, 1993, p. 41), a policy that denied them treatment would have saved about $5 billion. Viewed in isolation, this is a substantial amount of money. But in the larger context, saving such an amount would have a negligible effect on the overall situation, reducing national health care costs from $900 billion to about $895 billion. It is unlikely that the American public, if reasonably well-informed about such a policy, would be persuaded of its economic significance.

On the other hand, a serious risk of unofficial, covert rationing of health care on the basis of old age is posed by a provision in President Clinton's health care plan that would link Medicare with the purchasing alliances that are to serve as the primary vehicles for reform. A seemingly minor, innocuous provision in the proposal would allow state governments to integrate Medicare beneficiaries into the purchasing alliances. As states exercise this option, many older people may end up in a system of health care that has a limited budget— such as a health maintenance organization (HMO) or preferred provider organization (PPO).

Older people, grouped with younger people in these budgeted plans, may very well become subject to a covert, informal system of old-age-based rationing. As doctors attempt to provide adequate care within the context of limited budgets, they are likely to be pressured by administrators and colleagues to not make available to their older patients expensive tests and medical specialists that they do make available to their younger patients.

The likelihood of such covert rationing is indicated by the experience of the British National Health Service. There, as documented by Aaron and Schwartz (1984), the pressures of a limited budget have resulted in older patients being routinely, although unofficially, denied tests and care made available to younger patients with the same clinical conditions. Indeed, the gatekeeper physicians in the British system often tell older patients that "nothing can be done" for them, medically, when such is not the case.

President Clinton's plan appears to be somewhat sensitive to this possibility of old-age-based rationing. It specifies that states "must demonstrate adequate risk adjustment methodologies to assure that plans have sufficient compensation to provide appropriate access to care" (White House Domestic Policy Council, 1993, p. 217) before they can fold Medicare beneficiaries into their alliances. This reliance on a bureaucratic statement of research methodologies, however, is not much of a bulwark. Indeed the validity and reliability of such methodologies, in general, has not even been established to date.

The President's proposal also requires that state alliances offer Medicare beneficiaries at least one fee-for-service option at no higher cost to them. In principle, this provides older persons with an escape route from exposure to the risk of rationing in a budgeted plan. But in practice, especially in rural areas and predominantly rural states, the sparse number of available physicians may be tied up in contracts with budgeted groups of health care providers. Even where this is not the case, strong corporate marketing campaigns are likely to attract many older people to sign up with a group of health care providers rather than remain in a traditional fee-for-service plan.

There are no obvious reasons for folding Medicare into purchasing alliances. If the aim is to reduce Medicare costs, integrating Medicare beneficiaries into the alliances is less direct and may be less effective than the direct price controls that are implemented under Medicare now, which could be extended further.

If purchasing alliances prove to be an effective strategy for reforming American health care, there will be plenty of time to integrate Medicare into their mechanisms. In the meantime, the federal government could to continue to control Medicare reimbursement rates, while retaining its universal coverage and genuine access for older Americans. At the same time, Medicare can also serve as a "yardstick" against which we can measure how well purchasing alliances are doing in keeping costs down and providing quality services.

In any event, the grave ethical and moral implications of any formal or informal limitations on the volume of services provided to older people ought to be subject to the widest possible public debate and understanding and certainly not be the outcome—even unintentionally—of covert, unofficial rationing.

Financing Long-Term Care Insurance

Ironically, even as measures to contain Medicare costs have come into play and proposals to limit health care for older people are in vogue, proposals for substantially expanding public insurance to pay for long-term care of elderly persons and others with chronic diseases and disabling conditions have become well established on the public policy agenda. A coalition named the Long-Term Care Campaign—which claims to represent nearly 140 national organizations and is spearheaded by the 35-million member American Association of Retired Persons (AARP), the Alzheimer's Association, and the Families USA Foundation—has been lobbying for legislation that would established federal reimbursement for long-term care services, provided in nursing homes and in residential environments, regardless of the patient's financial means (McConnell, 1990).

More than 80 federal programs and a plethora of state and local public and private agencies, are sources of funding for long-term care services (Congress of the United States, 1988). But each source regulates the availability of funds with rules as to eligibility and breadth of service coverage and changes its rules frequently; patients are often ruled ineligible for funding through Medicare, Medicaid, and other programs. Thus, despite the many sources of funding, specific patients and caregivers may find themselves ineligible for financial help and unable to pay out-of-pocket for needed services. In one study, about 75% of the informal caregivers for dementia patients reported that they did not use formal services because they were unable to pay for them (Eckert & Smyth, 1988).

The Medicare health insurance program does not reimburse patients for long-term care, either in nursing homes or at home. Private long-term care insurance, in an early stage of product development, is very expensive for the majority of persons, and its benefits are limited in scope and duration. Only 3% of older persons have any private long-term care insurance, and only about 1% of nursing home costs are paid for by private insurance (Wiener, 1990). Even when the product matures, it is unlikely to be a panacea. A Brookings Institution study suggested that about 25 years from now, when all the "bugs" may be worked out, some 25% to 45% of elderly people would be able to afford private long-term care insurance premiums, and that private insurance benefit payments would account for only 7% to 12% of all nursing home benefits (Rivlin & Wiener, 1988).

Paying the costs of long-term care can be a catastrophic financial experience for patients and their families. The annual cost of a year's care in a nursing home averages $30,000 and ranges higher than $100,000. Equivalent care provided in a home setting is just as expensive when the in-kind, informal services provided by family and friends of a patient are included in as expenses. Although nursing homes originally developed as an alternative to home care, their financial costs have redirected great attention during the past two decades to home care as a possible cheaper alternative. But numerous demonstrations and studies have concluded that home care is not cheaper for patients who would otherwise be appropriately placed in a nursing home (Weissert, 1990).

Patients and their families paid over $29.5 billion out-of-pocket for long-term care services in 1992. The total national expenditure for long-term care was an estimated $85 billion. Expenditures on nursing homes were $65 billion. Home health care services provided by agencies participating in Medicare and Medicaid totaled $8.5 billion. Payments for related nonhealth home care services to other home care service providers accounted for an estimated $7.5 billion in additional expenditures. Out-of-pocket payments accounted for 44% of nursing home expenditures and 11% of home care expenditures (Sonnefeld et al., 1991).

Medicaid, the federal-state insurance program available to persons of all ages who qualify through classification as economically poor, does pay for long-term care in nursing homes (accounting for nearly 50% of total national nursing home expenditures). But Medicaid does not pay for the full range of home care services that will be needed in most cases. Most state Medicaid programs provide reimbursement only for the most "medicalized" services that are necessary to maintain a long-term care patient in a home environment; rarely reimbursed are essential supports, such as chore services, assistance with food shopping and meal preparation, transportation, companionship, periodic monitoring, and respite programs for family and other unpaid caregivers.

Medicaid does include a special waiver program that allows states to offer a wider range of nonmedical home care services, if limited to those patients who otherwise would require Medicaid-financed nursing home care. But the volume of services in these waiver programs is small in relation to the overall need (Miller, 1992).

Since 1989, a number of comprehensive long-term care bills have been introduced in Congress, with projected first-year expenditures ranging from $21 billion to $50 billion, depending on varied details regarding specific populations eligible and technical provisions regarding the timing, nature, and extent of insurance coverage. Because of such cost estimates, no major long-term care bill has come close to enactment, as yet.

President Clinton has proposed a new long-term care program for persons of all ages, to be administered by state governments as a federal grant-in-aid program. Its stated aims include (a) expanded home and community-based services, (b) improvement in Medicaid coverage for nursing home care, and (c) the establishment of quality and reliability standards for private long-term care insurance products, as well as tax incentives to encourage people to buy those products.

To be eligible for publicly financed services, an individual must meet one of the following conditions: (a) requires personal assistance, standby assistance, supervision, or cues to perform three or more of the following five activities of daily living (ADLs)—eating, dressing, bathing, toileting, and transferring in and out of bed; (b) presents evidence of severe cognitive or mental impairment as indicated by a specified score on a standard mental status protocol; (c) has severe or profound mental retardation; or (d) for a child under the age of six, who is dependent on technology and otherwise requires hospital or institutional care (White House Domestic Policy Council, 1993, pp. 171-172).

Medicare enrollees can qualify for the proposed home and community-based care program if they pay a $20-a-month premium for coverage and, of course, meet the criteria for determining that they have disabilities requiring care. For those whose incomes fall below the poverty line, however, there would be no premium payments at all.

The minimum benefits required to be provided by a participating state are "to each eligible individual a standardized assessment and an individual plan of care" (White House Domestic Policy Council, 1993, p. 172). Beyond that, the President's plan simply lists a broad range of services that can be financially covered by the program. States must continue to serve all individuals currently receiving home and community-based services under Medicaid. But whether the range and levels of services for other populations is maintained or enhanced appears to be up to each state.

Overall, the President's long-term care proposal is limited in its scope and impact. Its minimum requirements for services are skimpy. Its provision that a prospective service recipient must have limitations in three ADLs is a rather severe eligibility standard; most previous long-term care bills have set the standard at two. Net federal increases in expenditures on long-term care are not estimated to reach even a $20 billion annual level until the turn of the century. Whether even this limited proposal for long-term care, let alone a more fully funded and comprehensive approach with less severe eligibility criterion, will be enacted in the 1990s will be somewhat dependent on the politics of advocates for the aged and the disabled, within the broader politics of health care reform.

Health Care Reform and the Politics of Aging

What role will the politics of older people and some 50 national old-age interest groups (see Table 15.1) have on the efforts of President Clinton and Congress to achieve health care reform? Although journalists and other observers of American politics vastly overstate the political power of the "gray lobby" (see Binstock, 1992b, 1992c), there is little doubt that some aged persons and old-age organizations will have much at stake in the health policy decisions that lie immediately ahead and in attempts to affect them.

Further proposals to freeze or otherwise restrict reimbursements to hospitals, physicians, and other providers are unlikely to engender serious opposition from old-age interests. To be sure, selected organizational spokespersons have and will continue to point up complex indirect effects that such cost-containment measures may have on older people's access to health care. Yet the implementation and ongoing success of Medicare's prospective payments for reimbursing hospitals—instituted nearly a decade ago, despite initial outcries from aging advocacy groups—was an early indication that such changes are not of sufficient moment to most older people to become the basis for effective political opposition. The most recent indication was the ease with which Medicare reimbursements to health care providers were cut back, once again, in OBRA 1993.

On the other hand, the saga of the Medicare Catastrophic Coverage Act (MCCA)—its enactment in 1988 and its swift repeal in 1989—might suggest that major measures to increase and perhaps redistribute financial burdens among Medicare program participants are unfeasible, politically. Yet, as will be detailed later, the MCCA was an unusual case.

Medicare Part B premium rates have been increased continually over the years without political difficulty; this happened most recently in OBRA 1993. Other measures in the President's plan and alternative plans to increase and redistribute costs among Medicare insurees—by imposing, for example, higher premium rates, deductibles, and copayments on wealthier older people—would simply be

Table 15.1 National Old-Age Interest Groups, 1992 (selected)

Mass membership organizations
    American Association of Retired Persons (35 million members)
    Gray Panthers (70,000 members)
    National Alliance of Senior Citizens (2 million members)
    National Association of Retired Federal Employees (490,000 members)
    National Committee to Preserve Social Security and Medicare (5 million
      members)
    National Council of Senior Citizens (5 million members)
Advocacy organizations for special older constituencies
    Alzheimer's Association
    Associacion Nacionale Pro Personas Mayores
    Families U.S.A. Foundation (poor older persons)
    National Caucus and Center on Black Aged
    National Citizens Coalition for Nursing Home Reform
    National Foundation for Long-Term Care
    National Hispanic Council on Aging
    National Indian Council on Aging
    National Pacific/Asian Resource Center on Aging
    Older Women's League
Professional and trade organizations
    Alliance for Aging Research
    American Association of Homes for the Aging
    American Association for International Aging
    American Federation for Aging Research
    American Geriatrics Society
    American Society on Aging
    Association for Gerontology in Higher Education
    Gerontological Society of America
    National Academy of Social Insurance
    National Association for Home Care
    National Association of Area Agencies on Aging
    National Association of Foster Grandparents
    National Association of Meals Programs
    National Association of Nutrition and Aging Services Programs
    National Association of RSVP[a] Directors
    National Association of Senior Living Industries
    National Association of State Units on Aging
    National Council on the Aging
    National Senior Citizens Law Center

SOURCE: Adapted from Van Tassel and Wilkinson Meyer (1992).
a. Retired Senior Volunteer Program.

increments extending a 10-year trend through which Congress has reformed policies on aging to reflect the diverse economic situations of older persons.

The Social Security Reform Act of 1983 began this trend by subjecting to taxation one half of the Social Security benefits of individuals with incomes exceeding $25,000 and married couples with over $32,000. The Tax Reform Act of 1986, even as it eliminated the extra personal exemption that had been available to all persons aged 65 and older when filing their federal income tax returns, provided new tax credits to very low-income older persons on a sliding scale. The Older Americans Act programs of supportive and social services, for which all persons aged 60 and older are eligible, have been gradually targeted by Congress to low-income older persons. And the MCCA of 1988 continued this legislative approach in two respects, through progressive taxation provisions and its requirement that Medicaid pay the Part B premiums and cost-sharing expenses for Medicare enrollees who have incomes below the poverty line. (Although the former provision was repealed in 1989, the latter remains in effect.)

This trend was extended and reaffirmed in OBRA 1993. The legislation raised to 85% the proportion of Social Security benefits subject to taxation for individuals with incomes of over $34,000 and couples over $44,000.

But the relatively recent experience of enacting and swiftly repealing the MCCA has made some members of Congress particularly wary of policy measures that redistribute burdens to wealthier older persons. That legislation involved the first major expansion of benefits to older persons in 16 years. It provided insurance coverage for economically catastrophic hospital and physician bills, outpatient prescription drugs, and for some elements of long-term care. About one third of these new benefits were to be financed through increased premiums paid by all Medicare Part B enrollees and two thirds through a progressive, sharply escalating surtax levied on middle and higher income Medicare enrollees—about 40% of program participants.

During a period of nearly 2 years between the introduction of the bill and its enactment as law, neither Congress nor the aging advocacy groups floated "trial balloons" to enable older Americans to understand what sorts of benefits they would receive through the new MCCA and who would pay for them. Consequently, when the proposal finally did become a law, there was no popular constituency supporting it. But there was distinct opposition to it from those older persons who had to pay the most new taxes and who perceived that they already had private insurance coverage for the benefits provided through the new law (Holstein & Minkler, 1991). They were a small numerical minority, yet they were dispersed through every congressional district. When they protested vociferously against the act, Congress received no evidence of countervailing popular support for the new law (despite the fact that it was endorsed by AARP lobbyists).

Yet there are sound reasons to think that Congress could have withstood the protests of the minority of older persons who expressed their dissatisfaction with the MCCA. Indeed, following the repeal of the law, several congressional leaders publicly lamented that they had not had the courage to stand up to a small number of comparatively wealthy older constituents (Tolchin, 1989). Moreover, despite the clichés of journalists that suggest that politicians who harm or threaten old-age interests invariably suffer when they stand for reelection, the evidence clearly indicates that this is not the case.

A classic and representative example is provided by the 1984 election. In 1983, President Reagan and the Congress froze the cost-of-living adjustment on Social Security benefits and, for the first time, also imposed taxes on those benefits for wealthier recipients. Yet neither Congress nor Reagan suffered in the ensuing election. In fact, the President received far greater support from older persons than he had in 1990, and in virtually the same proportion as from younger age groups (Binstock, 1992b). Similarly, it is doubtful that any members of Congress or the President will suffer from a demonstrable "punishment" at the hands of older voters for the taxes and cutbacks on old-age programs in OBRA 1993.

The experience of the MCCA, however, does provide some lessons for assessing the politics of any major initiative for expanding public long-term care insurance. If such a program is to be enacted and endure, then it will probably require broad grassroots political support, with desires and demands articulated actively within congressional districts nationwide. Although some polls indicate that favorable sentiment has crystallized around the general principle of public long-term care insurance (McConnell, 1990), the principle masks many basic value issues that have just begun to surface in public discussion. Widespread debate on these issues will be required for a substantial proportion of Americans to understand and support the implications of any law that is to be enacted.

From the perspective of older persons, long-term care has been seen as a problem besetting elderly people, categorically. And the predominant, although not exclusive, element of interest in additional public insurance has been generated by an economic concern. That concern is the possibility of becoming poor through "spending down," that is, depleting one's assets to pay for long-term care and then becoming dependent on a welfare program, Medicaid, to pay nursing home bills. There is a distinct middle-class fear—both economic and psychological—of using savings and selling a home to finance one's own health care. This anxiety reflects a desire to protect estates, as well as the psychological intertwining of personal self-esteem with one's material worth and independence. But, as indicated earlier, the political weight of this type of concern is not substantial in today's climate of public policy discourse in which older persons are perceived as having more than their fair share of public resources.

If public long-term care insurance is to be enacted as an old-age entitlement, to serve older persons as a buffer against spending down, there are some fundamental moral and political issues that the American public will need to confront and resolve. Among these issues are: Assuming that we can improve laws for protecting spouses of long-term care patients from impoverishment, why shouldn't older people spend their assets and income on their health care? Why should government foot the bill? Why should it be government's responsibility to preserve estates? So they can be inherited? Should government take a more active role than at present in preserving economic status inequalities, from generation to generation? On what basis should some persons be taxed to preserve the inheritances of others? Should the taxing power of government be used to preserve the psychological sense of self-esteem that for so many persons is bound up in their lifetime accumulation of assets—their material worth?

Widespread public debate on such issues may very well fail to resolve them in a fashion that supports a major initiative in long-term care to protect older persons from paying for their care. Indeed, research findings are even beginning to show that the incidence and prevalence of the spend-down phenomenon may be grossly exaggerated by advocates for long-term care (Burwell, Adams, & Meiners, 1989). Moreover, it appears that many nursing home patients who are paid for by Medicaid become eligible for that program by sheltering and transferring their financial assets, rather than by spending down until they are poor (Moses, 1990). In this fashion, one can preserve his or her estate—and, perhaps, pass it on as a legacy—while having government pay for one's long-term care through Medicaid, a program intended for the poor.

To the extent that a major long-term care initiative is designed, like President Clinton's, to include persons with AIDS, younger disabled persons, and the mentally retarded and developmentally disabled, the challenges of developing broad political support will be even more complex. Program costs will be substantially greater and more difficult to predict. Some segments of the American public may be influenced by hostile stereotypes of persons with AIDS.

The constituency of younger disabled persons may continue their long-standing reluctance to be symbolically and politically identified with elderly people because of traditional stereotypes of older people as frail, chronically ill, declining, and "marginal" to society. Advocates for the disabled have continually rejected a "medical model" of long-term care, emphasizing their strong desires for autonomy, independence, and as much "normalization" of daily life as possible (see Binstock, 1992a).

Advocates for the aged and the disabled did work together, however, in the planning process for the White House initiative on long-term care. This is reflected in the facts that the Clinton long-term proposal carries forward the notion of age irrelevancy and incorporates many specific concerns that have been put forward by advocates for the younger disabled population over the years—such as the principle that clients should be able to hire and fire service providers of their choice.

Yet there are distinct signs that the unity of the two constituencies will not hold up under the pressure of other issues in the overall Clinton plan for reform. On the one hand, advocates for the younger disabled have expressed concern that persons with what they term "special needs" will receive short shrift in terms of attention and appropriate services within the acute care range of needs—as they receive their health care in the context of the limited budgets of HMOs, PPOs, and other health care provider groups that would be assembled for the purchasing alliances. On the other hand, old-age interest groups, particularly AARP and the National Committee to Preserve Social Security and Medicare (see McSteen, 1993), have become preoccupied with concerns about the acute care arena—particularly with what they regard as inequities between the insurance that will be provided to Medicare enrollees compared with the coverage that the President's plan proposes for most other Americans.

The chairwoman of AARP told Congress that her organization was deeply disappointed that the President's plan would not provide the same coverage for Medicare beneficiaries as it would for younger populations. More specifically, AARP has complained (a) that younger Americans will have a standard package of benefits that "is much, much better" than provided by Medicare, even considering the new coverage proposed for prescription drugs and long-term care, and (b) that the President's proposal sets limits on out-of-pocket costs—$1,500 a year for an individual and $3,000 a year for a family (Pear, 1993). The Medicare program has no out-of-pocket limits, and Mr. Clinton's proposal, as now drafted, would not establish such limits for Medicare. One suspects that AARP will continue to give its major attention to these issues in the months ahead. In short, what seems to be emerging is a loss of focus and unity on the issue of long-term care, by both advocates for the disabled and the aged.

As indicated by AARP's complaints, the White House may not have effectively secured the support of the old-age lobby for its overall package for reforming American health care. The long-term care initiative and the proposal for a Medicare benefit to cover outpatient prescription drugs apparently were expected to be sufficient bargaining chips to enlist the old-age interest groups—and by extension, elderly people—as strong supporters of the President's plan. And, to be sure, in the wake of publicly aired complaints from AARP, its chief lobbyist hastened to assert that the organization backs most of the Clinton plan (Rother, 1993). Yet the already voiced concerns about the comparatively thinner benefit package available to Medicare enrollees, as well as their comparatively higher out-of-pocket costs, could form the basis for strong organized opposition by the old-age lobby. This opposition could become especially vigorous if grassroots concern develops regarding the possibility that Medicare integration into purchasing alliances could mean unofficial rationing of health care on the basis of old age.

Even so, it is safe to say that the legislative fate of President Clinton's Health Security Plan—and other broad proposals for health care reform in the 1990s—will more likely be determined by the reactions and activities of interests that have much stronger bases of economic and political power than do older Americans—big business, small business, and organized labor; physicians and hospitals; pharmaceutical companies; medical equipment and supply manufacturers; and the health insurance industry.

References

Aaron, H. J., & Schwartz, W. B. (1984). *The painful prescription: Rationing hospital care.* Washington, DC: Brookings Institution.

Arnett, R. H. III, McKusick, D. R., Sonnefeld, S. T., & Cowell, C. S. (1986). Projections of health care spending to 1990. *Health Care Financing Review, 7*(3), 1-36.

Binstock, R. H. (1992a). Aging, disability, and long-term care: The politics of common ground. *Generations, 16*(1), 83-88.

Binstock, R. H. (1992b). Older voters and the 1992 presidential election. *The Gerontologist, 32,* 601-606.

Binstock, R. H. (1992c). The oldest old and "intergenerational equity." In R. Suzman, D. Willis, & K. Manton (Eds.), *The oldest old* (pp. 394-417). New York: Oxford University Press.

Binstock, R. H. (1993). Health care costs around the world: Is aging a fiscal "black hole"? *Generations, 17*(4), 37-42.

Binstock, R. H., & Post, S. G. (1991). *Too old for health care? Controversies in medicine, law, economics, and ethics.* Baltimore, MD: Johns Hopkins University Press.

Burwell, B., Adams, E., & Meiners, M. (1989). *Spend-down of assets prior to Medicaid eligibility among nursing home recipients in Michigan.* Washington, DC: Syste-Metrics/McGraw-Hill.

Butterfield, F. (1990, July 27). Silber taps public's anger to run a strong race in Massachusetts. *The New York Times,* p. A6.

Callahan, D. (1987). *Setting limits: Medical goals in an aging society.* New York: Simon & Schuster.

Congress of the United States, Congressional Budget Office. (1992). *The economic and budget outlook: Fiscal years 1993-1997.* Washington, DC: U.S. Government Printing Office.

Congress of the United States, Congressional Budget Office. (1993). *The economic and budget outlook: An update.* Washington, DC: U.S. Government Printing Office.

Congress of the United States, Library of Congress, Congressional Research Service. (1988). *Financing and delivery of long-term care services for the elderly.* Washington, DC: U.S. Government Printing Office.

Coulam, R. F., & Gaumer, G. L. (1991). Medicare's prospective payment system: A critical appraisal. *Health Care Financing Review, 13*(Suppl.), 45-77.

Daniels, N. (1988). *Am I my parents' keeper? An essay on justice between the young and the old.* New York: Oxford University Press.

Eckert, S. K., & Smyth, K. (1988). *A case study of methods of locating and arranging health and long-term care for persons with dementia.* Washington, DC: Congress of the United States, Office of Technology Assessment

Gornick, M. J., Greenberg, N., Eggers, P. W., & Dobson, A. (1985). Twenty years of Medicare and Medicaid: Covered populations, use of benefits, and program expenditures. *Health Care Financing Review, 7*(Suppl.), 22.

Hing, E. (1987). Use of nursing homes by the elderly: Preliminary data from the 1985 national nursing home survey. *Advance data* (No. 135). Hyattsville, MD: U.S. Department of Health and Human Services, National Center for Health Statistics.

Holstein, M., & Minkler, M. (1991). The short life and painful death of the Medicare Catastrophic Coverage Act. In M. Minkler & C. Estes (Eds.), *Critical perspectives on aging: The political and moral economy of growing old* (pp. 189-208). Amityville, NY: Baywood.

Lamm, R. D. (1987). A debate: Medicare in 2020. In *Medicare reform and the baby boom generation: Proceedings of the Second Annual Conference of Americans for Generational Equity* (pp. 77-88). Washington, DC: Americans for Generational Equity.

Lamm, R. D. (1989). Columbus and Copernicus: New wine in old wineskins. *Mount Sinai Journal of Medicine, 56*(1), 1-10.

Leon, J., & Lair, T. (1990). Functional status of the noninstitutionalized elderly: Estimates of ADL and IADL difficulties. *National Medical Expenditure Survey Research Findings, 4* (DHHS Pub. No. PHS 90-3462). Rockville, MD: Public Health Service, Agency for Health Care Policy and Research.

Liu, K., Manton, K. M., & Liu, B. M. (1985). Home care expenses for the disabled elderly. *Health Care Financing Review, 7*(2), 52.

Lubitz, J. D., & Prihoda, R. (1984). The use and costs of Medicare services in the last two years of life. *Health Care Financing Review, 5*(3), 117-131.

Lubitz, J. D., & Riley, G. F. (1993). Trends in Medicare payments in the last year of life. *New England Journal of Medicine, 328*, 1092-1096.

McConnell, S. (1990). Who cares about long-term care? *Generations, 14*(2), 15-18.

McSteen, M. (1993, October 21). Testimony before the Subcommittee on Health, Committee on Ways and Means, U.S. House of Representatives, 103rd Congress, First Session.

Mendelson, D. N., & Schwartz, W. B. (1993). The effects of aging and population growth on health care costs. *Health Affairs, 12*(1), 119-125.

Menzel, P. T. (1990). *Strong medicine: The ethical rationing of health care.* New York: Oxford University Press.

Miller, N. A. (1992). Medicaid 2176 home and community-based care waivers: The first ten years. *Health Affairs, 11*(4), 162-171.

Moses, S. A. (1990). The fallacy of impoverishment. *The Gerontologist, 30*, 21-25.

National Center for Health Statistics. (1989). National Hospital Discharge Survey: Annual summary, 1987. *Vital and health statistics* (Series 13, No. 99). Hyattsville, MD: Public Health Service.

National Center for Health Statistics. (1990). Current estimates from the National Health Interview Survey, 1989. *Vital and health statistics* (Series 10, No. 176). Hyattsville, MD: Public Health Service.

National Center for Health Statistics. (1993). Births, marriages, divorces, and deaths for September 1992. *Monthly vital statistics report* (Vol. 41, No. 9). Hyattsville, MD: Public Health Service.

Pear, R. (1993, October 25). Influential group says health plan slights the aged. *The New York Times*, p. 1.

Reischauer, R. (1992, November). *Mandatory spending through 2002.* Paper presented at the 45th Annual Scientific Meeting of the Gerontological Society of America, Washington, DC.

Rivlin, A. M., & Wiener, J. M. (1988). *Caring for the disabled elderly: Who will pay?* Washington, DC: Brookings Institution.

Ross, S. G. (1991, November). *The financial status of the Social Security and Medicare programs.* Paper presented at the annual meeting of the Gerontological Society of America, San Francisco.

Rother, J. (1993, October 31). Retiree group backs most of Clinton plan [Letter to the editor]. *The New York Times*, p. 16.

Schneider, E. L., & Guralnik, J. M. (1990). The aging of America: Impact on health care costs. *Journal of the American Medical Association, 263*, 2335-2340.

Schulte, J. (1983, April 26). Terminal patients deplete Medicare, Greenspan says. *Dallas Morning News*, p. 1.

Scitovsky, A. A. (1984). "The high cost of dying": What do the data show? *Milbank Memorial Fund Quarterly/Health and Society, 62,* 591-608.

Scitovsky, A. A. (1988). Medical care in the last twelve months of life: The relation between age, functional status, and medical care expenditures. *Milbank Memorial Fund Quarterly/Health and Society, 66,* 640-660.

Slater, W. (1984, March 29). Latest Lamm remark angers the elderly. *Arizona Daily Star,* p. 1.

Smeeding, T. M., Battin, M. P, Francis, L. P., & Landesman, B. M. (Eds.). (1987). *Should medical care be rationed by age?* Totowa, NJ: Rowman & Littlefield.

Social Security and Medicare Boards of Trustees. (1992). *Status of the Social Security and Medicare programs: A summary of the 1992 annual reports.* Washington, DC: U.S. Government Printing Office.

Sonnefeld, S. T., Waldo, D. R., Lemieux, J. A., & McKusick, D. R. (1991). Projections of national health expenditures through the year 2000. *Health Care Financing Review, 13*(1), 1-27.

Taeuber, C. (1990). Diversity: The dramatic reality. In S. Bass, E. Kutza, & F. Torres-Gil (Eds.), *Diversity in aging: Challenges facing planners and policymakers in the 1990s* (pp. 1-45). Glenview, IL: Scott, Foresman.

Tolchin, M. (1989, November 5). House acts to kill '88 Medicare plan of extra benefits. *The New York Times,* p. 1.

U.S. Senate, Special Committee on Aging. (1991). *Aging America: Trends and projections.* Washington, DC: U.S. Government Printing Office.

Van Tassel, D. D., & Wilkinson Meyer, J. E. (Eds.). (1992). *U.S. Aging policy interest groups: Institutional profiles.* New York: Greenwood Press.

Weissert, W. G. (1990). Strategies for reducing home care expenditures. *Generations, 14*(2), 42-44.

Wiener, J. M. (1990). Which way for long-term care financing? *Generations, 14*(2), 4-9.

White House Domestic Policy Council. (1993). *The president's health security plan.* New York: Random House.

Additional Sources

Binstock, R. H., & George, L. K. (Eds.). (1990). *Handbook of aging and the social sciences* (3rd ed.). San Diego, CA: Academic Press.

Binstock, R. H., & Post, S. G. (1991). *Too old for health care? Controversies in medicine, law, economics, and ethics.* Baltimore, MD: Johns Hopkins University Press.

Binstock, R. H., Post, S. G., & Whitehouse, P. J. (Eds.). (1992). *Dementia and aging: Ethics, values, and policy choices.* Baltimore, MD: Johns Hopkins University Press.

Blumenthal, D., Schlesinger, M., & Drumheller, P. B. (1988). *Renewing the promise: Medicare and its reform.* New York: Oxford University Press.

Day, C. L. (1990). *What older Americans think: Interest groups and aging policy.* Princeton, NJ: Princeton University Press.

Marmor, T. R., Mashaw, J. L., & Harvey, P. L. (1990). *America's misunderstood welfare state: Persistent myths, enduring realities.* New York: Basic Books.

Russell, L. B. (1989). *Medicare's new hospital payment system: Is it working?* Washington, DC: Brookings Institution.

Torres-Gil, F. M. (1992). *The new aging: Politics and change in America.* New York: Auburn House.

16

When the Phoenix Rises, Where *Will* She Go?

The Women's Health Agenda

CHRIS HAFNER-EATON

*A*rticles abound in current professional journals, women's magazines, and the general media regarding an entire spectrum of health problems facing women. In fact, the number may be at an all-time high due to the convergence of many social, political, and economic factors. Many of these articles espouse a belief that there is a single problem that should be solved, yet few of these concur about which problem should receive priority attention. An array of the women's health agenda might start with a list such as health care access; violence against women; breast, uterine, and ovarian cancer; heart disease; abortion; osteoporosis; eating disorders; menopause; cesarean sections; hysterectomies; infertility; clinical trial representation; new contraceptive methods; pre- and postnatal care; breast-feeding; long-term care; depression; AIDS; breast implants; homelessness; poverty;

family leave; child care; tobacco and chemical dependency, and more. The list goes on with varying priority order depending on the source. This lack of consensus stems from the fact that women's health problems are nearly as heterogeneous as women themselves, and from several underlying imbalances including more than a dozen years of blatant political neglect toward women's health; the predominance of men in medicine, basic science, and funding agencies; and the fragmentation of the once powerful women's movement. Additionally, the American public in general has had difficulty coalescing its beliefs regarding the need for or direction of health reform (Blendon, 1988; Litman & Robins, 1991). Thus the result is an abundance of problem issues, without concentrated or focused reform efforts. When reform has occurred, it has been categorical in nature, targeting only a segment of the population or one particular condition (consequently birthing the phrase "disease-of-the-month club").

Although it is true that some progress has been achieved recently, much work still lies ahead. Lest any readers interpret this chapter as pure ranting, a brief recognition of these accomplishments is included here to remind us of a few recent victories. First, we have moved forward in the area of research on particular health issues, such as osteoporosis, menopause, ovarian and breast cancer, and alternative contraceptives (Clancy & Massion, 1992; National Cancer Institute [NCI], 1992). Some preventive and patient care programs have regained former or higher levels of funding. For example, the Family Planning Program, Title X, was allocated a much needed $173.6 million for fiscal year 1993 (National Family Planning and Reproductive Health Association, 1992). Additionally, as of 1993, Title X is no longer bound by the "gag rule," prohibiting providers receiving Federal grants from counseling women on abortion options. In 1991, we witnessed the founding of the Society for the Advancement of Women's Health Research. The U.S. Congress passed legislation to establish national quality standards for mammography in 1992. Also, several states, including Oregon, have mandated that insurance plans include coverage for mammography and cervical cancer screening. Once again, the issue of a National Health Program has been raised as a serious political agenda item. And finally, after years of lobbying, we have an Office of Research on Women's Health within the National Institutes of Health (NIH) to reverse the systematic institutional research biases against women (Kirchstein, 1991). This office was charged with a tall mission of establishing priorities, planning and implementing research, advising other NIH programs, interacting with the scientific community and organizations involved in women's health, and developing initiatives to increase women's representativeness in research. As part of President Clinton's first 100 days, the Family and Medical Leave Act was enacted. This act enables families with newborn or adopted children or a seriously ill immediate family member to maintain their employment position and benefits during a leave. Of course, we also must recognize as a major step forward the recent cabinet appointments of Dr. Shalala as the head of the Department of Health and Human Services and Dr. Joycelyn Elders as the Surgeon General of the U.S. Public Health Service.

Why Have a Women's Health Agenda?

Before examining specific elements of any women's health agenda, it is important to emphasize what the past 12 years of conservative Republican administrations has meant for women. Although these administrations purported to run a minimalist government, many unprecedented extensions of government occurred, particularly to the detriment of women's health. Litman and Robins (1991) state this well by noting these years "were marked by major entreaties, both in policy and practice, which called for extensive government intrusion into the privacy of the home (e.g., abortion and family planning), the workplace (e.g., mandatory drug testing), as well as medical practice, including the physician-patient relationship itself (e.g., Diagnosis Related group-based prospective payment)" (p. 74). Although Litman and Robins are referring to both men and women, the relative impact of such control is felt more by women because of their central role in family planning and abortion, their likelihood of being part of a lower-paid, lower-autonomy, temporary or part-time workforce requiring compulsory drug testing, and their proportionately higher use of health services. In addition, there is little evidence to suggest that these administrations did anything but undermine so-called family values.

Some of the issues listed in this introduction are unique to women, but many are not. So why treat them any differently? This is not a conspiracy against men. Most women in this field like men, are friends with men, may be married to men, and want to improve the health of men as well. However, we have been working on that agenda since before formal medicine and health services research originated. Agendas are established by those in power, the media, and key financial stakeholders—few of whom have been female in previous years. So, whether intentionally through collusion or unconsciously through the norms of brotherhood, women's concerns have either not been raised or have been assessed lower priority. Policymakers, health services researchers, medical practitioners, and basic scientists must come to realize that women's bodies are not the same as men's bodies.

Today's medical model is still a male-oriented conceptual model. In *The Mismeasure of Woman*, Tavris (1992) skillfully illustrates the predominant use of the male body and mind as the norm or golden standard. Even in medical texts, bodies are clearly illustrated as male 69% of the time but as female only 11% of the time—with the remainder being gender neutral (Tavris, 1992, p. 96). Moreover, Smith (1993), a Fellow of the American College of Obstetrics and Gynecology, argues that "there is still no attempt to teach gynecology residents about the unique needs of women, their perspective as patients, or (silly though it sounds) how they are different from men" (p. 129). Government notwithstanding, the National Institutes of Health, as recently as 1990, allocated a mere 13.5% of biomedical research funds to women's health. The remainder of funds went to research entirely on men's health or research affecting both (Kirchstein, 1991). Women's different hormonal balance from men's means that pharmaceuticals used to treat jointly shared conditions might not work or, worse yet, could be seriously injurious if used as tested safely on men. The use of the male body and its reactions as the norm has detrimental consequences for women and many times for their children as well.

Women's socioeconomic and political postures in this nation are also vastly different from men's, and this has significant consequences for health. Women still earn only 69 cents for every dollar a man earns (U.S. Bureau of the Census, 1991b). College educations and professional degrees often improve but do not equalize the gap. A woman's lower income places her at risk not only for lower health status but also for not having private health insurance, life insurance, adequate sick leave, parental leave, and resources for child care. As Tavris (1992) notes, "divorce typically lowers a woman's standard of living by an average of 73%, and raises a man's by an average of 42%" (p. 109). The fact that women are more likely than men to be caring for children also influences their health needs practically and clinically. Also, women more frequently enter retirement with fewer resources and are widowed into near poverty or poverty. In addition, oppression of women through violence against women and children has continued virtually unabated, and with the current extreme economic tensions, has probably worsened. These are only a few of the socioeconomic elements that help define women as distinct and different entities.

Last, women are now directly represented by a record, albeit still small, number of women in Congress, which affects the political feasibility of health legislation. Also of key significance, we have a strong, educated female within the White House, working in probably the closest and most visibly active collaboration with the President ever witnessed. Hillary Rodham Clinton's major role as the health reform chair has set the stage for years of promising action on many topics beyond health care finance and organization. Her discernible strength, along with that of Drs. Shalala and Elders and Ms. Janet Reno further promotes and stimulates action on the part of other women. And looking into the future, the Congressional Caucus for Women's Health Issues introduced the Women's Health Equity Act of 1993, a package of 32 bills aimed at improving the health of America's women (American Public Health Association, 1993).

So the question is not "Why have a women's health agenda" but, rather, "Why don't we have a women's health agenda ready to lay on the table?" This is not to deny that broad-based groups such as the Older Women's League, the National Organization for Women, and the Women's Caucus of the American Public Health Association have formulated fine agendas. We need to thoroughly explore and assess these for their merits in light of their public health impact for women. The time has come to join these formidable forces and to actively bring these forward to the political and public health front lines.

Social Issues as Health Problems

Several problems, such as poverty, homelessness, and violence against women, may not immediately appear under the purview of "health." Indeed, many political scientists, sociologists, and social welfare professionals might view this inclusion as encroachment by the medical paradigm. However, using a public health rubric of population-based effects leaves no doubt that these conditions have dramatic and real impacts on the health status of large numbers of women. This approach of public health incorporates, but is not limited to, medicine as a tool to ameliorate problems. We must take a multidisciplinary, cooperative approach toward analyzing and addressing women's health.

However large the task, the overall standard of living for women must be raised to improve their health status. Repeatedly, the standard of living has been linked both directly and indirectly to health status and access to health care (Brook et al., 1983; Davis, Gold, & Makuc, 1981; Kasper, 1986; Navarro, 1991). Even if health care access were vastly improved, differences in social class and standard of living would probably overshadow this accomplishment. Additionally, women must be empowered to make their own informed decisions. This empowerment must be comprehensive and meaningful, as opposed to categorical and superficial. It must include choices over employment, housing, child care, and safety, as well as family planning, disease prevention, and health interventions.

Racial discrimination and police brutality against anyone is repugnant. Quite appropriately, the nation was outraged at police officers who passively watched the Rodney King beating by other officers in Los Angeles. More strikingly, however, few seem to even comment when an officer responds to a domestic violence call and fails to arrest the abuser (nearly always male) and fails to take the victim seriously.

Violence against women and their children increases after such incidents (Heise, 1992; Worscter & Orloff, 1992), yet little if any outrage is expressed regarding the passive role of the police, judicial system, or legislative government. The Federal Bureau of Investigation (FBI) states that every 15 seconds in the United States a woman is physically beaten by her male domestic partner. Almost one third of all female homicide victims are killed by their male domestic partners (Lazarus & Lanzerotti, 1992). Nationwide, when police are called to the scene of a domestic violence incident, only 4% of the time is the aggressor arrested. However, when mandatory arrest laws are implemented for domestic violence, the recidivism rate declines dramatically (Worscter & Orloff, 1992). Clearly, there is room for the federal government to encourage the passage of mandatory arrest laws and appropriate training of law officers at the state level.

Violence against women in the form of rape and sexual assault happens with shocking frequency. According to FBI statistics, a woman is forcibly raped every 6 minutes, and one in three American women is sexually assaulted during her lifetime (Lazarus & Lanzerotti, 1992). These events not only require immediate medical and psychologic care but also scar women for life. The health and well-being of these victims should be a major concern, as should preventing future occurrences of such violence. It is likely that societal problems such as this one will require years of social, cultural, educational, and legal intervention to address the core reasons for destructive dysfunctional behavior.

Competing for Preventive Health Dollars

Although the United States spent approximately $946 billion on health services in 1993 and expects to spend nearly $1.06 trillion in 1994, the provision of medical care is not the only health area that needs attention. In fact, many of women's health needs are in direct competition for scarce dollars with the provision of traditional medical care services. With less than 4% of our total health expenditures directly devoted to prevention and public health activities, our system is structured reactively instead of proactively (U.S. Department of Health and Human Services, 1993). Funding for health promotion and education, screening, and early treatment must be increased if we are to make any headway in terms of treating lifelong chronic conditions that are so costly. As Russell (1992) illustrates, these treatment costs must be analyzed systematically to balance the number of life-years saved against the costs of prevention programs. This process will assist in deciding which programs are to be logically emphasized. Where to get these funds becomes another issue. Societally, we must face the debate over the merits of high-technology interventions, end-of-life heroic treatment, and half-way technologies if we are to solve budgetary dilemmas. Systemic prioritization requires that health services be more intentionally organized, planned, and financed so that resources that are diverted from one area will go to a higher-priority service or activity. Such an explicit process is quite foreign to us as a nation and considered distasteful or immoral by many individuals. Although the Oregon Medicaid Initiative/Health Plan attempts to begin this process, the plan is focused on the most politically vulnerable portion of the population (Hadorn, 1991). Thus part of the criticism of the so-called Oregon Rationing Plan stems from the fact that the plan takes away from the poorest who have Medicaid already (overrepresented by women and children) to incorporate those who are uninsured (disproportionately men but also children). Prioritizing needs to include all persons, preferably at the national level so that equity is maximized in terms of income redistribution and risk sharing.

Our system must be willing to take aggressive preventive actions based on public health, epidemiologic, and statistical evidence, even when there is great resistance. The case of tobacco vividly illustrates this. Clearly, there is enough medical and public health evidence to take strong preventive action in the area of tobacco growing, advertising, and distribution, yet political and financial lobbying obstacles block the road. The Centers for Disease Control (CDC) found that 26.5% of childbearing-age women smoke. This figure is over double the national objective of 12% prevalence for the year 2000 (CDC, 1991). Tobacco smoking endangers not only the health of women via increased cancer and cardiovascular disease but also their unborn children (through lower birth weight) and children living with them (through the effect of secondary smoke on the respiratory system) (Rigotti & Pashos, 1991). Yet our nation financially subsidizes the growing of tobacco and has some of the most lenient advertising laws in the industrialized world (Horovitz, 1988). The tendency to wait until problems present themselves, instead of eliminating the cause or source of the problem, seems pervasive in many areas, such as family planning, sexually transmitted diseases, AIDS, cancer control, cardiovascular diseases, mental illness, and substance abuse.

The conflict between profit motive and health, as well as between crisis intervention and prevention, is also readily seen in more subtle contexts besides tobacco. For example, rarely are the medical and public health professions roused to comment on the conflict between the clear benefits of breast-feeding versus commercial formula manufacturer profits. Formula feeding of an infant costs between $600 and $800 per year—takes away income from women and their families, and distributes it as profit to corporations. Indeed, based on the industry's profit margin of 10%, the result is that nearly $2 million per day are reaped in profits by the formula manufacturers for a substitute for something that is produced naturally and for little cost by mothers. These costs do not factor in time and adequate water supplies or the energy necessary to heat or, if applicable, sterilize water. However, cost is not the most consequential health issue here. Research study after research study strongly demonstrates the positive health effects for breast-fed babies: one fifth the risk of urinary tract infections and serious illness; one third the risk of ear infections; one seventh the risk of allergies; lower incidence of sudden infant death syndrome, gastrointestinal infections, liver disease, Crohn's disease, celiac disease, diabetes, and dental malformations; and higher IQ scores (Auriccio, Follo, & de Ritis, 1983; Davis & Belle, 1991; Duffy,

Byers, Riepenhoff-Talty, Zielezny, & Ogra, 1986; Knishkowy, Palti, Adler, & Tepper, 1991; Lucas, Morley, Cole, Lister, & Leeson Payne, 1992; Metcalfe & Baum, 1992; Mitchell, Taylor, Ford, Stewart, & Becroft, 1992; Newman & Maissels, 1992; Piscane, Liberatore, Mazerrella, Scarpellino, & Zona, 1992; Pukander, Luotenen, Timone, & Karma, 1985; Rogan & Gladen, 1993; Strimac & Chi, 1986; Tudlehope, 1991; Virtanen et al., 1991; Yolken et al., 1992). For women, the direct health benefits of lactation are quite remarkable yet have received little media attention. Women who have lactated a total of 2 years have a 40% reduction in the risk of breast cancer; for women with 6 years total lactation experience, the risk is reduced by 66% (Layde et al., 1989; McTiernan & Thomas, 1986; Rueter, Baker, & Krolikowski, 1992; Yoo et al., 1992; Yuan, Yu, Ross, Gao, & Henderson, 1988). The highly efficacious contraceptive effects of lactation have been well documented for natural spacing of children (98% effective during the first 6 months and still highly effective beyond 1 year), but again, these results remain a relative secret (Gross, 1991; Lewis, Brown, Renfree, & Short, 1991; Majumder, 1991). In addition to these benefits, women who have lactated have lower risk of uterine cancer and the very deadly ovarian cancer (Cunningham, Jelliffe, & Jelliffe, 1991; Gwinn, Lee, Rhodes, Layde, & Rubin, 1990; McTiernan & Thomas, 1986). Few behaviors or miracle pharmaceuticals can boast such tremendous preventive health benefits, yet the public has hardly heard of these. "Breast versus bottle" has been promoted as basically a lifestyle choice when, in fact, the benefits of lactation for both women and children are far superior. Why has this discussion not been raised? The most significant and plausible reason lies in the inability of any single company or conglomerate to be able to economically benefit or "capture" the positive externalities of lactation.

Prevention in health services has become highly medicalized as a concept, even when a more holistic approach might serve us better and in many cases at lower cost. Whereas the model of self-help and women's health collectives advocates empowerment of women as the protagonists, medicine has often removed decision making from the female patient, replaced human communication with technology, and isolated the patient on the periphery. Examples include (a) the routine use of electronic fetal monitoring instead of either fetal stethoscopes or doptones (at a net cost of $675 million more per year than for monitoring high-risk cases only), (b) the promotion of breast imaging to the exclusion of efficacious self-palpitation, (c) the failure to actively promote breast-feeding as an infant's best nutrition and as a preventive measure for breast cancer (McTiernan, 1987), (d) the routine use of episiotomy in childbirth instead of perineal massage and support, and (e) the use of tranquilizing drugs instead of cognitive discussion and social support for psychiatric and coping adjustments (Crowe, Bjornson, & Sunkenik, 1992). Most recently, routine ultrasound in pregnancy has been scientifically questioned as both costly and ineffective for supposedly improving outcomes (Berkowitz, 1993; Ewigman et al., 1993). When outcomes are examined, any of our new technologies or procedures merely serve to separate provider and patient, unnecessarily add to the cost of "prevention," and remove control from women. Although many women-run collective health clinics have existed for several decades now, only recently have these been recognized as viable sources of care by the dominant medical profession (Woods, 1985).

Medical care in its strictest definition, provided by physicians, does benefit women, so this discussion should not be interpreted as a negation of any value. However, we need access to holistic and preventive information, the ability to help ourselves when feasible, choices of nonphysician alternative providers, and the resources to access the more formal medical care system when deemed necessary.

Access to Health and Medical Care Services

At least 14 million women of childbearing age lack any private or public coverage for health services, with an additional 5 million insured women in this age group lacking coverage for prenatal and obstetric services (Harvey, 1990). These women have lower access to health care services, both preventive and curative, and less continuity of care, both of which may have long-term impacts on their health status. Private health insurance mechanisms in the United States revolve around having job tenure and full-time employment in higher-paying industries and occupations. Although 56% of employed men have health insurance coverage through employment, only 37% of employed women have employment-based health insurance (U.S. Bureau of the Census, 1991b). Women's labor force attachments tend to be less continuous, in lower-paying industries and occupations, and, consequently, with fewer benefits than men's. And although Medicaid covers some women of reproductive age, it also leaves large gaps in coverage of women. Medicaid is inherently a categorically linked welfare program, with frequent changes in eligibility and reduced options for providers (who are willing to accept it). This patchwork coverage is sporadic and leaves many either unprotected against high medical costs or involuntarily tied to situations to maintain their coverage. Women may be forced to stay in jobs, marriages, or poverty simply to keep their health coverage.

Older women are less well protected by Medicare for the costs of their most prevalent illnesses compared to men (Sofaer & Abel, 1990). Although women live longer than men and constitute a disproportionate 67% of our 31.2 million elderly, they live years with chronic conditions and have a higher rate of use of nursing homes (U.S. Bureau of the Census, 1991a). These chronic conditions often require continuing outpatient prescriptions and long-term care, both of which are not covered by Medicare. Women are less likely to have supplemental Medigap insurance provided as retirement benefits and therefore must rely on Medicare alone or Medicare with Medicaid (National Center for Health Statistics [NCHS], 1990). Because Medicare is not designed to cover long-term care costs, these women are virtually uninsured for long-term care and must spend down their resources to qualify for Medicaid. Thus the current financing scheme leaves women less well protected, with higher uncovered or excluded services, longer periods of co-insurance, and greater out-of-pocket costs overall.

Although there is some consensus regarding the need for health care reform in our nation, this need should be expressed most vehemently by women. Women's higher need for and use of care, coupled with their lower protection against the costs, should provide even more support for major reform in payment and organizational structures within health services delivery.

Included within the purview of access to medical care is the provision of certain services that women want but sometimes have great difficulty obtaining either because of legal obstacles, financing, or inadequate supply of providers. These services include access to family-planning services and, in particular, abortion on demand. Free access to abortion is vital to the public's health. When abortion is limited or made illegal, women die unnecessarily (Stephanson, Wagner, Badea, & Serbanescu, 1992; Susser, 1992). The situation in the United States during the 1980s had disastrous repercussions on health, but the Clinton administration promises to restore the balance of women's rights. In the United States alone each year, more than 50% of all pregnancies are unintended, and half of these (1.6 million) are terminated through legal abortion (Zero Population Growth [ZPG], 1992). Nonetheless, the struggle between pro-choice and antichoice groups has grown in recent years. In 1977, the U.S. Supreme Court declared that states did not have to fund abortion through Medicaid. This left over 44 million women without financial access to abortion (ZPG, 1992). Since then, the high court has allowed states to set significant restrictions on a woman's choice of abortion. These limitations and obstacles have taken the form of parental consent laws, the barring of public facilities for abortion use, counseling and "informed consent" stipulations, and waiting periods (National Abortion Federation [NAF], 1992). Beyond the legal and financial restrictions facing women is the reduced supply of providers who are willing and trained to perform abortion. In 83% of U.S. counties, not a single physician is available to perform abortions (ZPG, 1992). Even in metropolitan areas, nearly 25% are lacking in abortion providers. Our nation's medical schools and residency programs are not picking up the slack either. In 1991, only 13% of all obstetrics gynecology (OB-GYN) residency programs required first-trimester abortion training—even though it is one of the most common forms of OB-GYN surgery (NAF, 1992; ZPG, 1992).

One possible mechanism to stem the surgical abortion financing and supply shortfall would be through access to a drug referred to as Mifepristone or RU486. RU486 is a pharmaceutical abortifact, developed in France but prohibited from importation into the United States until President Clinton signed the bill lifting this ban. Although this action was mainly a symbolic one, indeed, it sent a strong and vital message. This medical intervention can be used only very early in pregnancy and has a 96% success rate, which is nearly the same as the 97% of surgical abortion (National Women's Health Network [NWHN], 1992). This drug not only could improve access to and reduce the side effects of abortion, but it also shows promising potential for the treatment of several other health concerns. Research in other nations, where RU486 has been allowed for study and/or use, lends strong evidence that RU486 might be used successfully in treating, breast cancer, Cushing's syndrome, glaucoma, brain cancer, endometriosis, diabetes, and hypertension (Fund for the Feminist Majority, 1989; Grimes & Cook, 1992; NWHN, 1992; Rosenfield, 1992; ZPG, 1992). In the past, U.S. researchers have had no access to RU486 because Roussel Uclaf, the manufacturer, fears boycott by anti-abortion forces in the United States and because of the previous explicit prohibitions voiced by former President Bush. Currently, the state of Oregon has been approved as one of the first U.S. testing arenas for RU486.

Another area of access to health care where women are particularly disadvantaged is in the early detection of AIDS (acquired immunodeficiency syndrome) and HIV (human immunodeficiency virus). The CDC estimates that over 120,000 women in the United States are HIV-positive. Even more astounding, the number of AIDS cases in women is rising at a rate double that of men (Buehler, 1992; CDC, 1992). And AIDS was estimated to be the fifth leading cause of death in women ages 25 to 44 (Buehler, Hanson, & Chu, 1992). Yet health professionals worldwide are often slow to suggest HIV-detection tests to women and may be even slower to begin aggressive treatment regimens (Petros-Barvazian & Merson, 1992). This type of discrimination has and will continue to cost women months or years of their lives, in addition to unnecessary suffering. It also deprives them the opportunity of planning and preparing for a potentially shorter life span. Beyond women's lives are those of their children, those alive and yet unborn. It is estimated that in 30% to 50% of pregnancies in an HIV-positive women, the virus is transmitted to their children (American College Health Association, 1990). Thus the repercussions of nondiagnosis are far-reaching in terms of both male and female lives.

Personnel

Although women use significantly more physician and psychiatric professional visits, pharmaceutical prescriptions, and have more restricted activity days than do men, far fewer resources are devoted to them in research and in the training of new personnel (NCHS, 1992, pp. 1-5). Although we have made gains in both these areas, the gender ratios still lag far behind. For example, although 39% of new medical graduates are female, only 17% of the practicing physician population is female (NCHS, 1992). In obstetrics and gynecology, the women's health specialty, only 25% of practicing OB-GYN physicians are female. It is highly noteworthy that 60% of all female medical students report experiencing sexual harassment from various sources, including faculty, male students, and administrators or staff ("Why So Few," 1992).

The gender gap exists throughout the health industry. Females make up the vast majority of health care workers, yet they are employed in occupations that are relatively low paying. Ninety-five percent of all nurses are female. Moreover, on average, nurses earn only 20% of what the average physician earns. (Leavitt and Walsh

[1984, pp. 3-7] provide an excellent discussion of these topics in *Women and Health in America*.) The nursing profession also leaves nurses with little professional or legal autonomy and provides no mechanism to apply knowledge or experience should a nurse wish to continue on for a medical degree.

Because women consume more health care than do men, more female providers are necessary if we are to strive for women to have a real choice in obtaining appropriate care. This goes beyond feeling more comfortable with a woman provider. Women physicians have been shown to spend more time with patients and spend a greater proportion of this time both listening to and educating patients than do their male counterparts (Roter, Lipkin, & Korsgaard, 1991). Female physicians are also more likely to perform screening tests such as mammography and pap smears (Lurie et al., 1993). Improving the supply of female practitioners might not only ease female patients' anxieties but also improve the overall cognitive-technologic and preventive balance in medical care.

The statistics on women in research speak very clearly. In the highly acclaimed American Society of Clinical Investigators, fewer than 2% of the members are women. Also, women hold only 4% each of medical school chair and department head positions ("Why So Few," 1992). Many first-investigator awards for clinical studies, sponsored either by public sources, such as the NIH, or private ones, require investigators to be under an age cutoff or within 5 years of graduation. This stipulation biases awards against women because long years of doctoral or medical education are completed leaving little time to postpone childbearing. Thus women are forced to choose research or children, whereas men are not. And, as if the income disparity between men and women in the general population was not discouraging enough, women in medicine and science earn only 63 cents for every dollar earned by men ("Why So Few," 1992).

Medical Care as a Health Problem: On the Cutting Edge

Although many women cannot access the health care system at all because of lack of insurance, cultural barriers, transportation, and so on, there are millions who are subjected to iatrogenic conditions through unnecessary and excessive medical care. It is true that millions of women do benefit from the skillful care they receive. Frequently, however, when medicine has been actively involved in women's health, it has been violently so. The use of radical surgical techniques to "cure" women of their ills has long been the center of debate. Where lumpectomies and chemotherapies for breast cancer are now the norm for the one in eight women who will get breast cancer during their lifetimes (American Cancer Society, 1992; NCI, 1992), radical, disabling mastectomies were the treatment of choice 20 years ago. Currently, one in four babies is surgically removed from its mother via cesarean section, a rate that is considered at least double what it should be, if not triple (Gould, Davey, & Stafford, 1989; Tussing & Wojtowycz, 1992). Hysterectomies are performed routinely to cure a variety of "abnormalities," yet between 27% and 50% of these are considered to be clearly unnecessary (Consumer's Union, 1992; Crowe et al., 1992; Scully, 1980; Smith, 1993, pp. 1-9). An equally startling statistic is that a full 30% of all women will have a hysterectomy before age 65—the majority between the ages of 25 and 44 years (Crowe et al., 1992). The routine use of procedures such as episiotomy, which may permanently leave scar tissue, numbness, and sexual dysfunction is a prime example of overintervening in a natural process. Estimates place this common medical procedure at 90% over what is medically required for healthy outcomes (Lieberman, 1987, pp. 1-20). Smith (1993) provides a scathing critique of obstetric and gynecologic practices in *Women and Doctors*. This controversial monograph recites case after case of women who have been fraudulently told that they require major gynecologic surgery to "correct" problems such as infertility, endometriosis, fibroids and the like that later have been proven nonexistent. In isolation, each of these statistics may not appear overtly startling because inappropriate treatment occurs in men as well. However, the fact that so many of these procedures can be performed only on women and the disproportionate number of male practitioners performing them leads to some questioning (Leavitt & Walsh, 1984; Smith, 1993, pp. 84-91).

Perhaps the traditional provider-patient relationship, combined with male dominance in the medical profession and lack of research on these women's health issues has evolved into the current state in a nonintentional fashion. Still, the results equate to manipulation and invasion of women's bodies that should be rectified.

A Potential Women's Health Agenda (not in order of priority)

- Eliminate the gender bias in drug testing and all clinical trials. Require appropriate representation of women in any trial that may result in any bigender implications.

- Pass the Freedom of Choice Act and fund "abortion on demand."
- Encourage the passage of state "mandatory arrest laws" in cases of domestic violence and violence against women.
- Encourage the importation of RU486 for cancer chemotherapies and abortion randomized controlled trials and practice.
- Pass a comprehensive benefit, single-payer National Health Insurance to gain control over health costs and open financial access to all universally.
- Include comprehensive services in a national health insurance to equally cover diseases that affect women. Do not have large co-insurance for preventive items such as pap smears or mammograms. Do reduce the financial impact that long-term care and chronic disease have on women when they require years of follow-up visits and prescriptions. Coverage should be included for alternative providers that women may prefer, such as midwives.
- Sever the umbilical cord between employment and health insurance completely so that women and men are free to pursue a wider range of opportunities and businesses may compete in international markets. This may be achieved through the use of a tax-financed, government-administered national health insurance.
- Expedite the approval of new contraceptives, therapies for breast cancer, ovarian cancer, osteoporosis, depression, and other conditions particularly prevalent in women through a strengthened Food and Drug Administration workforce and NIH requests for proposals.
- Require chemical dependency programs receiving federal grants to open up programs for pregnant substance abusers and all women.
- Eliminate tobacco advertising, and phase out tobacco-growing subsidization.
- Endorse and enforce the World Health Organization/United Nations International Children's Emergency Fund (WHO/UNICEF) code of marketing of breast milk substitutes, including the elimination of advertising, free samples, and gifts to health workers and facilities.
- Increase public spending for health education campaigns for AIDS, tobacco and chemical dependency, violence, family planning, cardiovascular diseases, and cancer.
- Pass strong gun control measures to reduce the most violent threats to women.
- Encourage more women to choose medicine, basic science, and policy as fields of study through the provision of scholarships, mentorships, and training institutes.
- Focus attention on domestic growth simultaneously with changing our regressive taxation policies. Deal with our enormous economic inequities through programs such as the Conservation Corps.

- Revitalize and institutionalize the concept of true fairness and equity in America, not only by gender but also by ethnicity, sexual orientation, and marital status.

Conclusion

Undoubtedly, this priority list appears looming because of its size and the difficulty in achieving some of the individual items. Nonetheless, we must begin somewhere. Women's health affects everyone—children, men, and, of course, women themselves—through the wide array of roles that women fulfill in society. Some of the priorities are merely a matter of political will. Having a president, secretary of health, and surgeon general who each are willing to take a stand on issues will make a difference to health care action. In many cases, the scientific evidence is there to back them. In other cases, research will have to be initiated, funded, performed, and evaluated. The United States must make this commitment to ensure that all members of society may participate to their fullest capacity.

Although government commitment is necessary to make health changes, it certainly is not sufficient, especially for the more controversial issues. Grassroots action will be needed to raise consciousness and build support for these issues. Women and men who are knowledgeable must take on the task of educating and directing motivated individuals so that we are not drowned out by a small, but extremely vocal and politically active minority. Gaining momentum may be, at first, slow and arduous. Still, the support of the federal administration will help to reinforce the belief that these efforts will realize true gains in women's health. Demonstrated gains, such as the rapid passage of previously blocked or vetoed legislation (e.g., the Family and Medical Leave Act), will help to provide this necessary positive feedback to community and grassroots organizations.

Organizations and individuals working on particular health issues should be willing not only to work together but also to compromise on the order in which priorities are addressed. It is critical that we unify instead of fighting against potential allies. Perhaps trade-offs will be necessary, but in the end, we will all achieve much more through codified action plans. Finally, the public health paradigm must be maintained throughout the political process. Public health approaches that are multidisciplinary will help to balance the issues of equity and freedom in light of improved health for the female and male citizenry. Prioritization of the problems to be addressed first should be based on a critical examination of which issues affect the largest number of lives and how severely, not who holds the greatest political clout.

References

American Cancer Society. (1992). *Cancer facts and figures, 1992 (breast cancer, uterine cancer, ovarian cancer)*. New York: Author.

American College Health Association. (1990). *Women and AIDS: Information fact sheet*. Baltimore, MD: Author.

American Public Health Association. (1993, November). Optimism accompanies women's health legislation to Congress. *The Nation's Health*, p. 5.

Auriccio, S., Follo, D., & de Ritis, G. (1983). Does breastfeeding protect against the development of clinical symptoms of celiac disease in children? *Journal of Pediatric Gastroenterology and Nutrition, 2*, 428-433.

Berkowitz, R. L. (1993). Should every pregnant woman undergo ultrasonography? *New England Journal of Medicine, 329*(12), 874-875.

Blendon, R. (1988). The public's view of the future of health care. *Journal of the American Medical Association, 25*, 3587-3593.

Brook, R. H., Ware, K. E., Rogers, W. H., Keeler, E. B., Davies, A. R., Donald, C. A., Goldberg, G. A., Lohr, K., Masthay, P. C., & Newhouse, J. P. (1983). Does free care improve adults' health? *New England Journal of Medicine, 309*, 1426-1434.

Buehler, J. W. (1992). The surveillance definition for AIDS. *American Journal of Public Health, 82*(11), 1462-1463.

Buehler, J. W., Hanson, D. L., & Chu, S. (1992). The reporting of HIV/AIDS deaths in women. *American Journal of Public Health, 82*(11), 1500-1505.

Centers for Disease Control. (1991, December 11). Cigarette smoking among reproductive aged women—Behavioral risk factor surveillance system, 1989. *Journal of the American Medical Association, 266*(22), 3111-3112.

Centers for Disease Control. (1992). Update: Acquired immunodeficiency syndrome— US, 1991. *Morbidity and Mortality Weekly Report, 41*, 463-468.

Consumer's Union. (1992, July). Wasted health care dollars. *Consumer Reports*, pp. 435-448.

Clancy, C. M., & Massion, C. T. (1992). American women's health care: A patchwork quilt with gaps. *Journal of the American Medical Association, 268*(14), 1918-1920.

Crowe, M., Bjornson, E., & Sunkenik, J. D. (1992). Some common and uncommon health and medical problems. In J. Pincus & W. Sanford (Eds.), *The new our bodies, ourselves: Updated and expanded for the 1990s* (pp. 598-599). Boston, MA: Boston Women's Health Book Collective.

Cunningham, A. S., Jelliffe, D. V., & Jelliffe, P. (1991). Breastfeeding and health in the 1980s: A global epidemiologic review. *Journal of Pediatrics, 118*(5), 659-666.

Davis, D., & Belle, D. A. (1991). Infant feeding practices and occlusal outcomes: A longitudinal study. *Journal of the Canadian Dental Association, 57*(7), 593-594.

Davis, K., Gold, M., & Makuc, D. (1981). Access to health care for the poor: Does the gap remain? *Annual Review of Public Health, 2*, 159-182.

Russell, L. B. (1992). Opportunity costs in modern medicine. *Health Affairs, 11*(2), 163-169.

Scully, D. (1980). *Men who control women's health: The mis-education of obstetrician-gynecologists*. Boston, MA: Houghton-Mifflin.

Smith, J. M. (1993). *Women and doctors*. New York: Dell.

Sofaer, S., & Abel, E. (1990). Older women's health and financial vulnerability: Implications of the Medicare benefit structure. *Women's Health, 16*, 47-67.

Stephanson, P., Wagner, M., Badea, M., & Serbanescu, F. (1992). The public health consequences of restricted abortion. *American Journal of Public Health, 82*(10), 1328-1331.

Strimac, J. N., & Chi, D. S. (1986). Significance of IgE level in amniotic fluid and cord blood for the prediction of allergy. *Annals of Allergy, 61*, 133-136.

Susser, R. (1992). Induced abortion and health as a value. *American Journal of Public Health, 82*(10), 1323-1324.

Tavris, C. (1992). *The mismeasure of woman*. New York: Simon & Schuster.

Tudlehope, D. (1991). Breastfeeding practices and severe hyperbilirubinaemia. *Journal of Paediatric Child Health, 27*, 240-244.

Tussing, D. A., & Wojtowycz, M. A. (1992, June). The cesarean decision in New York State, 1986: Economic and noneconomic aspects. *Medical Care, 30*(6), 529-540.

U.S. Bureau of the Census. (1991a). *1990 census tapes* (Series A) [Machine-readable data file]. Springfield, VA: U.S. Department of Commerce, National Technical Information Service.

U.S. Bureau of the Census. (1991b). *1990 Current population survey* [Machine-readable data file]. Springfield, VA: U.S. Department of Commerce, National Technical Information Service.

U.S. Department of Health and Human Services, Health Care Financing Administration. (1993). Health Care Financing Administration annual expenditure estimates: Early release of 1992 data. *1993 data compendium*. Baltimore, MD: U.S. Department of Health and Human Services, Health Care Financing Administration, Bureau of Data Management and Strategy.

Virtanen, S. M., Rasanen, L., Aro, A., Lindstrom, J., Sippola, H., Lounama, T., Touisaneu, L., Tuomilehto, J., & Akerblom, H. (1991). Infant feeding in Finnish children, < 7 years of age with newly diagnosed IDDM. *Diabetes Care, 14*(5), 415-417.

Why so few women doctors in research? (1992, June 22). *American Medical News*, p. 3.

Woods, N. F. (1985). New models of women's health care. *Health Care Women International, 6*, 193-208.

Worscter, N., & Orloff, L. (1992, November). *Mandatory arrest laws as a response to domestic violence: A double edged sword*. Paper presented at the 120th Annual Meeting of the American Public Health Association, Washington, DC.

Yolken, R. H., Peterson, J. A., Vonderfect, S. L., Fouts, E. T., Midthum, K., & Newburg, D. S. (1992). Human milk mucin inhibits rotavirus replication and prevents experimental gastroenteritis. *Journal of Clinical Investigation, 90*, 1984-1991.

Yoo, K. Y., Tajima, K., Kuroisk, T., Hirose, K., Yoshida, M., Miura, S., & Murai, H. (1992). Independent protective effect of lactation against breast cancer: A case-control study in Japan. *American Journal of Epidemiology, 135*(7), 726-733.

Yuan, J. M., Yu, M., Ross, R., Gao, T., & Henderson, B. (1988). Risk factors for breast cancer in Chinese women in Shanghai. *Cancer Research, 48*, 1949-1953.

Zero Population Growth Nonprofit Organization. (1992, Fall). *Abortion in America: Special report*. Washington, DC: Author.

17

Assuring Access to Health Care for Homeless People Under National Health Care

MICHAEL R. COUSINEAU
JOHN N. LOZIER

*H*omelessness is one of America's most vexing social problems (Baxter & Hopper, 1982; Rossi, 1989). Although precise quantification of the problem is impossible, it is obvious to even the most casual observer that the past 15 years have seen an explosion in the number of persons living on the streets, in their cars, under bridges, and in emergency shelters. Women and children are the fastest growing segment of the homeless population, and members of racial minorities make up a large majority of homeless people, belying the old stereotype of a skid row populated by older White male alcoholics. Credible estimates of their numbers reach into the millions. Unseen millions more find precarious refuge in the homes of friends and family members.

Because of the role of health problems as both a cause and a consequence of homelessness, homeless people have an enormous stake in the efforts to solve the American health care crisis. However, compared to other groups who are better organized, homeless people risk being overlooked in efforts to reform the financing and delivery of health services in the United States. Obviously, the provision of health insurance for all people should be seen as one strategy to prevent homelessness. But this chapter assumes that mass homelessness will not be solved in the near future. Rather, health care reform strategies must take into account the unique challenges in bringing health care services to people who are impoverished and homeless. Our chapter centers around three points:

1. Homeless people have special needs and use the health care system differently from those who have stable housing. Improving their health status will require a unique, comprehensive, and multidisciplinary response that includes a wide range of services.
2. Given these special needs, unregulated managed health care plans will not be able to deliver health care in a way that promotes access to a wide range of services for homeless people.
3. The transition to a national or statewide health program should maintain, and in some places expand, the role of traditional safety net providers, public health departments, and outreach programs that provide health care for the homeless.

Health and Homelessness

Health care concerns figure prominently in the etiology of homelessness. Consider the case of a minimum-wage earner who is uninsured and becomes sick or injured. Without health insurance, the individual will likely delay seeking care until the problem worsens. The health problem may lead to the loss of employment, and then the family must struggle to obtain health care from an overcrowded and underfunded public health system, hospital emergency rooms, or clinics. Diverting family resources from food, other necessities, and, finally, rent to pay for physician visits, medication, or lab tests places the family at risk for eviction and homelessness. This scenario is very typical and underscores the role of health care reform in preventing people from becoming homeless in America.

But whereas health problems cause homelessness among some, the social conditions of life on the street cause disease and death among those already homeless. Homeless people live in crowded shelters, in run-down hotels, or on the street where they have little access to bathrooms, regular meals, and privacy. These conditions expose homeless people to communicable disease and put them at risk for injuries caused by accidents and acts of violence. Several studies document that homeless people suffer from many of the same health problems as people who are not homeless, although disease rates are higher than expected (Institute of Medicine, 1988). Common problems include upper-respiratory infections, trauma, dermatitis, hypertension, gastrointestinal disorders, and peripheral vascular disease (Brickner, 1990; Wright & Weber, 1987). The recent surge in the rate of tuberculosis (TB) in American cities can be traced, in part, to the rise in homelessness (Centers for Disease Control, 1991; McAdam & Brickner, 1990). Chronic mental health and substance abuse problems also disproportionately affect homeless people (Fisher & Breakey, 1986; Koegel, Burnam, & Farr, 1988; Leshner, 1992). Homeless children, sensitive to the stress of constant moves, sleep deprivation, and inadequate nutrition, are twice as likely to suffer from acute and chronic illnesses and depression. Many are developmentally delayed and at increased risk for child abuse and neglect. Depression is also common among the many young women who head homeless families; yet they seldom have adequate access to mental health services and social support (Bassuk & Rosenberg, 1988; Wood, Valdez, Hayashi, & Shen, 1990).

Access Problems

Although they experience higher morbidity and mortality rates, homeless people often lack the most basic elements of access to health care: knowledge of the health care system, health insurance, transportation, and even a quarter for a phone call (Robertson & Cousineau, 1986). Without access, individuals and families often neglect health problems while they search for food, shelter, and money. Homeless people often mistrust the system due to prior bad experiences or mental illness. Moreover, transiency makes continuity of care difficult. Financial access remains the most formidable barrier to care. Because many homeless people are unemployed or work part-time in low-wage jobs that do not provide health benefits, it is not surprising that most do not have health insurance. Few if any have the cash required to make a physician visit, and in spite of their indigency, the majority are not covered by the federal/state Medicaid program. Of the patients served by the federally funded health care for the homeless programs in 1991, 14% were covered by Medicaid and only 2% had Medicare (Bureau of Primary Care, 1992). Most homeless adults are ineligible for Medicaid because they are not categorically linked to entitlement programs, particularly Aid to Families with Dependent Children (AFDC) and supplemental security income (SSI). Only a few states extend coverage to unattached indigent adults, which must be paid with state-only funds. Moreover, many of those who are eligible for AFDC and SSI are not enrolled at the time they seek care at clinics and outreach sites, suggesting the difficult challenges in enrolling homeless people in any type of organized health care system.

Avenues of Care for Homeless People

Health Care for the Homeless Programs

Over the past 6 years, we have learned that the traditional health care delivery system is limited in bringing health care to homeless people. These inadequacies have resulted in the emergence of specialized health care for the homeless providers, beginning with the demonstration program announced in 1984 by the Robert Wood Johnson Foundation and the Pew Memorial Trust. Building on the success of these programs, the United States Public Health Service has funded 120 health care for the homeless programs in 49 states, the District of Columbia, and Puerto Rico. Currently, $58 million is appropriated for the program. These projects are based in a variety of settings including public health departments, community health centers, clinics, hospitals, and other freestanding nonprofit organizations. In 1991, 1.7 million services were provided to 427,547 people, of whom 62% were minorities and 15% were children or runaway youths (Bureau of Primary Care, 1992). The development of these unique health care for the homeless programs has not eliminated the need for public and private community-based organizations who have traditionally cared for the indigent, and they merit a brief description here.

Public Health Departments

The increased morbidity and mortality associated with homelessness are primarily the products of environmental exposure to agents of disease and injury and of behaviors associated with the life conditions of homeless people. These properly require the intervention of public health departments, including surveillance, screening, and treatment of TB and other communicable disease; maternal and child health; home visits by public health nurses; care for the chronically mentally ill; and indigent substance abuse treatment. The role of health departments is crucial, as illustrated by a recent outbreak of shigella in Los Angeles shelters. The outbreak brought a countywide response by the health department that provided access to free treatment at public health clinics, provided treatment information to physicians, educated shelter staff about the signs and symptoms of the disease, and instituted surveillance and other preventive strategies. Similarly, since TB has reemerged as a deadly threat to public health, local health departments nationwide are reinvesting in TB control, after a decade when their TB control infrastructure collapsed due to cuts in federal funding.

Community Health Centers

Community health centers (CHCs) are designed to provide comprehensive primary care to medically underserved populations regardless of their ability to pay, and many homeless people find care at CHCs. In some communities, CHCs are the sole source of health care for the community. Many federally funded health care for the homeless programs operate as a part of community health centers, although other CHCs are not invested in the deliberate outreach efforts, multidisciplinary care, or case management that make homeless health care effective. Over the past 15 years, changes in federal-funding priorities have made CHCs more dependent on Medicaid and Medicare, and this coupled with an increase in the number of uninsured make CHCs more difficult for homeless people to access. Nevertheless, CHCs remain a critical line of defense against homelessness by providing access to affordable and comprehensive primary, secondary, and ancillary health care.

Public Hospitals

Public hospitals are indispensable providers of all levels of care in many urban and rural communities. In many states, public hospitals provide the bulk of care to the indigent. In California, for example, the state's public hospitals and health centers account for 77% of care to the state's indigent and Medicaid population. Public hospitals provide critical backup and ancillary services, secondary care, and hospital care to outreach efforts. Sadly, the busy emergency rooms of both public and private hospitals remain an important source of primary care for many homeless people who are unable to gain access to less expensive and more appropriate sources of care.

New Ways of Delivering Care

Health care for the homeless programs are designed to facilitate access by homeless people to primary care and a comprehensive set of related services. Outreach to a person who might not otherwise seek care is a common element in these programs, with staff members aggressively but patiently seeking out people on the streets and in other places where homeless people may be found. But responding to basic acute and chronic illness of homeless people requires considerable flexibility in the approach to health care delivery, including a multidisciplinary staff and a comprehensive set of services. Most do not rely on physicians and, instead, use nurse practitioners, physician assistants, nurses, and community health workers to provide primary care (Doblin, Gelberg, & Freeman, 1992). The majority employ social workers, health educators, outreach workers, patient advocates, peer counselors, and substance abuse specialists, who respond to a wide range of medical psychological, and social needs of homeless people. Working together, outreach teams provide care in medically equipped vans or in specially designed clinics in shelters and drop-in centers. Other teams use less formal settings, such as hotel rooms, closets, and even bathrooms. Regardless of where care is rendered, outreach efforts provide the first point of entry into the traditional systems of care. Teams assist people in gaining access to specialty and ancillary care, in finding food, clothing, and housing, or in obtaining other health services, such as Women Infant Child (WIC) food supplements or food stamps, childhood screening and treatment services, and prenatal care. Teams provide patients with bus tokens, give them maps to welfare offices, and explain rights and responsibilities in applying for public assistance programs. Some projects even employ community organizers who advocate on behalf of the population in general, by identifying common problems and challenging public health and public assistance bureaucracies to be more responsive to the needs of homeless people.

Importantly, psychosocial and support services are not seen simply as dispensable add-ons to the basic medical care but, rather, as critical elements in the treatment plans and essential for the resolution of the health problem at hand. Consider peripheral vascular disease, a widespread health problem among homeless people. This condition is caused by the accumulation of fluids in the lower extremities leading to circulatory problems and occasionally to lesions of the skin. Treatment requires bed rest and sometimes antibiotics and hospitalization. But this condition is caused by prolonged periods of time standing in lines and walking and is exacerbated by poor nutrition and cold weather. Simply treating the problem without responding to the conditions that precipitated them will likely result in the condition's returning.

Thus health care teams not only provide medical care but assist their patients in finding a shelter bed or motel room, a meal coupon, or transportation. This social orientation is an alternative concept of primary care more consistent with a public health rather than a traditional medical model, and it has relevance not only to homeless people but to other groups of people with special problems, such as those suffering from HIV-related disease, families with substance abuse problems, newly arrived immigrants, pregnant women with high-risk conditions, and the chronically mentally ill. However, there have been no attempts to systematically study these practice patterns, to understand the strengths and weaknesses of different applications of the model across projects, and to understand how they could be incorporated in a managed-care environment.

The Impact of a Shift to Managed Care on Access to and Quality of Health Care for Homeless and Other Low-Income People

The experiences of the national health care for the homeless programs provide important lessons to efforts at reforming health care in the United States. Managed health care, with its promise of cost containment and an emphasis on prevention and primary care, appears to be a key element of several plans for health care reform. There are common elements in any managed-care approach, whether it is delivered through tightly regulated and globally budgeted plans or through competition. They include assumed financial risk by a qualified plan, capitated payments, access to a specific benefit package, and a closed panel of providers. We know very little empirically about the benefits or risks associated with the enrollment of homeless people or other special populations in managed health care plans. Some studies of the Medicaid population show that the poor do not have better health outcomes under managed care when compared to fee-for-service care (Ware et al., 1986). These suggest that the homeless will also not benefit from managed care. Enrollment in a managed-care plan presumes a certain level of stability in the consumer's life that will enable him or her to navigate among a more limited set of health care resources. Homelessness assumes profound instability: extreme transiency, poor nutrition, lack of income, and competing demands. Safety net programs, including the federally funded health care for the homeless programs, emphasize outreach, easy access to multidisciplinary care, case management, mental health care, and substance abuse treatment that are effective in overcoming this instability in order to improve health status.

Thus national health reform proposals that rely on managed competition raise several questions with respect to homeless people. We discuss each of these in turn.

Would Homeless People Be Covered?

Universal coverage is a basic principle in most health care reform proposals, and achieving this principle will be essential to ensure access for the homeless. Managed competition, also, promises to cover everyone, including those now enrolled in Medicaid and Medicare and the uninsured, using government general funds generated through several new taxing options. But to achieve universal coverage, local and state governments will be faced with difficult questions of how to extend enrollment to those who have no or, at best, a fragmented attachment to the system of community-based human services. Who would be responsible for enrolling people into plans, and what vehicles would be used for identifying and enrolling people before they get sick? And how, in a competitive environment, will the states prevent adverse selection of enrollees? As a beginning, states should break the link between health coverage under Medicaid and eligibility for public assistance entitlement programs. This would eliminate an important barrier to coverage that now exists for homeless people. In addition, outreach and education would have to be expanded to assist homeless people to understand their options in choosing and enrolling in a health care plan. Enrollment could occur in clinics, hospital emergency rooms, and even shelters and drop-in centers. But efforts designed to reach the hundreds of thousands of people who have little or no contact with the human service system would be costly and have unpredictable outcomes. Once homeless people are reached, many would have little information about the plan that would best serve their needs. A broader class of human service workers without ties to the managed-care industry would have to be empowered to assist families in understanding benefit packages, location of providers, copayments, restrictions on use, and disenrollment procedures. Such information would be vital for homeless people given their transiency, their unfamiliarity with the health care system, and their competing demands to meet basic needs. However, the ongoing costs of such efforts could offset the savings of shifting from fee-for-service to managed care.

If, on the other hand, enrollment is tied to the marketing devices of managed-care companies, those companies marketing to lower-risk families by offering additional benefits and charging higher premiums would put their plans out of reach of homeless people, who will depend on government subsidy for the cost of a basic plan. Moreover, many companies will not want homeless people, who have multiple health problems, high rates of mental illness and substance abuse, and serious social needs that would make them costly high users of services. The perception might also prevail that the presence of homeless people would jeopardize their efforts to attract middle-class families into plans. This adverse selection in a competitive environment may, over time, result in many homeless people in underfunded plans relative to their needs for care. On the other hand, some managed-care plans looking for large-volume enrollment may market to homeless and other low-income people knowing that they could restrict use by limiting access to providers. California experienced a statewide scandal involving unregulated marketing of managed care for the Medicaid population in the early 1970s. Thousands signed over their Medicaid cards to managed care but later were unable to obtain the benefits outlined in the plan. More recently, advocates and providers in Los Angeles, New York, and other large cities have complained about the presence of managed-care companies with Medicaid contracts who market their plans to AFDC recipients living in shelters. In many cases, these companies have provided insufficient and at times fraudulent information about the benefits and restrictions under the plan. Many times, beneficiaries turn over their

Medicaid cards but are unaware that they can no longer go to the clinic or physician they want. Strong regulation and constant monitoring of enrollment procedures would be required to guard against adverse selection and marketing abuses. In short, efforts to enroll homeless people into managed-care plans will be difficult, costly, and without guarantee of success.

Would Enrollment Ensure Access Quality and Continuity of Care?

Geographic Accessibility

Whereas a family with stable housing in a neighborhood with a sufficient number of providers is likely to benefit from capitated managed health care, enrollment in a managed-care plan would not insure access to health care services for many homeless people and their families. Primary care providers may be located in communities that are not geographically accessible to shelters and transitional housing programs. Homeless people are very transient, and chances are that a person who enrolls in a plan with a primary care physician in one community is likely to move to temporary housing in another within 30 days or less. Specialists and ancillary services may be available only in certain locations, thus requiring long bus rides from where homeless people are living.

Case Management: A Key to Success

Many homeless people would be unable to maneuver within the network of providers without assistance. Good case management is a key element in the quality and continuity of health care for homeless people. In fact, nearly half of the encounters in the national health care for the homeless program were case management designed to meet social needs and assist homeless people in gaining access to specialty care, ancillary services, detoxification, residential substance abuse services, and mental health care. But management in a capitated environment is designed as a gatekeeping mechanism, which, for the more stable population, will guard against inappropriate use. But for the homeless, gatekeeping will impose barriers that keep people out of needed services. Thus responding to the needs of homeless people may come into conflict with the basic incentive structure inherent in capitated managed-care programs that are designed to limit, not promote, access. In confronting these barriers, homeless people simply give up trying to gain access to their own system and seek care at emergency rooms and public and private free clinics, who then will be unable to bill for the services they provide. Fragmentation of medical care will result, quality of care will suffer, and the health status of the patient will decline.

Services Important to Homeless People

To achieve health status improvement, managed-care companies would have to provide a range of services important to homeless people. However, it is doubtful that these organizations would provide the comprehensive response to such problems as communicable disease transmission and other public health concerns. Few would be able to manage the psychiatric needs of the chronically mentally ill homeless and cover inpatient detoxification and other chemical dependency problems that are present at high rates among the homeless. In addition, key to the success of health care for the homeless programs are outreach and case management. But many of these services are costly, and managed-care companies wanting to limit expenditures are unlikely to provide them voluntarily.

Multicultural and Culturally Sensitive and Multiple-Lingual Staff

Health care for the homeless programs have provided services to people from a broad cultural and ethnic background. From the earliest days of the Robert Wood Johnson demonstration projects, we learned the importance of assembling health care teams that can understand the cultural diversity found among homeless people. Teams must incorporate bilingual and bicultural staff and use forms and educational materials that are written in languages commonly spoken among homeless people in a particular community. Having a multilingual and multicultural staff will be critical to the success of any health care plan's efforts to assure equity in access to homeless people. However, reform designed to achieve universal coverage and cost containment must provide the statutory requirements and the funding needed to recruit, train, and retain both culturally and medically competent staff.

expand the current network of health care for the homeless pro-grams authorized under the Stewart B. McKinney Act. Access and quality of care could also be improved by coordinating funding that now supports community-based primary health care and mental health and substance abuse services.

Finally, considering the health of homeless people challenges us once more to better understand and confront the health-destroying conditions of poverty itself. It compels us to embrace a broader definition of health that would allow the convergence of health care reform efforts with those designed to solve the nation's critical affordable housing problem, ensure adequate nutrition for all people, and improve education and job training. In the near future, for example, this could be accomplished through health policy initiatives and jointly funded programs involving several federal departments. In the long term, the health care dollar must be applied more broadly to ameliorate the conditions of impoverished Americans and to help end poverty in America.

References

Bassuk, E. L., & Rosenberg, L. (1988). Why does family homelessness occur? *American Journal of Public Health, 78,* 783-788.

Baxter, E., & Hopper, K. (1982). The new mendicancy: Homelessness in New York City. *American Journal of Orthopsychiatry, 52,* 393-408.

Brickner, P. (1990). *Under the safety net.* New York: Norton.

Bureau of Primary Care. (1992, November). *The national health care for the homeless program.* Paper presented at the annual meeting of the American Public Health Association, Washington, DC.

Centers for Disease Control. (1992). Prevention and control of tuberculosis among homeless persons. *Morbidity and Mortality Weekly Report, 41*(RR-5), 13-23.

Doblin, B., Gelberg, L., & Freeman, H. (1992). Patient care and professional staffing patterns in McKinney Act clinics providing primary care to the homeless. *Journal of the American Medical Association, 267,* 696-701.

Fisher, P. J., & Breakey, W. R. (1986). Mental health and the social characteristics of the homeless: A survey of mission users. *American Journal of Public Health, 76,* 669-678.

Institute of Medicine, Committee on Health Care for Homeless People. (1988). *Homelessness, health and human needs.* Washington, DC: National Academy Press.

Koegel, P., Burnam, A., & Farr, R. (1988). The prevalence of special psychiatric disorders among homeless individuals in the inner city of Los Angeles. *Archives of General Psychiatry, 45,* 1085-1092.

Leshner, A. (1992). *Outcasts on Main Street: A report on the Task Force on Homelessness and Severe Mental Illness.* Washington, DC: U.S. Public Health Service.

McAdam, J., & Brickner, P. (1990). Tuberculosis in the homeless: A national perspective. In P. Brickner (Ed.), *Under the safety net* (pp. 234-249). New York: Norton.

Robertson, M. A., & Cousineau, M. R. (1986). Health status and access to health services among the urban homeless. *American Journal of Public Health, 76,* 561-563.

Rossi, P. H. (1989). *Down and out in America: The origins of homelessness.* Chicago: University of Chicago Press.

Ware, J. E., Brook, R. H., Rogers, W. H., Keeler, E. B., Davies, A., Sherbourne, C. D., Goldberg, G. A., Camp, P., & Newhouse, J. P. (1986). Comparison of health outcomes at a health maintenance organization with those of fee-for-service care. *Lancet, 3,* 1017-1022.

Wood, D., Valdez, R. B., Hayashi, T., & Shen, A. (1990). Homeless and housed families in Los Angeles: A study comparing demographic, economic and family functioning characteristics. *American Journal of Public Health, 80,* 1049-1053.

Wright, J. D., & Weber, E. (1987). *Homelessness and health.* New York: McGraw-Hill.

18

Health System Reform in the Nineties

PAULINE VAILLANCOURT
ROSENAU

We in the United States have embarked on the largest health reform in our history. This chapter surveys some of the most important dimensions of that transformation. Although it is too early to come to any conclusions about the long-term results, we can examine the potential short-term strengths and weaknesses of various health care reform projects. Several substantive areas are discussed, including the government's role, patient participation, provision of services, maintenance of quality, and cost control. Lessons learned from the experience of other countries, especially Canada, are also indicated.

Health care reform is likely to provide a new balance between the public and private sectors. It must also define a role for the states. It reconsiders health system resources such as the ratio of primary care physicians and specialists. Antitrust legislation may also be revamped to permit hospital efficiencies. Tort reform may be included, and this would reduce malpractice insurance for MDs. Health care reform emphasizes prevention, and this refocuses our attention on long-term health considerations. This is a substantial change from the recent past where short-term budgetary preoccupations often meant increased long-term health care costs. The role insurance companies play in the health system may also be modified over the course of health care reform.

The comparative health systems perspective chosen here offers needed perspective, although it will not supply answers to all health system problems in the United States. For example, no country or state provides adequate, affordable long-term care to a heterogeneous, diverse, aging population (see Binstock's chapter in this volume). Some programs are, however, better than others, and this yields indicators as to the direction reform might best take.

Government's Role: Planned Versus Competitive Market Mechanism

Balancing public- and private-sector responsibilities is central to health reform today, and seeking a compromise between regulation and competition is not easy (see the Beauchamp and Ambrose chapter in this volume). In recent decades the rhetoric of public policy and of American political philosophy has called for minimizing governmental activity. The U.S. health care sector of the economy is largely for-profit. It includes marketing, advertising, administration, and insurance, and all these increase costs. Nevertheless, 40% of every dollar spent comes from the government, for the most part through Medicare and Medicaid.

No consensus exists today on the proper balance of public- and private-sector activity in the health sector; thus health reform proposals diverge widely. Managed competition, the dominant model in the United States today, seeks to incorporate the best of both worlds—competition between plans but close regulation by the federal government over the terms of marketing. The single-payer system, on the other hand, depends more on regulation than on market competition to provide efficiency. Medical savings accounts (also called medical IRAs) are another option that would retain the current private-sector dominance of the U.S. health system.

Confidence in market competition has not produced a health care system of which the United States can be proud in every respect. Access and cost still pose problems. If these are a priority, the adequacy of the competitive market mechanism in the health sector needs to be questioned. In an effort to avoid the ills of planning and government regulation, the Reagan and Bush administrations fell victim to the opposite error of permitting laissez-faire competition in a sector of the economy that might profit from considerable regulation and monitoring. Although it may not be true for every sector of the economy, comparative analysis of the experience of other countries suggests that active government intervention and planning in the health care sector may be associated with better outcomes. Why might this be the case?

First, economic principles that apply to the demand, supply, and price relationships in competitive commodity production differ from those in the health sector where increased suppliers sometimes lead to increased prices and where market-sector behavior does not conform to conventional economic theory. For example, the nature of hospital demand curves is not that generally expected by economists (Roemer, 1986, pp. 104-105). If a city has two hospitals, the costs of hospitalization are greater than for cities in which there is only one (Rosenthal, 1980). The price of brand name drugs increases when generic products become available (Frank & Salkever, 1991), whereas in theory the opposite should be true.

Unplanned, market-driven systems assume competition advances the collective interest and this is questionable in the case of health care. For example, although it is in society's interest to have vaccines available for child immunization, the incentives to producers and distributors are limited because they are single-dose products and demand is not elastic (Freeman & Robbins, 1991). Here the "marginal private costs and marginal social costs diverge, calling for some form of intervention. In such cases of market failure the free market doesn't provide the optimum level of output of the good" (M. Intriligator, personal correspondence, February 21, 1993).

Health care reform responds to these limitations. If accountable plans and networks of providers are a part of health system reform, these plans are not allowed to compete on the substance of the standard basic benefits package of medical care: This is settled by law. Many proposals designate the power to modify the standard health care benefit package to a national health board or Federal health commission. Competition, by law, would involve only the price of the benefit package(s).

Second, the profit motive offers theoretical incentives to work hard and produce (supply) just enough of a product (demand) at the lowest price possible. But highly competitive markets on occasion encourage cheating and may even reward dishonesty in cases where competition becomes so great that organizational survival is jeopardized. Corruption, fraud, and deception are not incompatible with the logic of extreme versions of the free-market philosophy. Government and oversight might discourage such activities, but within absolutist expositions of laissez-faire market economics, government intervention is absent by design. "Let the buyer beware" is the watchphrase. Consequences for life are potentially more serious in the health services sector, with some exceptions, than in other commodity sectors. No systematic studies of this phenomenon have been undertaken, to my knowledge. But anecdotal evidence abounds, and this suggests that rigorous studies would be appropriate: the case with Silicone (Dow-Corning) breast implants (Hilts, 1992, p. A8), the dubious data generic-drug producers and Halcion sleeping pill manufacturers (Upjohn) presented to the FDA (Gupta, 1991; Kolata, 1992), fraudulent bills submitted by private mental hospitals to insurance companies (Kerr, 1991), provider unbundling and "padding" practices (Pear 1991, p. A1), and hospital overcharges in the case of 99% of accounts processed (Rosenthal, 1993).

Most health care reform proposals provide for increased government intervention to contain dishonest practices in the provision of health services and this might reduce costs by reducing illegal practices. To the extent that an organization's survival is threatened by competition, incentives for cheating need to be discouraged. In the case of Clinton's proposed Health Security Act (Title IV Medicare and Medicaid, Subtitle A, Part 5) sanctions are envisioned for failure to comply with statutory obligations concerning the quality of care (Title V, Quality and Consumer Protection, Subpart E). In fact, a high degree of oversight is not always required once the norms have been incorporated into medical practice.

Third, the "expectation that freely operating markets will produce the socially optimal allocation of resources, rests on assumptions about the nature of markets" that may not hold in the health sector (Bice, 1988, p. 373). The free-market model assumes that the individual knows what he or she wants and that he or she can make comparisons between the various services offered, deciding on the basis of comparison which is the best choice. It is the responsibility of each individual to be attentive to his or her own interest. In the field of health, this not always possible because providers almost have a monopoly on highly specialized knowledge and skill. The consumer seldom has all the information necessary to make an informed choice between the alternatives offered in the medical marketplace. Many health care reform proposals provide for consumer education, including information on the performance of health providers. Section 5013 of Clinton's Health Security Act is an example.

The free-market model assumes the absence of externalities, namely that "one's consumption decisions affect only oneself" (Bice, 1988, p. 375), and such an assumption is dubious in the health sector (Roemer, 1986, pp. 107-109). In the United States, it has long been the case that, if an individual falls seriously, chronically ill his or her family may be destitute. The free-market model assumes independent producers/suppliers can enter and leave the market depending on demand, and this is also questionable. The training of providers (doctors and nurses) is lengthy and costly, making it difficult to leave the profession. The technical knowledge involved in production and supply is equally difficult to acquire. These are not "competitive" fields, and the number of competing sellers is limited. Next, the free market assumes that "suppliers bear the full cost of producing their products" (Bice, 1988, p. 375) and this is not always the case in health care. Producers depend on government-subsidized information and research and testing programs (Leary, 1993). If producers (providers) err, they do not have the resources to fully compensate victims. Government must assume the long-term responsibility for such mistakes once a single producer (company) has exhausted its resources and its insurance liability limit. Finally, consumers do not bear the full costs of purchasing medical care, and this also reduces the relevance of the free-market model. A range of insurance companies and other payers are involved.

The very existence of health care reform suggests that the anti-government and deregulation rhetoric has been moderated, and a larger role for public institutions is now possible. The government has never been entirely absent from the health sector (see Intriligator in this volume), and it has played a significant role as both insurer-payer and as collector. But for the reasons outlined above, expanding this role may be judicious, especially if it can restore balance by encouraging cost containment without promoting excessive, destructive forms of exaggerated competition that might sacrifice quality of care and threaten health outcomes.

Coordination and Patient Participation

Although close management and patient participation are central to most efficient health systems in the world today, both of these organizational dimensions have been neglected in the United States or they have been implemented in a one-sided fashion.

Managed Care and Integrated Health Services: Serving Patients as Well as Providers

Health care management has a potentially important role to play in health services reform (see the chapter by Cousineau and Lozier in this volume). The term *managed care* can be used in two different ways. It refers to the active coordination of quality and continuity of care. But, especially in the United States, it has also come to refer to the monitoring of physician and hospital performance. In this sense it is utilization review and has a cost containment purpose. States have experimented with managed care and many HMOs testify to its relevance. Care management can be both an effective force for rationalization by assuring efficient use of resources and promoting continuity of care if patient interests, as well as provider concerns, are taken into account (Hembree, 1985). But if care managers are to contribute to system performance at the broader level, they need to be independent of providers and insurance companies. Few health care reform proposals seek to solve this problem because they generally leave care management to the various providers and accountable plans.

Most health care reform proposals envision organized, integrated prevention services as central to the basic package of health care to be delivered by the various health plans. Such a coherent set of services is the basis of managed care itself. But the organizational infrastructure assumed is usually very thin and is often left to the mercy of the plan organizers. Other countries do better: The Quebec health care system in Canada provides an example of care management defined in the broadest terms. It brings together a range of government supported legal, medical, and social services (Vayda, 1986, pp. 241-245), including health care management within local community health and education centers. These CLSCs (local community service centers or *Centres locaux de services communautaires*) provide a full range of public health services: health promotion, prevention, early diagnosis, and some treatment (Desrosiers, 1986).

Ideally, care managers would work in such organizational settings. They would have access to a range of integrated resource units including occupational medicine; immunization clinics; prenatal and postnatal care; family planning; community intervention programs; home health services; health education courses; welfare services; crisis counseling; mental health outpatient services; psychological assistance; family counseling; doctors house-call (home) visits for those in need of such services (children, the elderly, and those with communicable diseases); and day care for the young, the old, and the disabled. Care managers could facilitate access to the health care system for patients and see that all medically relevant information about past treatment of a patient as available to those making current medical decisions. They could coordinate services for the patient and oversee referrals to nonmedical personnel or social services where required.

There is no reason that case management could not take on this type of role within the health care reform in the United States. Many HMOs constitute a preliminary step in the direction of integrated health care. But, as long as health care is for-profit with a short-term perspective, the first goal will remain that of survival in a highly competitive environment. Any broader, long-term concern for the patient, even when it is cost conscious in intent, must necessarily be secondary.

Patient Participation

Because ultimately the health of each individual cannot be enhanced without his or her consent, health care reform needs to envision a broader role for the individual patient in his or her health decisions. It often makes sense and even saves resources to ask people what they want. Why provide something they not only do not want but are opposed to and will not use? For example, why provide nursing home care to someone who would prefer to live in his or her own home, and could do so at less cost to society, if he or she was offered essential services, including partial home help, transportation to stores, and medical appointments? A continuum of lifestyle options for the elderly should be offered rather than the present wasteful situation in the United States where most elderly individuals are either fully independent and autonomous or assigned to costly custodial care facilities. It is hoped that health care reform will include provisions for the extensive development of home- and community-based services for those with disabilities and make these available to those who want them and for whom they are effective alternatives to institutional arrangements.

Clinton's Health Security Act, the most comprehensive of the health care reform proposals in many respects, seeks to assure consumer satisfaction by instituting a national consumer survey to be carried out under the auspices of the National Quality Management Council (NQMC) (Section 5004). The survey, by law, must include the hard-to-reach: those who fail to enroll in a health plan, those who have resigned from a plan, and those who are members of vulnerable populations. The questions that remain are, what can be learned from the survey in terms of patient needs and how will that information be employed to revise and improve health care delivery?

The rights and freedoms of individuals and those of society need to be balanced. Citizens should have the right to refuse treatment if their decision does not have negative consequences for their dependents or unfairly impose great costs on society. Where medical treatment is of unknown value (more often than we care to admit), patients should, if they wish, make the final decision. Information in an easy-to-understand format needs to be available to inform their decisions.

For the moment, medical care in many instances is as much an art as a science, and this raises the question of patients choosing their own physician. The doctor-patient relationship can be enormously personal and very important to some people, even if only for psychological reasons. Health care reform can be structured to preserve it without adding to the cost. Canada's system is an example. It also preserves another individual freedom that is taken for granted in the United States, namely, the rights of the physicians. Physicians in Canada are not obliged, except in emergencies, to accept all patients who seek them out. The result is an emotional security that the patient-doctor relationship is voluntary and consensual on both sides. Managed competition proposals often reduce patient choices of a doctor limiting them to the selection of a doctor whose services have been contracted for by a plan. Sometimes an optional, high-cost plan will offer systemwide choice, but at much greater cost.

Although more studies of patient preferences and their impact on health services need to be undertaken, it appears that patient participation in medical decisions may even reduce costs. Thus those concerned with health care costs may want to lobby for it. Many women opt for midwife deliveries at home rather than the more expensive physician-assisted hospital deliveries. Some patients may prefer earlier discharge from the hospital, if given a choice. Would they choose a less aggressive treatment over a more expensive, often painful, medical procedure even though the risk of an earlier death were greater? Sometimes this is the case (Wennberg, 1990). That patients are kept alive without hope of recovery or an acceptable quality of life suggests a need for consultation as well as the need to expand hospice care.

Empowering patients can have surprising and positive results, even in terms of medical care, and few health care reform proposals adequately consider this. Patient participation is often responsible and efficacious. For example, experiments with the administration of pain medication after surgery revealed that patients self-administered a lower dose than that routinely prescribed by physicians to a control group. And in another example, patient participation in decision making increased compliance with medical prescription.

Provision of Services

Historically in the United States, the provision of health services has developed without much thought to the overall process and how the various elements of the health system are interrelated. A number of health care reform proposals attempt to bring order to what has been haphazard in the past by establishing accountable plans to organize health services networks and cooperative alliances to constitute cooperative purchasing units. Cost containment is central to such efforts.

Paying for Services: Financing Health Care

Health care reform has brought forth new suggestions for mechanisms to pay for health services. Insurance companies have played a major role as payers in the United States in recent decades. Their performance has met with serious criticism (Light, 1994). Clinton's Health Security Act would control costs through government regulation of health insurance premiums. This legislation and several other reform proposals would require a community-rating system (where premiums are the same for each member of a population) and end experience ratings that permit an insurance company to increase rates, even cancel policies, for those who develop medical problems that require high-cost treatment (see the chapter by Lu Ann Aday for a lucid explanation of these concepts).

Single-payer health system reform proposals would eliminate the insurance companies' role entirely. From the Canadian single-payer experience, it appears that this organizational form, where the national government sets fees and covers costs out of general sales and income tax revenues, has important cost advantages. For example, because of its simplicity of administration it saves as much as 20% (Woolhandler & Himmelstein, 1991). In Canada, administration costs are only 2% of each health care dollar. The U.S. government comes close to matching this with its regulated programs such as Medicare (2.2%).

Physicians: Primary Care and Specialists

Many health care reform proposals seek to increase the proportion of primary care physicians because it helps to contain costs. In the past, some specialists in the United States increased their fees despite having fewer patients in order to meet their "target income" level. The proportion of specialists to primary care physicians is far greater in the United States than in other countries where health care costs are lower.

Several mechanisms are available to increase the proportion of primary care physicians. The number of medical residencies for specialists could be reduced. Clinton's Health Security Act proposes that this strategy be implemented beginning in the year 2003 (Title III, Section 3012). Most reform proposals set up a national medical board at the federal government level that would have the power, among other duties, to "designate for each academic year the number of individuals nationwide who . . . are authorized to be enrolled in eligible programs." A program for retraining specialists as primary care physicians is also included in the Health Security Act (Title III, Section 3062b). Other proposals employ educational fellowships for those willing to be primary care physicians. Doctors might be encouraged in this direction through payment incentives that improve the financial compensation for primary care.

Historically, Great Britain's primary care physician reimbursement system provided an example of how payment incentives can be cost efficient, access to specialists minimized, and physicians encouraged to be "concerned with the welfare of the patient" (Blishen, 1991, p. 117). Primary care physicians are paid by a capitated system (a set fee amount per patient basis), and they serve patients who choose them and who are resident in their geographical area. Several practicing physicians may work in the same area according to population needs. Patients, therefore, have some freedom in selecting a physician. A physician's income depends on the number of patients on his or her list. Newly licensed primary care physicians are assigned to areas where there is a need. Specialists work in hospitals and are available only by referral from general practitioners.

Hospitals: Global Budgets and Policy Design

A range of health-related hospital services are included in most health care reform proposals, including inpatient hospital services, outpatient hospital services, and emergency room facilities. The organization and provision of these services varies. The Health Security Act assigns it to corporate and regional accountable plans that would contract with already existing facilities in their geographical region. Whatever reform proposal is implemented, hospice care for the terminally ill is likely to be included as a cost effective alternative to hospitalization.

Hospital performance might be improved through global budgets but the managed competition model usually rejects this approach to cost containment. Experience in the single-payer system of Canada indicates that expenditures on the unproductive, nonessential features of hospital services are minimized with global budgets. One of the benefits of this type of hospital financing is that doctors retain autonomy: There is less pressure in Canada to discharge patients prematurely and doctors do not have to justify clinical decisions to nonmedical personnel.

Health economists worry that if adopted in the United States global budgets might lower quality of care in hospitals, creating barriers to admitting patients by providing incentives for hospitals to understaff or to hire less expensive employees and by encouraging hospital administrators to run deficits in the expectation that they will be bailed out by government funding in the end. Their concerns are reasonable, but their observations are limited to, for example, HMOs that must try to survive in any way they can in an environment of extreme competition. Critics' fears are realized when hospitals are underfinanced because the global budgets allocated are inadequate. Where global budgets are more realistic, as in most of the Canadian provinces, occupancy rates are high and waste is minimized.

Hospital services at the community level need to be designed to encourage coordination and cooperation among hospitals. Antitrust laws need to be revised to encourage this. Some reform proposals would permit hospital coordination, including mergers, cooperation on purchase and utilization of high technology, hospital exchange of price information, and joint administration and provision of some services. Enhanced efficiency, less waste, and duplication could result. Regional divisions of labor could be developed for purchasing high-tech equipment and for the delivery of associated professional services. Hospitals would probably still be forbidden from agreeing on prices, however.

Quality and Costs: Appropriateness Research and Tort Reform

There are advantages to considering quality and cost containment together. Health care costs are best reduced in coordination with an understanding of appropriateness and efficacy. If efforts are made to reduce them independently or on the basis of market competition mechanisms, there is a risk that appropriate and efficacious medical acts will be cut along with everything else. The problem remains, however, to determine what is appropriate and efficacious and that is not always easy. It may be difficult or impossible to determine where treatment is appropriate because random assignment to the "no care" alternative in prospective studies would mean injury and death. But in most cases, research is feasible and it would shed light on questionable medical procedures.

Unexplained differences in practice styles in the United States and worrisome geographical variations in the use of medical procedures suggest that what works and does not work is often decided on the basis of untested assumptions (Wennberg, 1987). Where studies have been undertaken, changes in medical practice sometimes result. For example, very few people have their tonsils removed today, even though tonsillectomy was a common procedure in the past.

Efficacy of many medical procedures is not taken for granted by health care reform proposals and most are committed to allocating resources to determine appropriateness and efficacy of medical treatment. Clinton's Health Security Act seeks to assure quality performance through the establishment of a National Quality Management Program, a "performance-based program of quality management and improvement designed to enhance the quality, appropriateness, and effectiveness of health care services and access to such services" (Title V, Subtitle A, Section 5001). The goal is to collect data and to learn "more about what works and doesn't"; which medical acts may be of "less value than once believed"; which doctors, hospitals, and so on are producing better results; and which cost less (Zelman, 1993, p. 12). The NQMC, made up of 15 members appointed by the President, will include those representing government, employers, plans, the States, health providers, and academic health centers. It will also include individuals "distinguished in the fields of public health, health care quality, and health services research" (Section 5002). Consumers (i.e., patients) are not represented on the NQMC, either directly or through their alliances. This may be because it is assumed that patients have no competence in this area of quality performance, but for reasons outlined in Section 2 of this chapter, consumer input may be quite relevant.

Cost containment efforts often assume that quality is held constant when payment for services is reduced. Although this is possibly true, it is not necessarily the case and should not be taken for granted. Cheaper is not always better. There is some evidence that cost containment efforts are administratively expensive and may contribute to a decline in quality of care. For example, implementation of prospective payment systems such as DRGs in the United States has meant that elderly Medicare patients are more likely than before the DRG system was implemented to be "discharged home in an unstable condition" (Kosecoff et al., 1990; Rogers et al., 1990, p. 1989). No matter what health care reform proposal is adopted, it is important that quality not be allowed to deteriorate if insurance premium caps come into play in future years or as costs are reduced in other ways.

Malpractice

In the United States, physicians have felt obliged to overtreat patients in order to assure that they are adequately covered in case of a malpractice suit. This form of excessively aggressive medical care wastes resources and may not benefit patients. In addition, it has added substantially to the cost of medical care.

Many health care reform proposals include federal-level tort reform designed to reduce physician costs of medical malpractice insurance and decrease the probability of overtreatment. The mechanisms involve installing mandatory alternative dispute resolution systems (ADR), essentially mediation and arbitration. The Health Security Act specifies that a certificate of merit, signed by a medical specialist, would have to be filed before any medical malpractice liability action could be brought to court. Sanctions would be instituted for submitting false allegations. A number of reform proposals limit attorney's contingency fees. The dollar amounts for "pain and suffering" are set at $250,000 in one proposal.

The Canadian model offers an interesting, but different, example of reducing medical malpractice insurance costs. Few nonsalaried lawyers work in the area of malpractice legal cases in Canada and both malpractice insurance costs to doctors and payments to those seeking compensation for medical mistakes are lower than in the United States. A national physicians' malpractice insurance fund, instituted by the Canadian Medical Association, provides legal services for members. This organization hires lawyers, mediators, and trained arbitrators (on a salary basis) to represent doctors in cases of alleged negligence, ignorance, or incompetence. Contingency-fee suits, in which lawyers share awards with those injured, do not exist. Most complaints are settled out of court through the informal mediation process. Although these approaches might not be appropriate in the United States, they do lend perspective on our own attempts at tort reform.

Cost Containment and Long-Term Accounting

Cost containment is central to health system reform. The questions remain: "Whose costs are being contained?" and "at whose expense?" For example, switching drugs from prescription to over-the-counter status has been advocated as a cost containment mechanism. The costs to insurance plans that reimburse only for prescription drugs will be contained. But in the absence of evidence of declining insurance premiums and reductions in fees, it is clear that the situation is more complicated than it first appears. Are costs being contained or are they being shifted from insurance plans to consumers (Rosenau, 1994)?

Health reform that emphasizes medical prevention encourages long-term cost estimates rather than a short-term, immediate savings focus, as was the case in the past. In accounting terms, this suggests factoring into the equation the budgetary consequences not just for the coming fiscal year but for the future. This would mean, for example, that opportunistic budget-balancing savings of a few dollars in the short-term, obtained, for example, by cutting nutritional supplements for pregnant women or nutritional supplements for newborns, would not be acceptable. Such a "cost savings" during the Reagan-Bush years resulted in malnourished mothers who were more prone to give birth to deformed and physically and mentally handicapped babies. Undernourished infants are more likely to be cognitively and behaviorally underdeveloped (Dutton, 1986, pp. 46-50). In some cases these disadvantaged children end up being taken care of by the state for decades. The Clinton administration's vaccination program for children is a positive example. The expenditure is justified because spending $3.00 in the short-term will result in $10.00 saved later because fewer children would need hospital care (Greenhouse, 1993, p. D1).

The health consequences of changing the accounting basis of cost calculations of health care are substantial in the reform process. Even costly programs may turn out to be cost-effective if the long-term view is considered. For example, Clozaril costs a great deal ($6,000-$9,000) per year per patient, but the program could be a net savings to society if an individual with schizophrenia, so treated, could be reintegrated into a normal life situation and function well enough to find employment and become self-sufficient. The same principle applies to rehabilitation programs. And another example, studies in the past 5 years provide evidence that treating the emotional and psychological status of patients improves medical outcomes substantially, independently of medical treatment (see Goleman, 1991, for a summary). Controlled studies indicate that the cost of counseling and psychological care was more than made up for by shorter hospital stays, increased productive months and years of life, and so on. Health reform might provide for physician training to alleviate patient stress and for counselors to organize and provide psychological support for patients.

Conclusions

Many of those actually involved with patient care on a day-to-day basis, and those who witnessed the situation in county hospitals and emergency rooms describe the U.S. health crisis as one of national emergency. Almost all health care reform proposals will extend health care to the whole population. (See the chapters in this volume by Lu Ann Aday and Joyce Lashof for an explanation why even this may not be adequate to improve the nation's health.) Almost all health care reform efforts seek to rearrange expenditures in order to reap the full value of what is already an astonishing dollar commitment to health. Options include proposals that are administrative and conceptually simple and straightforward, such as the single-payer system (see E. Richard Brown's chapter in this volume) and Medicare expansion (see Michael Intriligator's chapter in this volume). Clinton's Health Security Act is considerably more complex. It proposes to regulate insurance premium increases and control the cost of pharmaceuticals.

The goal of health system reform should be to provide quality health care to all citizens at minimum cost. Illness and disease are not cost-neutral. They represent lost potential and are a deficit on any society's balance sheet. Universal medical coverage may not assure each individual of the possibility of realizing his or her full potential, but it is one important prerequisite.

It is likely that some form of managed competition will be adopted in the United States. But there is room for caution. Will such legislation create a two-tiered health system, a minimum package for the poor and a higher quality health plan that only those with considerable income can afford? Will it leave undocumented immigrants without access to the health system except in emergency situations? Will it preserve an important role for private insurance companies without requiring that they reduce their expensive administrative costs? Health care reform in the 1990s will be complex. It will touch the lives of each and every citizen. If it is a failure, the consequences will be extremely serious for all of us. If it is successful, it will provide the basis for building in the future and ultimately for a healthy population in which each of us can develop and contribute to the best of our ability.

References

Bice, T. (1988). Health services planning and regulation. In S. Williams & P. Torrens (Eds.), *Introduction to health services* (pp. 373-406). New York: John Wiley.

Blishen, B. (1991). *Doctors in Canada*. Toronto: University of Toronto Press.

Desrosiers, G. (1986). The Quebec Health Care System. *Journal of Public Health Policy, 7*(2), 211-217.

Dutton, D. (1986). Social class, health, and illness. In L. Aiken & D. Mechanic (Eds.), *Applications of social science to clinical medicine and health policy.* New Brunswick, NJ: Rutgers University Press.

Frank, R., & Salkever, D. (1991). *Pricing, patent loss and the market for pharmaceuticals.* Working paper, National Bureau of Economic Research, Cambridge, MA.

Freeman, P., & Robbins, A. (1991, Winter). The elusive promise of vaccines, the American promise of vaccines. *The American Prospect, 4.*

Goleman, D. (1991, November 29). Doctors find comfort is a potent medicine. *The New York Times*, pp. C1, C8.

Greenhouse, S. (1993, February 15). President gambles on spending. *The New York Times*, p. D1.

Gupta, U. (1991, September 17). Generic drug makers scramble as patents near end. *Wall Street Journal*, p. B2.

Hembree, W. (1985, July/August). Getting involved: Employers as case managers. *Business and Health*, pp. 11-14.

Hilts, P. (1992, January 18). Strange history of silicone held many warning signs. *The New York Times*, pp. A1, A8.

Kerr, P. (1991, November 24). Mental hospital chains accused of much cheating on insurance. *The New York Times*, pp. A1, A28.

Kolata, G. (1992, January 20). Makers of sleeping pills hide data on side effects, researchers say. *The New York Times*, pp. A1, A9.

Kosecoff, J., Kahn, K. L., Rogers, W. H., Reinisch, E. J., Sherwood, M. J., Rubenstein, L. V., Draper, D., Roth, C. P., Chew, E., & Brook, R. H. (1990). Prospective payment system and impairment at discharge. *Journal of the American Medical Association, 254*, 1980-1983.

Leary, W. (1993, January 26). Companies accused of overcharging for drugs developed with U.S. aid. *The New York Times*, p. C6.

Light, D. (1994). Life, death, and the insurance companies. *The New England Journal of Medicine, 330*(7), 498-499.

Pear, R. (1991, December 20). Federal auditors report rise in abuses in medical billing. *The New York Times*, pp. A1, B6.

Roemer, M. (1986). *An introduction to the U.S. health care system* (2nd ed.). New York: Springer.

Rogers, W. H., Draper, D., Kahn, K. L., Keepler, E. B., Rubenstein, L. V., Kosecoff, J., & Brook, R. H. (1990, October 17). Quality of care before and after implementation of the DRG-based prospective payment system. *Journal of the American Medical Association, 264*, 1989-1994.

Rosenau, P. V. (1994). Rx to OTC switch movement. *Medical Care Review, 52*(2).

Rosenthal, E. (1993, January 27). Confusion and error are rife in hospital billing practices. *The New York Times*, p. C16.

Rosenthal, R. (1980). A model in which an increase in the number of sellers leads to a higher price. *Econometrica, 48*, 1575-1579.

Vayda, E. (1986). The Canadian health care system: An overview. *Journal of Public Health Policy, 7*(2), 205-247.

Wennberg, J. (1987). The paradox of appropriate care. *Journal of the American Medical Association, 258*(18), 2568-2569.

Wennberg, J. (1990). Outcomes research, cost containment, and the fear of health care rationing. *The New England Journal of Medicine, 323*(17), 1202-1204.

Woolhandler, S., & Himmelstein, D. (1991). The deteriorating administrative efficiency of the U.S. health care system. *New England Journal of Medicine, 324*(18), 1253-1258.

Zelman, W. (1993). The Clinton plan: With malice toward none and health security for all. *Journal of American Health Policy, 3*(6), 9-13.

Index

About the Authors

Lu Ann Aday is a Professor of Behavioral Sciences and Management and Policy Sciences at The University of Texas School of Public Health in Houston. She has conducted major national and community surveys and evaluations of national demonstrations on access and has published extensively in this area, including 10 books dealing with conceptual or empirical aspects of research on equity of access to medical care.

Paul M. Ambrose holds the MA degree in psychology from Connecticut College. He has worked as a research psychologist for Grumman Data Systems Corporation, as a project manager at National Evaluation Systems, and as a policy analyst and statistician with the New York State Department of Health. He is Project Director of the Governance Project within the health care financing reform initiative (New York) sponsored by The Robert Wood Johnson Foundation, and is the coauthor of the governance report, *Managed Contradiction: Implementing the Clinton Health Plan.*

Dan E. Beauchamp, Ph.D., is a political scientist (Johns Hopkins University, 1973) and taught health politics at the University of North Carolina for many years. In 1988, he moved to New York to serve as Deputy Commissioner for Policy and Planning, the New York State Department of Health, where he led the development of the department's proposal for Universal New York Health Care (UNY Care). He returned to the university in 1992 and is now Professor and Chair, Department of Health Policy and Management, School of Public Health, at the University of Albany in Albany, New York. He is the author of many articles and two books on health policy and the ethics of public health. He has been coprincipal investigator of two major grants of The Robert Wood Johnson Foundation on health care finance reform.

Linda A. Bergthold is a Principal of William M. Mercer Incorporated in Washington, DC, where she consults on health care reform and benefit design. Author of a number of journal articles, she recently published *Purchasing Power in Health: Business, the State and Health Care Policies* (Rutgers University Press, 1990). From February through May of 1993, she was on leave from Mercer to the White House Health Care Task Force, where she was a special consultant on benefits coverage.

Robert H. Binstock is a Professor of Aging, Health, and Society at Case Western Reserve University, Cleveland, Ohio. A former President of the Gerontological Society of America, he has served as the Director of a White House task force on older Americans and as chair and member of a number of advisory panels to the U.S. government, state and local governments, and foundations. He is the author of more than 100 articles on politics and policies affecting aging. His 17 books include *Too Old for Health Care?*, *Dementia and Aging: Ethics, Values, and Policy Choices*, five editions of *America's Political System*, and three editions of the *Handbook of Aging and the Social Sciences*.

E. Richard Brown is Director of the UCLA Center for Health Policy Research and Professor of Public Health in the UCLA School of Public Health. He received his Ph.D. from the University of California, Berkeley. He has studied and written extensively about a broad range of health policies, programs, and institutions, with particular emphasis on issues that affect the access of low-income people to health care. His most recent research focuses on health insurance coverage and the effects of lack of coverage on access to health services. He served as a senior consultant to the President's Task Force on National Health Care Reform, for which he cochaired a work group on low-income families and individuals. He also developed bills in the California Legislature and in the United States Senate, where he was health policy adviser to Senator Bob Kerrey.

Michael R. Cousineau is the Associate Director of the UCLA Center for Health Policy Research and a faculty member at the School of Public Health. He is the former Executive Director of Homeless Health Care Los Angeles, a community-based organization providing health care and related services to homeless people. He has conducted research on access to health care and substance abuse services for low-income and homeless people, urban encampments, and public hospitals. He is a consultant to the National Health Care for the Homeless Council. His articles have appeared in *Evaluation Review, American Journal of Public Health,* and *Health Care Financing Review.* His current research includes understanding variations on the rates of uninsurance in California and on the impact of managed care on homeless people.

Colleen M. Grogan is an Assistant Professor of Health Policy Resources and Administration at Yale University. She received a Ph.D. in health policy research at the University of Minnesota. After a year of independent research in the People's Republic of China, she was a postdoctoral fellow in the program on economics of aging and health services at the University of California, Berkeley. Her current research focuses on federalism and health and welfare policy. Her specific health policy interests include state Medicaid policy, health care expenditures and cost containment issues associated with aging, and comparative health systems.

Chris Hafner-Eaton is an Assistant Professor of Health Care Administration in the Department of Public Health at Oregon State University in Corvallis. She has published articles in several journals, including the *Journal of Ambulatory Care Management* and the *Journal of the American Medical Association.* Her research interests encompass access to health care for the underserved (for acute, chronic, and long-term care), health care finance, women's and minority health issues, health policy, and comparative international health systems. She has worked in hospitals, county and community clinics, private voluntary organizations, and private health service research institutes in Europe, the United States, Latin America, and the Far East.

Russell L. Hanson is an Associate Professor of Political Science at Indiana University, Bloomington. He is the author of *The Democratic Imagination in America: Conversations With Our Past* as well as several articles on state policy-making in the United States. Along with John Hartman, he is currently investigating the impact of differential benefit and eligibility policies on the migratory behavior of poor people, with the aid of a grant from the Institute for Research on Poverty at the University of Wisconsin—Madison.

Michael D. Intriligator is a Professor of Economics and Political Science at UCLA, where he is also the Director of the Jacob Marshak Interdisciplinary Colloquium on Mathematics in the Behavioral Sciences and is affiliated with the Center for International Relations. He is the author of *Mathematical Optimization and Economic Theory* and of *Econometric Models, Techniques, and Applications* and a coauthor of *A Forecasting and Policy Simulation Model of the Health Care Sector*. He has published more than 60 journal articles and more than 90 other publications in the areas of economic theory, econometrics, health economics, and strategy and arms control. In the area of health economics, he has served as a member of the Prospective Payment Technical Advisory Panel of the Health Care Financing Administration, U.S. Department of Health and Human Services, and as a consultant and expert witness for government agencies, corporations, and associations.

Joyce C. Lashof currently is Dean Emerita and Professor of Public Health, University of California, Berkeley. She was Dean of the School of Public Health at Berkeley from 1981-1991. She received her M.D. degree from the Medical College of Pennsylvania in 1950 and is board certified in internal medicine. She has combined a career in academic medicine—holding faculty appointments in preventive medicine at the University of Chicago, the University of Illinois, and Rush Medical College—with a career in public service. She then entered government service, first as Director of Public Health for the State of Illinois (1973-1977), then as Deputy Assistant Secretary for Health Programs, Department of Health, Education, and Welfare (1977-1978), and as Assistant Director, Office of Technology Assessment, U.S. Congress (1978-1981). Dr. Lashof has been President of the Association of Schools of Public Health (1987-1989). She also has been active in the American Public Health Association (APHA) for more than 20 years and served as President (1991-1992).

Philip R. Lee, M.D., is the Head of the U.S. Public Health Service and Assistant Secretary for Health in the Department of Health and Human Services. He has served with distinction as Director of the Institute of Health Policy Studies, School of Medicine, at the University of California, San Francisco, for the past 21 years. He has also frequently advised federal and state health groups and served on numerous advisory boards and planning committees. In 1985, then-San Francisco Mayor Dianne Feinstein named him as the first president of the city's Health Commission, which was the governing body in the city/county health department that included public health, mental health, and substance abuse services, as well as the San Francisco General Hospital (the major AIDS care facility in the city) and a 1,000-bed long-term care facility.

John N. Lozier is the Executive Director of the National Health Care for the Homeless Council, an association of 24 direct service providers in cities around the country. He holds an M.S.S.W. from the University of Tennessee and an AB from Brown University. His career has involved establishing service projects and advocacy organizations for prisoners, families, and homeless people.

Cathie Jo Martin is an Assistant Professor in the Department of Political Science at Boston University. She is currently writing a book titled *Mobilizing Business for Social Welfare Initiatives: The Case of National Health Reform*, funded by The Robert Wood Johnson Foundation, that describes the business movement to put health reform on the national agenda. Her dissertation, funded by the National Science Foundation, culminated in *Shifting the Burden: The Struggle Over Growth and Corporate Taxation*, published in 1991. She received a postdoctorate fellowship to work with the MIT commission on Industrial Productivity, which produced *Made in America*, published in 1989. She is currently involved with a Woodrow Wilson Center working group on fiscal policy in America. She taught at Northwestern University from 1988 to 1990, where she held a joint appointment in the political science department and the Center for Urban Affairs and Policy Research.

J. Peter Nixon is a Policy Analyst for the Service Employees International Union (SEIU) in Washington, DC. Prior to joining the staff at SEIU, he worked as an analyst in the Department of Employee Benefits of the AFL-CIO. He is the author of a number of monographs and articles about health care reform, most recently "Health Care Reform: Making It Work for Low-Income Communities," which was published in the inaugural issue of the *Georgetown Journal on Fighting Poverty*.

Mark A. Peterson, Ph.D., formerly an Associate Professor of Government at Harvard University, moved to the University of Pittsburgh in fall of 1993, where he is an Associate Professor in the Graduate School of Public and International Affairs and the Department of Political Science. His publications include *Legislating Together: The White House and Capitol Hill From Eisenhower to Reagan* (1990), as well as "Momentum Toward Health Care Reform in the U.S. Senate" (1992) and "Political Influence in the 1990s: From Iron Triangles to Policy Networks" (1993), both in the *Journal of Health Politics, Policy and Law*, of which he is now editor. He has worked on health policy in the U.S. Senate as an American Political Science Association Congressional Fellow.

Milton I. Roemer, M.D., is an Emeritus Professor of Health Services at UCLA's School of Public Health. He has served at all levels of health administration, from the U.S.-county level to the World Health Organization. He is the author of more than 440 articles and 32 books—most recently, a two-volume series titled *National Health Systems of the World*. He wrote *Ambulatory Health Services in America* and is the recipient of the Sedgwick Medal, public health's highest award.

Pauline Vaillancourt Rosenau is Associate Professor at the School of Public Health, The University of Texas—Health Science Center at Houston. She is author of several books including *When Marxists Do Research* and *Post-Modernism in the Social Sciences*. Recent publications have appeared in the *American Behavioral Scientist, Medical Care Review, Journal for Health Politics, Policy and Law, International Journal of Technology Assessment, International Political Science Review, Millennium, Policy Currents, Comparative Political Studies, Current Perspectives in Social Theory, Paradigms, Social Research*, and *Review*. Her current research focus is comparative health systems in developed countries, especially Quebec, Canada and the United States. Her scholarly work also includes biomedical ethics and policy, the new gene technology, and pharmaceutical regulation and policy.